D0983754

Dearest Wilding

Edited, with an introduction and annotations,

by Thomas P. Riggio

Dearest Wilding

A Memoir

By YVETTE EASTMAN

with Love Letters from Theodore Dreiser

University of Pennsylvania Press
Philadelphia

Printed in the United States of America

Library of Congress Cataloging-in-Publication Data

Eastman, Yvette Szekely
Dearest Wilding : a memoir : with love letters from Theodore Dreiser / by Yvette Eastman ; edited, with an introduction and annotations, by Thomas P. Riggio.
p. cm.
ISBN 0-8122-3311-5
1. Dreiser, Theodore, 1871-1945—Relations with women.
2. Dreiser, Theodore, 1871-1945—Correspondence. 3. Eastman, Yvette Szekely—Relations with men. 4. Novelists, American—20th century—Biography. 5. Love-letters.
I. Dreiser, Theodore, 1871-1945. II. Riggio, Thomas P. III. Title.
PS3507. R55Z62 1995
813' . 52—dc20
[B} 95-1821
CIP

Designed by Carl Gross

Contents

Illustrations

Introduction

Yvette Szekely Eastman's memoir is the latest, and arguably the most revealing, of a number of books written by women who knew Theodore Dreiser. Biographers eventually will have to explain why Dreiser, for all his unsavory reputation as a careless philanderer, has inspired more such reminiscences than any other American writer. Helen Dreiser, Margaret Tjader Harris, Dorothy Dudley, Ruth Kennell, Clara Jaeger, Louise Campbell, and Vera Dreiser have all added to the record of the novelist's life. *Dearest Wilding*—the title comes from a term of affection Dreiser used to address the author—surely provides the most intimate account. This is attributable to Mrs. Eastman's considerable narrative skills, to her eye and memory for vivid details, and to the quality she says she most admired in Dreiser—the "detached, nonjudgmental yet compassionate acceptance" of what life brings.

Dearest Wilding records the journey that took eight-year-old Yvette Szekely from an upper-middle-class scholar's home in Budapest to the intellectual and artistic centers of urban America in the 1920s and 1930s. The key moment of Mrs. Eastman's memoir is her fateful meeting with Dreiser in 1929. She was then a sixteen-year-old schoolgirl and he a famous friend of her mother. Although the narrative ends with Dreiser's death in 1945, this is more than an account of their sixteen-year relationship. Mrs. Eastman's attempt to understand the nature of her bond with Dreiser forced her back even further, to her early childhood in Hungary, to memories of her erudite and famed but distant father who did not accompany her to America, and to the formative experiences and subsequent psychic hungers that made the aging writer so important a part of her life.

Mrs. Eastman's youth, tied as it was to Dreiser and his circle, provided her with a privileged view of a special phase of modern life. Her distinction comes in part from the circumstances that placed her, from an early age, among the most noted figures in twentieth-century cultural history. In retrospect, she was fortunate to come to the United States with a mother—the "Margaret" of the story—who had, as Mrs. Eastman says, "a way of being where the action was, more especially if the situation held people of fame and importance or a cause she could support."

The causes of the period were many, from progressive political action to now obscure struggles for literary freedom. Beginning in 1929, Dreiser, then fifty-eight years old and at the height of his fame as a writer, invited Margaret Monahan and her two daughters to the popular Thursday evening soirees at his Rodin Studios apartment on West 57th Street and later to his country home, called Iroki, at Mount Kisco, New York. By this point Dreiser had put behind him the relatively impecunious lifestyle of his Greenwich Village days and had moved uptown to the posh apartment where, in his own inimitable way, he participated in the whirlwind pace of the late 1920s. A typical evening might find young Yvette in the same room with such writers and critics as Sherwood Anderson, John Cowper Powys, Floyd Dell, Edgar Lee Masters, and Claude Bowers; the banker-producer Otto Kahn; Freud's American translator, A. A. Brill; the actress Miriam Hopkins; the columnist Alexander Woollcott; and the multifaceted intellectual Max Eastman, whom she would later marry. Naturally, there was something intoxicating in this company for one so young. At first shy, she soon became a familiar presence among the artists and authors who had made New York their mecca in the nineteen-teens and twenties. Mrs. Eastman's portrait of Dreiser and his set is of course a valuable primary source in literary history. I might add that it is likely to be among our last such documents from this period.

In the thirties Dreiser addressed himself to the social and political challenges of the decade, and he became deeply involved in compiling a massive philosophical-scientific study on the nature of existence. Mrs. Eastman's memoir offers a view of the less public side of his life that has largely eluded biographical accounts. It presents an evocative and colorful picture of those times rendered with a fine eye for the texture of everyday life. Mrs. Eastman captures especially well the poetry and tensions of the teenager in all her naïveté and youthful adventuring, "in love with love, with poetry, and with the lover-father in this celebrated man." It is a very human document about a young woman enthralled by the celebrity and magnetism of a writer who was sixteen years older than her father. Her portrait of Dreiser, not by any means idealized, is of a complex man who was often troubled, suspicious, unfaithful, and jealous but who also cared and was supportive and not just for selfish ends.

Dearest Wilding is the first installment of a full-fledged autobiography, which culminates in Yvette Szekely's marriage to Max Eastman in 1958 and their years together until his death in 1969. That story employs a large canvas and includes detailed portraits of many public figures of the postwar years. *Dearest Wilding* has a design of its own, resembling a traditional bildungsroman, which follows the course of a life back to certain primal encounters. For Mrs. Eastman, the entire scheme of her life was radically altered by her experience with Dreiser. Their relationship, which began as a strange, even clumsy seduction, finally became, as Mrs. Eastman presents it, more like the supportive friendship that might exist between a father and daughter. She describes it best in a passage from her larger work:

> ["Dearest Wilding"] is a memoir of growing up and declaring independence, using my relationship with Dreiser as a centerpiece, walking with stubborn, unseeing innocence, straight into buffeting headwinds. It is primarily about a young me, how I saw TD and his impact on me, his effect on my life. It is also about my relationship with my mother. She and TD stand out as centers of influence and conflict—a sort of triangle with TD pulling me away from my mother and toward a wider world, and in the background my father for whom TD was somewhat of a substitute.

Mrs. Eastman's decision to allow Dreiser's letters to accompany her story makes the memoir more personal and more valuable as a historical record. This book is something of a publishing event, as it includes the first collection of Dreiser's love letters. Although researchers have had access to such letters among the Dreiser papers at the University of

Pennsylvania, they have rarely quoted from them, even in biographical accounts. Until now the letters in this book have been unavailable to specialists as well as to the general public. (Unfortunately, only a handful of Mrs. Eastman's letters to Dreiser have survived, and these appear in the memoir itself.) Readers will discover that Dreiser never wrote mere love letters. He often included reflections on his surroundings, on "life," politics, his writing, and the famous and the unknown whom he encountered. The letters also reflect the heady last days of the twenties, the reform-minded thirties, the toll the war took on the German-American novelist during the late thirties and early forties, and the concerns of his last years. They are, of course, primarily a mirror to Dreiser's various moods—the wistfulness, joy, loneliness, and tenderness that often warred with the less appealing qualities. In this they supplement Mrs. Eastman's account as only such private papers can.

Having had the privilege of reading the manuscript of Mrs. Eastman's complete autobiography, I can only hope that she publishes it sometime soon. For now we have *Dearest Wilding,* a splendid addition to our knowledge of the private life of one of the most challenging personalities in American literary history. It is all the more valuable for having been written by someone who knew Dreiser well and has had the time, now nearly a half century, to reflect on him and on her younger self.

THOMAS P. RIGGIO

Editorial Note

In 1993, the University of Pennsylvania acquired the letters that Dreiser had written to Yvette Szekely between 1929 and 1945. The total count of these letters is 229; none has been published previously. Although a complete edition of the letters would have served scholarly purposes, it became clear in preparing the letters for this volume that a compromise was in order. Omitted are letters that either repeat the contents of other letters or are lesser notes of invitation, holiday greetings, and the like—all of which would simply take up space and detract from the readability and general high quality of the correspondence. Readers who desire to examine the remaining letters can do so in the Special Collections Department of the Van Pelt–Dietrich Library Center at the University of Pennsylvania.

Letters are printed in full with no bracketed emendations or interpolations. Any ellipses in the letters are Dreiser's own. The guiding principle for holograph and typed letters has been that they be printed as they were received. The chief exception to this rule comes in the positioning of the place of origin, the date, and the complimentary close, all of which have been regularized. The reasons for the rule are, first, to preserve the private character of the letters and, second, to provide the reader with a feel for Dreiser's idiosyncracies of expression.

Readers will not experience any difficulty with this format. Dreiser tended to be consistent in his peculiarities, so that he establishes norms of his own that the reader quickly begins to recognize. For example, his misspellings include the almost constant reversal of the correct positions of *i's* and *e's*; he regularly omits the apostrophe and the question mark; and certain misused words (e.g., his steady use of "your" for "you're") are easy enough to decipher. For the sake of clarity, I have provided periods where Dreiser omitted them at the end of a page.

Errors of fact and special markings are recorded in the notes. The few cases of illegible words, as well as the location of all marginalia, are also explained in the notes. When words were inserted above lines, they have been included in the text without comment.

The letters are arranged chronologically and placed after the end of the memoir. The notes are used to identify references in the letters to people, events, and documents that the reader may find obscure. Names in notes to each section are identified only the first time they occur in that section.

T. P. R.

Acknowledgments

For its generosity and cooperation, I am grateful to the University of Pennsylvania, which has granted permission to publish the Dreiser letters written to me.

For reading first drafts and for careful criticism, I am indebted to Peggy Brooks and Ken McCormick. Great appreciation is also due to my friend Robert Giroux for his continuing support and editorial suggestions. I am particularly indebted to Jacqueline Kennedy Onassis, who first suggested publishing the letters and whose untimely death I continue to mourn. For his encouragement and valuable criticism, I owe much thanks to Richard Lingeman. For editorial work, copyediting the manuscript, typing the letters, and deciphering TD's handwriting, I thank Lee Ann Draud. I am especially grateful to Thomas Riggio, whose abiding and substantial interest, support, and help finally brought this book to fruition.

Y. E.

Dearest Wilding

How sharp the point of this remembrance is.
William Shakespeare
The Tempest

Prologue

On the morning of Saturday, December 29, 1945, I was working until noon as part of the skeleton staff of the Department of Welfare on 57th Street. Arriving early, I stopped in the building cafeteria for coffee and was joined by Juliette, a co-worker and friend.

"Did you see the paper this morning?" she asked and laid the *New York Times* on the table, front page up.

THEODORE DREISER DIES AT AGE 74
Author of "An American Tragedy"
Leader in Realistic Fiction
Succumbs in Hollywood

I stared back at the image of him on the printed page in disbelief, my mind protesting, "It can't be. I just got your letter two days ago; it is here in my handbag." Stunned, even frightened, I felt at thirty-three the sixteen-year supporting prop crumble from under me. I had never allowed myself to prepare for this.

I waited, stricken, at my desk for twelve o'clock, when I could leave. I took TD's recent letter from its envelope, hoping to find an answer and an explanation: "here I am again . . . dont forget me . . . think of me . . . Love as ever." The words were still alive contradicting the newspaper's "DIES . . . Succumbs."

Los Angeles
Dec—1945

Yvette Dear: Thanks so much for your letter of Dec 6. You always write so wisely and so kindly and so tolerantly, so much so that you make life seem so much better than it often truly is—so much so that often I think of you as the most tolerant and generous of all the people I have met. . . . here I am again, this time with a check for $15[00] which is your Xmas present since you know best what you want to buy. And when I get more, I'll send you more. Meanwhile dear dont forget me. I so much like to hear from you & to feel that you still care. And as I dream if a certain windfall arrives you are to come out here or at least you are going to get the means so to do, as well as my wish that you will be moved to favor me that much.

And meanwhile think of me. And here is my merry Xmas to you.

Love as ever
TD

I had cashed the check into a ten- and a five-dollar bill, folding them small to tuck into a special corner of my wallet so as not to spend them on necessities. They were to be for *something special.*

By noon it was raining, a steady, weeping rain. I turned east, walking past the Rodin Building on 57th Street, where he used to live, past Carnegie Hall, past the Russian Tea Room, across Fifth Avenue to Madison, into the rain, my face and hair rain wet, tear wet. I walked block after block, seeing remembrance pictures in my head. For good or bad, he had been the dominant figure in my life from the time when at age sixteen I stood on tiptoe like a young bird in the nest, hoisting my wings. He taught me to fly without fear because I believed he would swoop down to lift me up if I were to fall. What for him may have started out as lust for one more fledgling developed into a spiritual and emotional bond between us—unbroken, continuous—that grew strong enough to withstand, for all those sixteen years, the irregular comings together. This surrogate father and first lover took up enormous space in my mind and heart.

As a palliative and maybe as a denial that he was dead and that I would never see him again or receive any more letters, I regressed to the childlike belief that up there, above this rainy sky, he was looking down at me and my tears in the fancy Madison Avenue flower shop buying roses, taking from my wallet the little folded squares of a ten and a five. For *something special.*

Nine days later, reading a copy of the funeral services that his wife, Helen Richardson Dreiser, had sent me was like watching the ceremony through the knothole of a high fence. All that was left to me were memories and TD's many letters that I had kept over the years. They have remained for me souvenirs of an important part of my life. *Dearest Wilding* is my attempt to share these memories and letters—and at least a part of Dreiser—with a new generation.

1

First Memories

It is an October morning in 1928 on New York's 91st Street, and I will soon be sixteen. In the sun-washed spacious living room of the sprawling apartment, where I live with my mother, Margaret, my younger sister, Suzanne, and our housekeeper-cook, Zsuzsi, I am sitting astride an arm of the sofa reading a letter to Suzanne and me from our father in Budapest:

> I am thinking of you who, as little girls, were torn from the homeland to the vast America. You probably don't find this to be so extraordinary, so especially sad as I do. Still, what we here in ancient Europe believe in, prefer, want, is to have the children with their father as well as their mother, or at least growing up near enough to him to benefit from his guidance and protection.

As I fold the letter, I do not find it "especially sad." I had lived in Budapest with both my parents for only three years after their marriage—she at eighteen and he at twenty-five. After their divorce, I jumped to obey whenever my mother threatened, "If you don't put your toys away right now and wash your hands *I'll send you back to your father!"*

Father's letter has an undertone of complaint, an accusation directed at my mother, but it brings back to me a corner apartment building that wrapped itself around a corner along a Danube embankment. My father, too impatient to wait for his small daughter's short legs to mount, one at a time, the several steps to the elevator, tucked me upside down under his arm like a package and bolted up the stairs with my head dangling near his hip and my feet under his chin.

Some things I remember; others were told to me; and some I simply understood.

The polished brass plate on the entrance door to our apartment on the fourth floor read "Dr. Székely Artúr." Except by friends and intimates, he was addressed as "Sir Doctor"—a doctor of law, economist, author, contributor to literary and liberal journals, the Secretary of the Chamber of Commerce and Industry, and the director of Hungary's Inter-Commerce Bureau. My father: the then twenty-eight-year-old intellectual and aesthete who had the books in his library custom bound in maize-yellow linen or leather, who savored his after-dinner cigar while leafing through his slim volumes of Baudelaire and Verlaine. He had wide-open hazel eyes and thin, straight-line lips, one corner of which often lifted in a characteristic half-smile, for which he was dubbed by his associates and colleagues "Dr. Supercilious Smile." When he laughed his shoulders shook, and the sound I heard was like escaping steam. His kisses on arrivals and departures felt cold-damp on my child's mouth, the kind I would wipe dry with the back of my hand, but his tenderness leaked out to me when he let me taste a little corner of a sugar cube he softened brown with his demitasse before popping it into my mouth. Although his lap did not invite small children, I think he felt more warmth and affection than he was able to show. I remember him more as a cordial father than as a playful daddy.

"Torn from the homeland." What was left of it for me after seven years were flash cards of recall: a country at war; nannies wheeling prams along the Corso at noon past luxury hotels and restaurants that spilled Johann Strauss's music onto the sidewalk tables; vendors hawking their wares on the promenade, holding their bright bouquets of balloons and pinwheels; how wrinkly uncomfortable it was whenever the cuffs of my short white socks slid back into my shoes. And, yes, I remember the nanny unbuttoning the three-button dropseat of my underwear and making long s-s-s-s sounds to encourage the sprinkling as I squatted in the park above the dandelions. Early December brought chocolate brooms and switches tied with red ribbon for Saint Nicholas Day on the sixth, followed by the white and silver of Christmas

Eve: two little girls standing behind tall, closed double doors until the doors were opened to the sight of a ceiling-high Christmas tree, whose lighted candles made a quiet quivering glow that prompted their voices to lower to a whisper. Then, walking toward the tree, as in a procession, our child-soprano voices sang "Stille Nacht, Heilige Nacht." Someone put a match to the sparklers we held, and they burst into a shower of stars.

* * *

As dawn's blue-white daylight crept into our room, my sister lay sleeping in her crib. I slid out of my bed, tiptoed into my parents' bedroom, and crawled into my mother's bed. I laid my head on her bosom and felt the rise and fall of her breathing, the warm skin smelling like flowers, the softness on both sides where the breasts divide. I was four, and I was afraid that she might disappear. My hunger for her love was such that I needed to hear the sound of her voice to feel safe. When in anger she yelled at a servant, the loudness frightened me and made me anxious, as did her out loud crying that muffled my father's murmurs whenever they fought.

One day, lending truth to my fears, my mother did disappear for a time from the bounds of my small world, taking my sister with her. I was desolate. The divorce court gave me into the custody of my father. His cool-headed, orderly mind could not continue to live with a mercurial temperament that raced capriciously between seductive behavior and volatile histrionics. For my mother's part, she felt put down by his imperious, deprecatory attitude, his abrupt, impatient manner. There were distractions to dry her tears when he left. She had a way of being where the action was, more especially if the situation held people of fame and importance or a cause she could support. She became active in the "cause" of Count Mihály Károlyi's Party for Independence. When the monarchy collapsed in 1918 and Hungary was declared a republic with Károlyi its president, my mother, his staunch supporter and friend, was appointed Secretary of Welfare. With my sister she had taken up residence in the Ritz Hotel, then the Budapest headquarters for the postwar ministrations of the American Red Cross. Besides her political activities, she was also a Red Cross volunteer and, while serving as such, fell in love with an American army colonel who was planning to return to his wife and children in Chicago.

Eighteen-year-old Margaret and twenty-five-year-old Artúr Székely in Budapest just after their marriage in 1913.

Suzanne *(left)* and Yvette Szekely with their governess in Budapest.

"The children may not be taken out of the country without the father's consent," ruled the court that granted my parents' divorce. "Visiting rights: one half-day each week." When, after one of these "visits" of a March afternoon, I was called for to be taken back to the home of my stern paternal grandmother with the black velvet band circling her throat, my father was informed that some hours earlier my mother had checked out and boarded the train to Paris with both his children. Later he learned that she had booked passage aboard a ship bound for New York. Her destination: Chicago.

* * *

August 1921: My sister and I are in the back seat of a long red convertible that is driving along Brooklyn streets with its top down. My mother sits in front next to the young man at the wheel. The hot summer breeze combs back her hair as the car slows around a noonday traffic circle. A hurdy-gurdy rolls out the tune of "Margie." In a restaurant at a table with a white tablecloth, the nice looking young man with the crewcut and reddish-blond moustache turns to us and says, "I think it's time now for you to call me 'Daddy.'"

Three days later and five months after arriving in "vast America," Roy Phelps Monahan, age thirty; occupation: attorney; country of birth: United States of America, became our stepfather in a marriage solemnized by the city clerk of King's County, Borough of Brooklyn. Mother and children are now American citizens.

For six weeks we live in four rooms with newly bought furniture on a tree-lined street. Mr. Monahan brings home presents—a teddybear with electric eyes that can be turned on and off, a toy safe with a combination lock like real ones—and is rewarded with my calling him "Daddy," which my sister refused to do. His visiting father goes to early morning Mass every day in the Catholic church nearby, where we children attend the parish school.

At the end of the six weeks there are loud, angry voices, and late one afternoon Mother is standing in her nightgown bracing herself against the dining room wall. "Don't you touch me!" her voice rings out. Nearby stands Mr. Monahan.

"Hurry! Go find a policeman!" she calls to me. I run out and through streets where I had never before walked alone. At a busy intersection I find a policeman directing traffic. I take his hand and beg: "Please, please come. My mother . . . my mother."

Back at the house Mr. Monahan meets us in the hall. He and the policeman exchange words, and the policeman leaves. Then Mr. Monahan leaves, to return only once to collect his clothes and ties, which my mother has cut into strips with scissors. Movers come and take back the furniture bought on the installment plan but leave us two mattresses. While we sleep on them, the gas our mother has turned on seeps through the door cracks, bringing neighbors in. Seeing our mother lying there with eyes closed, not responding, they urge me to run to the church and bring the priest. When I come back with him, he tells me to kneel and pray, and, squeezing my eyes tight for emphasis, I recite all the prayers I learned in school. When I get to "and blessed is the fruit of thy womb Jesus," I visualize an apple or orange. My mother's head turns from side to side, her chest rises, and I hear the sound "mmmm." Life has come back.

* * *

It is four o'clock of a 1922 Saturday afternoon in the lobby of the Hotel Laclede on 15th Street off Union Square. Sitting around reading their newspapers, puffing cigars, playing cards, or dozing-snoring with mouths parted are some of the residents—mostly idle, unattached older men living on pensions or disability allowances. We live there too, and they like seeing us children around most evenings and on the weekends when we aren't in Saint Ann's School on 11th Street or in after-school care in Grace Church across the street, waiting for our working mother to pick us up at six o'clock. They save and give us the "funnies" from their newspapers: "Maggie and Jiggs," "Little Orphan Annie," "Mutt and Jeff." Among them are the retired, almost-blind naval officer Captain McAllister and his wife, Jamie, and Mr. and Mrs. Bidwell. Because Mrs. Bidwell is an actress and is seldom around, it is to Mr. Bidwell that our mother turns for the favor of "keeping an eye on the children" when she has to be out.

On one of these weekend afternoons, when we are alone playing in the lobby, Mr. Bidwell approaches. "We are going to have a birthday party for one of my children who live with their grandmother. It will be this afternoon upstairs in our rooms. You must come up for cake and ice cream and games."

When later we tapped on his door and he let us in, there was no one else in the darkish suite, with its glass doors separating a bedroom from the living room. "The other children have not yet arrived," said Mr. Bidwell, "but come and sit on the edge of the bed and I'll tell you stories until the party starts." He was in his pajamas and got into the bed. In a little while he said to my six-year-old sister, "Go down to the desk clerk and ask him for the right time." As soon as she left, Mr. Bidwell took one of my hands and placed it on top of the bed blanket over a hard bulge and then pulled me under the covers, removed my pants, and started kissing me. I froze with panic, fear, revulsion. I lost my voice.

When he heard my sister knock—back with the "right time"—he quickly pushed me out of the bed and said, "This is a secret game. You must never tell about it or something terrible will happen to you." Afraid to tell my mother, I only begged her not to ask Mr. Bidwell to look after us when she went out. I couldn't answer when she asked, "Why?"

* * *

The day our mother fainted on the street in front of the hotel and was taken to Saint Vincent's Hospital, Jamie McAllister contacted Mrs. Klauber, an old acquaintance of our mother's mother, with whom we had stayed for some days on arrival in America before going to Chicago. She had been a pupil of Franz Liszt and gave piano lessons in one of the row of ocher-colored frame houses with wood-railed porches in the Bronx, where she lived with her husband and two grown sons, both of whom were musicians in a band.

"Can you take the children for awhile?" Jamie asked.

Mrs. Klauber agreed to take my sister but did not want both children. The McAllisters decided to let me stay in the hotel with them during this emergency, but when some days later I got sick with acute bronchitis and robbed them of their sleep with my all-night coughing, Captain McAllister said, "You had better go to the hospital where your mother is." Like a blind Charlie Chaplin with waif, we, holding hands, trudged off to the hospital, where I was admitted to the children's ward. My mother, on a different floor, was lying in a straitjacket.

When I was well again and ready to leave but had no place to go and nothing to do in a ward with sick children, Mrs. Klauber persuaded a friend of hers from Brooklyn who was a widow to take me. In that household of middle-aged strangers and daily trips to the cemetery I wilted and was returned to the Klaubers, where my sister had become a household pet. My sister was a pretty child with dark auburn hair and big brown eyes, and the Klaubers dressed her in a sailor suit and stood her on the oak dining table, where their son Eddie, the saxophone player, taught her to dance the Charleston.

After we had consumed many bowls of sugared sour cream and quartered oranges at a corner of the kitchen table; marveled at the movie marquees with their blinking bulbs and offerings of Charlie Chaplin, Our Gang, and vaudeville; and been exposed to Christian Science, my mother was finally discharged from the hospital and again materialized for me. Besides my sister, she was the only one so far in my life who was important to me—the only one I wanted, needed, depended on. Although she did not bend down to my height and visit in my world, she was seductive. Her fortunes improved after she got out of Saint Vincent's. After she designed and made a nightgown for Jamie McAllister as a Christmas gift, Jamie suggested that she present herself as a recently arrived Paris designer of ladies' underwear. Dropping the "z" and the "l" from Szekely, she became "Madam Sekey" and succeeded in building a reputation in that specialty with earnings that were commensurate with her success.

We moved to a real apartment—two rooms and kitchen on the ground floor of a corner building on 103rd Street and Central Park West. I attended the neighborhood public school and the Presbyterian Sunday School and played games in the street with the other kids on the block—"Red rover, red rover" and "double dutch" jump rope: "Flat to let inquire within, when I move out let Ethel move in." When Ethel moved in, one of us held on to the wheelchair into which her brain-damaged brother, Lars, was strapped. While Ethel skipped until she "missed," we tenderly wiped the ever-drooling saliva from Lars's chin. The day after twelve-year-old Ernest Grant, his blond hair slicked and darkened brown with water, knocked on our door and offered me the present of a book, the chalked big letters on the red brick wall across the street announced ERNIE LOVES YVETTE. This made me a little famous among the eleven and twelve year olds, and although my mother found the message shameful, I felt for the first time a satisfaction of acceptance and belonging among a group of children my age.

When we moved around the corner to an apartment on Central Park West, where my mother had her own bedroom and we children had ours, she bought an ivory-white set of children's furniture—twin beds with storybook characters painted on their headboards—a four-poster bed for herself, and Windsor chairs and an upright piano for the dining-sitting room. A woman to clean and cook dinner came every day and a piano teacher once a week. My mother's friend, a Dr. Ward, frequently stayed overnight.

The influence of the Catholic school on my need to conform and be accepted meant that my openness to prayer as a means to obtain rewards or to stave off disasters had been firmly in place for some time. Every night I would kneel by my bedside and, after saying the Lord's Prayer and Hail Mary and requesting blessings on my mother and sister, amen, I would plead with my almost-asleep sister to get out of bed and say her prayers. This was not simple: in addition to being too sleepy, she couldn't have cared less about prayers. She refused to get out of bed and kneel. I was so afraid that if she didn't say her prayers I would find her dead in the morning that I begged and bargained: "All right, you don't have to kneel. Just sit up and say them." That prayers might be effective even if said lying down was, to me, outside the realm of possibility. I would crawl into her bed and, with my body, prop her into a sitting position and let her off with just one prayer—either the Lord's Prayer or the "Now I lay me down to sleep." Only after that could I go to sleep without worrying.

When summer returned, a two-hour train ride took us to Milford, Connecticut, where, as paying boarders, my sister and I were left in the care of a Hungarian family on its Orange Road "Sunset Farm." Mr. and Mrs. Bodnar were in their late forties, he with a luxurious reddish-blond moustache that I was not to forget, and she with a plain Grant Wood type of face—stern, thin brown hair pulled back and knotted into a bun.

One of her foremost preoccupations was to make her unattractive sixteen-year-old daughter, Irene, look desirable and marriageable to one or another young member of the clergy at the Hungarian church in Bridgeport. To this end, Irene was given singing lessons, silks and patterns for home sewing of party dresses, and one of the first permanent waves, which took seven hours to administer in a Bridgeport department store. On the farm two frame houses separated by a wide patch of lawn fronted the country dirt road that led from Milford to beyond. One house held mainly the summer dining room and kitchen, the other the guest bedrooms. There being no indoor plumbing, I sometimes helped Irene empty the guest chamberpots into a large enamel pail with a lid. When it was full and very heavy, Irene carried it to the three-seater wooden outhouse near the barns across the wide courtyard, in the middle of which stood a pump on a flagstone pedestal with hooks for water pails and a dipper. Wandering around freely were the clucking hens, crowing roosters, squawking geese, and waddling ducks—all of them pecking, fluttering, flapping. I stared with curiosity each time Mrs. Bodnar imprisoned one of the geese between her thighs and, with her hands and a long finger, stuffed a bowlful of mush into its forced-open beak, mouthful after mouthful, and massaged it down the long feathered neck. After she killed a chicken, its decapitated head with closed eyes lay quietly on one side of the grass while its body thrashed about in wild jerks away from it.

Behind the courtyard were the barns where the hired man, Miklos, milked the cows and led them to and from the pasture. There were horses and a pigsty. Miklos smelled of them all. He had little shoe-button brown eyes and pock-indented skin through which only the black dots showed of a beard that could get no further. He liked to take the dog, Dexter, to hunt woodchucks in the after-supper evenings.

One evening I asked to go along. We walked a bit down the road against the fading light. Dexter ran ahead, turning every little while to see if we were following. Miklos stopped to light his pipe and to spit. Abruptly, the dog stopped by the side of the stone wall that separated the road from the field beyond. He sniffed twice and sneezed. His hind quarters trembled as he began pawing, digging against a firm rock. He whined, and his tail whipped back and forth in a kind of rhythm. Miklos went closer. The dog gave a plaintive yelp and continued to paw the earth faster and harder. When there was enough of a hole, Miklos removed the rock and there was the head of a live woodchuck, its long front teeth chattering—with fright? rage? The dog barked—short, high, thin barks. His head jerked forward each time. He couldn't quite get at the woodchuck, whose neck was held fast between stones. Miklos chuckled and made teasing clucking sounds. As the dog made another move toward the woodchuck, Miklos took him by the collar and, holding it fast, slowly pulled him toward the rat-shaped head until his nose was but a few inches from it. He whined—scared. His eyes rolled to look at Miklos, and he pulled back in retreat so that his head almost slipped through the collar, the back of his neck wrinkled into deep folds that held the collar tight against itself and against the hand that was holding it. The woodchuck's eyes blinked, narrowed into slits, opened wide, bulged from its head, and shone like tiny headlights in the deepening dark.

Miklos pulled from his pocket a short rope with his free hand. It had a noose tied to one end of it, and he slipped this over the woodchuck's head. He let go of the dog, and with the long end of a stick he carried he tightened and poked the knot into place. He removed one of the stones pressing against the animal's neck and, with a sudden jerk of the rope, held the dangling woodchuck high in the air, its short legs clawing frantically into the dark nothing. The dog kept barking and jumping toward it. Miklos would tease by lowering the stick but still keeping it out of the dog's reach. When he jumped for it, Miklos jerked it high in the air. Tobacco juice trickled through his slightly open mouth and drooled down on his chin. He spat and made sucking noises to the dog, which kept barking and circling and jumping as the rope lowered and raised and lowered and the woodchuck chattered and clawed the air, its eyes now closed. At one point, Miklos tripped and the rope dropped. The dog sank its teeth into the back of the woodchuck's neck and shook it in a sort of frenzied way. Miklos, regaining his balance, beat the dog loose of its grip. The body of the woodchuck hung still. Around the neck the fur was darker and the hairs spiky, but I could still hear its metrical chatter. For a second the chattering stopped.

Miklos looked at the woodchuck and then poked it with his pipestem. The chattering resumed. The rope was lowered and raised and lowered until we reached back to the courtyard. The dog, his tongue lolling out of the side of his mouth, looked up, waiting. Miklos looked at the woodchuck, which hung still, its belly heaving ever so slightly, and, raising it high and with a swinging motion, tossed it to the dog, which picked it up and shook it, dropped it, picked it up again and shook it some more before lying down and guarding the small heap between its paws.

I felt sorry for the woodchuck, but I did not connect its death with the cruelty. I thought that's what happens to all woodchucks when they're hunted and get caught—and that's how dogs behave. But after this, I grew a hatred for Miklos and kept away from him.

In the course of the three summers we spent on the farm, I grew to be thirteen years old and was slow in "putting away childish things," but the grown-up things were again unpleasantly happening to me.

One afternoon, on my way into the house, Mr. Bodnar beckoned me over to where he was lying on the porch chaise, taking his siesta after the midday meal. When I came near enough, he pulled me down next to him, kissed me on the mouth, and held and fondled my budding breasts. His tongue and big moustache in my mouth and his calloused hand plunging down the neck of my blouse froze me, and I couldn't move until he stopped when he heard footsteps approaching from the yard. I could not say anything, tell anyone. The silence of fear. I tried to avoid being near him when no one else was around, but I sensed he was lying in wait for me. It happened again twice.

Back home we lived for two years in one of the rapidly growing new residential developments in Astoria, Long Island City, on a freshly plowed, short little street that called itself "Third Avenue," at whose dead end rose a midget of a grassy mountain christened "Bunker Hill," where we played warring Indians. Our house was one of a row of attached two-story, one-family brick dwellings with a backyard large enough for a clothesline, a tree, and one or two spring crocuses. We had a French live-in housekeeper-cook, Andrée; a French teacher, Mlle. Campiche, who came once or twice a week to take us on some cultural outing or to her New York Lexington Avenue apartment for tea and little sandwiches; and a piano teacher, who came to the house once a week. On Saturday mornings we took lessons from a fencing master, Louis Senac, in his 57th Street salle d'armes. I attended a Lutheran Sunday School, was confirmed in a white voile dress, and devoured Jules Verne's *Around the World in Eighty Days* and Alexandre Dumas's *The Count of Monte Cristo.*

I became conscious of the fact that other neighboring families, other households, were quite different from ours. Mothers stayed home, did the cooking, and made costumes for the children's parties, and fathers came home from their offices at the end of the day. On Sundays they visited relatives or received them. We had French Andrée, who didn't speak English, was almost six feet tall, and had to shave a dark beard from her cheeks and chin every morning. Despite the powder she dabbed over it, the darkness came through. Whenever the oceanliner *The Leviathan* docked in New York harbor, she would gather us together and take us to the pier in Manhattan, where we would board the ship and spend the afternoon amid the tarts and cakes and whipped cream while Andrée disappeared for a couple of hours with her friend, the first-class pastry chef.

Our mother was now thirty years old, and her friends were, for the most part, men. Unlike other girls' mothers, she didn't have a special woman friend, a confidante, someone to "go shopping" with. The fact was, she often declared, she didn't like women. There were a few whose politically liberal positions she shared or who were the wives of men she knew or who were artistically recognized in their fields with whom she socialized, but not in a woman-to-woman kind of way. Among these were Marcelle, the wife of Joseph Wood Krutch, drama critic of *The Nation,* and the celebrated feminist and pacifist, Mme. Rosika Schwimmer. Remembering "tea" in her apartment, I see a room mostly in colors: the silver tea service and fragile tea cups on hemstitched doilies framed by the shadow darkness of late afternoon before lamplighting. By assimilating through osmosis more than by understanding the issues involved, there formed in my consciousness a dividing line between what and who one was expected to be for and against from among the people and things my mother and her friends discussed. Good names were Clarence Darrow, Nicola Sacco and Bartolomeo Vanzetti, Robert La Follette, Heywood Broun; some of the bad names were Ku Klux Klan, Al Capone, the Daughters of the American Revolution.

Even before we moved to Astoria, my mother's intimate friend, Dr. Ward, was replaced by a Dr. Havas, and now a new man in her life, an architect, was about to move in with us. None of these men attempted to be a father to us. They were just there, and they were just "nice." I hardly paid attention, busy as I was playing Indians on Bunker Hill, trading marbles, doing homework, fencing, and ringing doorbells on the block to sell stamps for tuberculosis, which I pronounced *"toobercoolosis."* When the architect moved in, we had to find a larger place to live. In January 1927, three months after my fourteenth birthday, we moved back to Manhattan at 9 West 91st Street. It was a five- or six-story building with a roomy cage elevator run by an elevator man whose only pretension to a uniform was a cap with a visor. He was also the janitor, and his name was George. There were two apartments to each floor on either side of the elevator, each running the full length of the building.

Our mother had by this time established a fine enough reputation as a designer to be engaged to make up the Spring and Fall lines for nationally known firms like Vanity Fair, Munsingwear, and others. This made it necessary for her to travel to their factories in other states for at least a fortnight a few times a year. Since she was as extravagant as she was resolute and talented and as impetuous and possessive as she was generous, and in addition was witty, hysterical, and a dexterous bluffer, our next five years seesawed between feast and fine purple and the dispossession slip under our entrance door. Considering herself a journalist as well as a designer, our mother wrote and sent articles and "interviews" to newspapers and magazines in Budapest; thus, she joined the foreign press correspondents at their gatherings in New York.

Replacing Andrée as our live-in housekeeper-cook was Hungarian Zsuzsi, who never felt the need to learn English beyond "yes," "no," and "please"; thus, speaking to her in her own language was unavoidable in order to communicate. The kitchen was her castle, and no one was allowed to touch anything there without her permission. As a nod to democracy, our mother—too often, we thought—made us help Zsuzsi dry the dishes after dinner. Mondays and Tuesdays a laundress, Mrs. Chernowitz, came to wash and iron, and every so often a seamstress would come to sew and mend in the dining room where the sewing machine was kept. All the stations were covered, and our mother was free to come and go and travel when she had to.

Although we didn't share in each other's activities, I was fiercely attached to my sister. I loved her because she was a part of my life, like my mother and the home we lived in together. She was too young then for me to consider an equal, a friend to confide in. I knew she was my mother's favorite, but my feeling about that was not jealousy of Sue but rather resentment of my mother's unfairness. I could ask her for permission for us to go to the movies on a Saturday afternoon and she would refuse, but if Sue asked she always gave her consent. I learned to get Sue to do the asking.

Six years after we came to "vast America," in the course of which our mother dutifully informed our father how the children were and sent him snapshots of us regularly, she decided on a return visit to Budapest with her children. On arrival, the railroad station, like all big stations in European capitals, smelled of smoke and iron and was in motion all over: porters wheeling luggage trolleys or strapping suitcases onto their backs, travelers arriving and departing and being embraced, voices calling, and whistles blowing.

Artúr Székely in 1927 when Yvette and Sue Szekely visited him in Hungary while on vacation.

When our father came to the hotel, he seemed to be not as tall as I knew him at the age of eight. He limped and used a cane, the result of an accidental fall. He was now forty years old. The face I had not forgotten was rounder and fuller, and his head was balding. He and my mother were formal with each other and did not associate socially during this visit. He would call for us at prearranged hours almost every day and take us to his home, where he lived with his wife, Anny, and their four-year-old son, Thomas. By the end of our visit, the experience fused into one enormous feast, street lights along the river bank shining back and shimmying on the Danube, cafés, restaurants, graveled walks, cobblestones, wide avenues, and the smell of chestnut trees. We had been together and high-teaed and dined with a large assortment of relatives and their friends.

* * *

On my sixteenth birthday my mother was thirty-three years old. She was about five feet tall and small boned and wore her short brown wavy hair parted on the side or in the center. Her brown eyes looking out from her refined, narrow, chiseled face revealed her passionate partisanship, the certainty that she was decisively for or against something—never in the open zone. She didn't frequent hairdressers or cosmeticians for her smooth, unblemished skin; she applied only powder from the round orange Coty box printed with powder puffs. She did, however, care for her elegant, small, expressive hands and had her nails manicured, although never painted. Her tailored dresses and suits were of the best quality silk, wool, or linen, and their color or flare or the show of cleavage that they allowed kept them from looking severe. She wore no jewelry of any kind except for her wedding ring. She was excitable; arrogant when she found fault; and shrill as she recounted a grievance, accusation, or plea, the flush on her bosom deepening to dark rose.

Midafternoon guests began to arrive for the birthday party. My sister and I; my best friend, Margie Stengel; and three other school friends were the only young people. All the others were around my mother's age and older. Many were the habitués of the "open house," a sort of salon Mother created in our apartment Sunday afternoons and evenings for her circle of friends, which included artists, writers, singers, composers, and critics. How she came to be the center for these gatherings I can but ascribe to her talent for beguiling with a warm, insistent hospitality and her attraction to people of renown. Zsuzsi always had mountains of good home-cooked food prepared for the weekends, and today there was a special cake with sixteen candles.

My reflection in the mirror looked back at me with just "regular brown-eyes" eyes and short brown hair, not curly enough and not straight enough, I thought. I wished my nose were narrower and my height taller, but with my even features, slim good figure, and shapely legs, all seemed adequate to escape lament or applause.

It was at this time that my mother began finding fault with my small vanities: combing a curly strand of hair forward, above one eye, instead of pulling it back off the face; wanting silk stockings and Cuban heels; reading *Son of the Sheik.* I felt she was more and more disapproving of me at a time when I craved acceptance and exclusive interest and was ready to attach myself with devotion to anyone who might offer it. I felt helpless in the face of an uncanny way she had of tricking me into an admission of some wrong by pretending she already knew it as a fact. Increasingly, it seemed to me, she would find reasons to get angry at me and yell, and I, shrinking from confrontation and from the knife-edge of her raised voice, fanned her fury by saying nothing to reassure her—only smiling. Neither of us knew that the smile was not an insolence but a form of hysteria that I had no control over. It was after such clashes that I wanted to pack my toothbrush and move out. Yet between these adolescent storms of rebellion, our little family of three depended on one another. We were attached. My only wish as I blew out my sixteen birthday candles was that I had passed last Friday's Latin test in Mr. Henry's class. Margie and I had a special "thing" for the tall, red-haired, rather good-looking Mr. Henry, whom we followed after school into the subway and stared at from a distance until he got off at his station.

One Saturday afternoon I stood by our apartment's front door with my hand on the knob. A storm cloud that hung low over my mother and me just then, some big or small grievance, drove me to announce that I was leaving home, moving out. Without a packed bag or a plan other than that I would hide out in a friend's house in New Jersey where no one would be likely to look for me, I took a last glance at the living room that faced me. I saw my mother sitting in a corner armchair by the window, suddenly and ominously quiet. Before that there had been a seismic clash of wills. Seeing me now about to open the door, she seemed to feel helpless to stop me. Looking at me from where she sat, she said in a weary, uncharacteristically matter-of-fact tone, "Well, before you go, I have something to tell you."

"What?" I asked sullenly, taking a few steps into the room, stone certain that whatever she had to tell me would not stop me from leaving.

"I am not your real mother. Your mother was a French prostitute who abandoned you."

For a moment, the words didn't penetrate. It was what I imagine a sudden knife stab is like before it starts to hurt and bleed. I saw only her soft wavy hair and brown eyes that now looked so disturbed. As I stared at her, incredulous, bewildered, she went on.

"I first met you when you were nineteen months old, a pathetic, neglected-looking, unkempt, dirty little child, your stomach bloated from a poor diet of mainly potatoes. You had rickets."

I saw in my mind the picture of a tiny girl with matted dark hair, separated from her mother by the jostling street crowds of the French Revolution, just as in the movie *Orphans of the Storm.*

"I picked you out of the gutter," I heard my mother say. "I bathed you and diapered you and nursed you back to health." A wave of gratitude swept over me.

"I supported you, made sacrifices for you. Is this the thanks I get? Is this how you repay me?"

My pity for the little girl dredged up a sense of debt so enormous that it dwarfed my will to leave. I can't go now, ran a thought; I have a debt I must pay. Too shaken to ask questions, afraid of answers, I just watched my mother rise from her chair and leave the room.

It was a grey-white winter afternoon and slowly getting dark. I stood by a window looking out on an excavated lot across the street where building construction was going on. Workmen stood around a little bonfire. I fixed on its orange glow, and there filed past me, as in a parade, scenes from my sixteen years: the night-filled room in a Chicago rooming house, my five-year-old sister in the double bed with our mother, who was telling her the story of how it was when she was born—what a lovely baby, they had all said, how loved. Having no story to tell me when I asked made me feel left out as I lay alone on the extra cot.

The same Chicago room on another night. Our mother has gone out for the evening, leaving us children in the care of the landlady. We make up a game, standing by the front window, counting Checker cabs passing by on Washington Boulevard. Later one of them stops in front, and two men are carrying the limp body of our mother into our room. One of the men, the driver, leaves. I watch with fright and anxiety as the landlady and the other man hover over her, trying to revive her. One of them holds a bottle of smelling salts to her nostrils. Her head begins to turn from side to side. She moans. Her eyelids begin to flutter, and her flushed chest begins to rise and fall. More moans. The man says something we can't hear to the landlady and then leaves. He is the Army colonel our mother followed to Chicago, and this evening he tried to tell her their affair was over. Our mother's hysteria could feign death to get what she couldn't have. Lying in bed that night, worrying what would happen if my mother died, I wrought a child's instant solution to erase the unbearable thought: when she was dead I would cut off one of her arms at the elbow and hug it against me on my pillow all night, every night, keeping it—keeping *her*—with me always.

I had no such solution, not any solution now. My mother was not my mother, my sister was not my real sister. I was an outsider in my own family, and the truth was starting to hurt, more especially because I felt wrenched from my sister, whom I loved. Turning from the window, feeling as though I had swallowed a piece of lead, I looked at the familiar objects in the room as if I had never seen them before: my mother's box of Melachrino straw-tipped cigarettes next to the ashtray I gave her for Christmas, the red poppy embroidered on a sofa cushion, the etching hanging to the left of the bookcase—objects so familiar, so everyday that I had stopped seeing them, now stood out in high relief. At dinner in the dining room I fell into a dumb silence. The next day I went to school as usual. I told no one.

Some time later, looking for a postage stamp in a drawer in my mother's desk, a half-folded letter not in its envelope lay in full view. It was written in French in neat, evenly slanted strokes with rounded o's and a's. I started to read the part facing up: "Be a second mother to my child! If you will be as good to her as you have been cruel to me, she should be assured of a happy life." It was signed "Marthe Meylan." I slammed the drawer shut as if fearful of being caught red-handed at something, but those lines haunted me then and consumed me with curiosity.

2

Enter TD: 1929–30

One January evening in 1929 Sue and I came home around nine o'clock from an evening of dinner and school homework with Margie and her sister, Betty, to find no one at home. We sat on the hall bench by the elevator waiting for Mother. In a little while a taxi stopped in front of the house, and our mother came in followed by a tall, bulky man whose ruddy cheeks hung loose, making jowls where they reached his chin, under which there bunched a wad of skin, which gave him a long, fleshy face. I thought he looked old enough to be someone's grandfather. Our mother invited him to "come up and meet the children." Once in the apartment, he seated himself on the living room sofa and gazed on us with his deep-set eyes, blue-grey and intent under the visor of heavy brows. One eye looked straight ahead, the other just a little to the side, giving the effect of a magnetic force that draws and holds attention. He had a high-domed forehead and thin white hair combed back; a sort of power from him floated around the room. Sue and I, in our school middies, kneesocks, and saddle oxfords, came forward and were introduced to a Mr. Dreiser. Not knowing who he was—our divorced mother had many men friends—I don't think we were terribly interested. We shook hands politely and answered a few get-acquainted questions, then excused ourselves and retired to our rooms.

It was not until the next day that our mother told us he was Theodore Dreiser, America's foremost novelist, whom she had just interviewed for a Budapest newspaper the evening before, after which

Theodore Dreiser and Yvette Szekely as
they looked in 1929 when they met.

he had taken her out for dinner. She told us he was famous and celebrated, the author of *An American Tragedy,* which was acclaimed as the greatest American novel. My out-of-school reading then embraced William Henry Hudson's *Green Mansions,* Jacob Wasserman's *Caspar Hauser,* Rabelais's *Gargantua and Pantagruel,* Upton Sinclair's *Boston,* Erich Maria Remarque's *All Quiet on the Western Front,* and, of course, the thumb-printed, corners-curled softcover copy of *Lady Chatterley's Lover* that was now being passed around surreptitiously in the school cafeteria for a "no more than two days lend" by a classmate who had received it from her sister in London.

After his brief stopover at our house, my mother began to be invited—along with the other writers, painters, publishers, scientists, actors, actresses, poets, singers, dancers, concert artists, and literary critics who attended—to Dreiser's renowned open-house Thursday evening receptions at his Rodin Studios apartment at 200 West 57th Street. There, in a thirteenth- and fourteenth-floor cathedral-like duplex, Dreiser lived with Helen Richardson and their tall white Russian wolfhound, Nick. He suggested that my mother "bring the children," and once or twice before Easter Sue and I were taken along; but it was six months before we were invited regularly to these gatherings as well as to "just us" dinners at home and at their country estate, Iroki (meaning "beauty" in Japanese), at Mount Kisco, New York.

My mother took me shopping for a dress to wear to my first 57th Street party. In a little Broadway dress shop, we found a princess-line aqua silk dress with a gently draped cowl neckline. Sue, being only thirteen, had not graduated to this yet. That evening, on the Central Park West streetcar to Columbus Circle, the few blocks walk to the southwest corner of 57th Street, and up the elevator to the thirteenth floor, I felt expectant but also apprehensive, it being the first time that I had been to an adult party at the home of a celebrity.

A maid in black uniform and white tea apron opened the door. We entered a spacious foyer, to the left of which was a staircase to an upper story. Facing us on a wall by the stairs hung a caricature of Theodore Dreiser as a seated Japanese feudal baron in an elaborately patterned costume, and near it a striking red pastel drawing of a wild-eyed, windblown youth. To the right of the foyer was an enormous room, two stories high, with studio windows. At one end was a Steinway piano, and on the adjacent wall hung a full-length oil painting of Dreiser by Wayman

Adams. In the middle of the vast room—now filled and humming with people in both formal and informal dress—was a long and deep-seated free-standing sofa. Its arms were as high as its high back, and the seating part was not far from the floor. Someone remarked, "To sit on it is to lose your personality." Beyond it, toward one of the cathedral windows, stood Dreiser's gargantuan writing desk, converted from his famous songwriter brother's piano. On it were the usual pen and pencil cups, letter openers, and ornate little boxes for paperclips and rubberbands.

My eyes zeroed in on a doll: a doll that was an American Indian standing about a foot tall, holding closed the blanket draped on his shoulders. Under the blanket, he wore a shirt with a small print design. His swagger-brimmed felt hat could be lifted off to show his coarse black hair, parted in the middle and worn in two hanging braids. His high-cheeked, stern, walnut-brown face with its horizontal frown lines and watchful eyes surveyed all within his vision. I still retained a flicker of delight in dolls, especially if a hat or a shoe was removable.

The rest of that room held some high-backed chairs that looked as if monarchs might have sat on them. Off this room was a dining room. I don't know what the others were drinking, but Sue and I had lemonade. I was too ignorant to know who many of the seventy-five or more guests were, among them the authors, editors, and critics Burton Rascoe, Ernest Boyd, Claude Bowers, Max Eastman, and Arthur Davison Ficke. I had heard of "Dr. Brill," the noted psychoanalyst, and was aware that the banker Otto Kahn had some connection with the Metropolitan Opera. I knew about Miriam Hopkins because she was a movie actress, and I *did* read Alexander Woollcott's newspaper column. Sherwood Anderson's name was also very familiar because I had heard so much talk about his book *Winesburg, Ohio.* On meeting John Cowper Powys, I saw a small, dark, gnome-like presence whom I could easily imagine as storm-windy and romantic, stepping with fiery intensity through fog on the moors.

That evening I did not feel like an independent me but as one of a pair with my sister, and we together as my mother's daughters. I watched the people clustered around Mr. Dreiser, which was what Sue and I called him, who was sitting on one of those baronial chairs, his mood jovial as he argued and laughed and seemed to be enjoying his party. He appeared to me less startling than that first night he came to our house, and now I was impressed by his fame. Voices hushed to silence when Mr. Dreiser asked Helen to sing to the piano accompaniment of a guest. She sang in her warm, husky voice "Sometimes I Feel like a Motherless Child," bringing out all the wistful, sad longing in that spiritual. After this gathering and another like it, we saw Mr. Dreiser just once more—when he and Helen came to our house for dinner—before Sue and I went to spend our Easter vacation in St. Louis, where our mother was designing the Spring line for one of the big lingerie manufacturers.

A green plush smell permeated the overnight train to St. Louis, and friendly black porters in white jackets were deftly making up its dark-curtained sleeping berths. Sue and I, traveling alone, matched fingers—"odds or evens"—for an "upper." After our first day in the Hotel Warwick and a visit to the St. Louis Zoo, I was hospitalized with an abscess in my throat where tissue remained from an earlier tonsillectomy. I lay in a room to myself, where the young sandy-haired Dr. Soule came a few times a day. He was tender and comforting, and I was sad to leave the hospital when it was time to go.

At my mother's suggestion, I sent Mr. Dreiser a picture postcard of the hotel, marking our window with an "X" and closing with the standard "wish you were here." He answered with wishes for a speedy recovery and the promise of an Easter present when we returned to New York. Although the "Easter present" was a box of candy for both Sue and me, I was impressed and felt flattered to have a letter from him addressed to me. Also, I was surprised.

On the train back to New York, my mother, Sue, and I were returning to our parlor car seats from lunch in the dining car when one of two strange ladies, elbowing and pushing their way through, said to me, "Your mother should be ashamed to allow a young girl to read a book like that!" I was holding *The Well of Loneliness,* by Radclyffe Hall, a then much-talked-about book that simply read to me like a good story with no particular message. It only enlightened me to the fact that there was a painful thing called "housemaid's knee," which was gotten from scrubbing floors.

One weekend before the closing of school for the summer we were invited to Iroki. Except when we were in his company, I did not think about Mr. Dreiser. My preoccupations were with the daily business of school and after-school projects with one or another friend from my classes as well as the concerns that come with being sixteen. The drive

The photograph of Yvette *(right)* and Sue Szekely that they sent to Theodore Dreiser in 1930.

to Mount Kisco was nothing short of glamorous: riding in the boat-long Chrysler Imperial with the top down, Helen in her picture hat and gauntlet gloves at the wheel, the space beside her filled with the commanding whole of Mr. Dreiser, and in the back seat my mother, Sue, and I, with the wolfhound, Nick, between us. Until we left the city blocks behind and were on the Bronx River Parkway, people walking on the sidewalks turned to stare at us as at a pageant.

Having become this better acquainted, addressing Mr. Dreiser as "Mr. Dreiser" felt too stiffly formal, but at the same time I did not feel "old enough free" to call this fifty-eight-year-old celebrity "Teddy," so Sue and I began to call him TD. We had no problem about calling Helen (who was a few months younger than my thirty-four-year-old mother) "Helen," however. She was tall and softly curved, with gold-flecked tea-colored hair worn girlishly to almost shoulder length. She had a broad, friendly smile and a lowish throaty voice that could, in

TD's presence, launch into an appealing chuckle or even babytalk when she called him "Toady." She wore floaty as opposed to tailored clothes, and her characteristic expression was either a seeking one—seeking TD's approval—or a hairbreadth anxious one, which seemed to inquire, "Is everything all right?"

Driving out of Mount Kisco's main street along the unpaved Old Road, we arrived at the high stone wall that encircled the thirty-five-acre estate. A split solid wood gate was painted a deep cerulean blue and swung open from the middle, halving the "O" of the carved IROKI letters that stood on its top ledge. Facing the main house, one saw its horizontal logs perched on a fieldstone foundation high enough to require a railed stone stairway to its front door. The pitched shaggy roof of bark-covered shingles slanted down at a steep angle to the very eyebrows of the odd-shaped windows, making the house look a little like the gingerbread house in *Hansel and Gretel.* A stained brown frame guest house, some several yards to its left, was connected to the main house by a rustic bridge.

TD's height and bulk made him look heavy but not fat, and he walked with a slight side-rocking loll. His manner toward Sue and me was playful, kidding—admonishing my thirteen-year-old sister to straighten up and urging me to turn cartwheels, at which I was pretty good—as he walked with us across a field to show us the little log cabin under the brow of a hill. He behaved toward us like an indulgent father or grandfather but without patronizing us or acting superior. I felt he liked us and enjoyed having us there, and we liked *him.* If the main house made me think of Hansel and Gretel, this little cabin was the real thing, with its sloping, A-shaped, thatched roof, now canvas covered, reaching almost to the ground, its tall stone chimney, and its cutouts for windows here and there with wood shutters like European peasants' huts. The log door was split so that the upper half could be opened independently of the bottom. Inside was a darkish room with a big open fireplace, a studio couch, a wood table, and some chairs. Outside, surrounded by tall waving grass and slim, lace-leaved hickory trees, a round tabletop made from wood slats was nailed to a table-height tree trunk. TD told us that the construction of the cabin was supervised by the stone and wood sculpture artist Wharton Esherick. Just after it was built, John Cowper Powys, the first one to sleep in the cabin, which reminded him of houses on the moors of his native Wales, had performed a rite, invoking the favors of charitable spirits. Parallel with the cabin, some hundred yards on a hillcrest with a view of the reservoir, was a more prosaic two-room grey clapboard house with a deck-like porch and overhang, and near it was a huge tepee on which TD's artist friend Ralph Fabri had painted a kaleidoscope of colors—symbols of clouds, sun, lightning, rainbow, and rain.

Theodore Dreiser in front of the log cabin at Iroki, 1930.

That night we ate dinner on bright-colored pottery plates in the big stone studio, half below ground level of the main house, where TD worked at his writing at the handsome long table Esherick had made for him. The room looked out to an artificial pond, young trees, and rolling hills beyond. Among other guests that weekend were, besides Fabri, who had had a hand in the construction of the house, another painter, Jerome Blum, and his wife, Frankie; Kathryn Sayre, who was doing research for TD; and Esther McCoy. After dinner, TD sat in his rocker by the log fire, folding, unfolding, and pleating a white handkerchief, stirring up conversation as though he were tossing out crumbs to a flock of pigeons for the pleasure of watching them peck. It was like a staged performance, in which whatever one person said to another was really intended to be heard by TD. I had the impression that, drawn by the magnetism of fame, they felt privileged to be part of the celebrated author's small intimate circle and that he needed the stimulus—that without the challenging discussion and interplay he'd be lonely, even a little sad.

W. A. Swanberg, who interviewed my mother in connection with his biography of Dreiser, said that "Margaret Szekely, who had come to this country as a representative of a Budapest newspaper but had switched to dress designing," was among the Hungarians who added an "international flavor" to TD and Helen's parties. This may be partially true, but he seems to have been completely taken in by her invention that TD "leaned" on her as his confidant, that she supplied his need for a mother, that "he would come and weep because Helen didn't understand him," and that he would often "frantically" telephone her in the middle of the night to ask if she had an extra bed for him. From what I observed, it was not true.

Among the people my mother met that spring was Nellie Seeds, wife of Scott Nearing, the political scientist and left-wing author. Nellie Seeds had established a school and children's camp, Manumit (meaning "to release from slavery or servitude"), on their farm in Pawling, New York, and it was there that my mother arranged to send Sue and me for the summer of 1929. Margie and Betty Stengel's parents did the same. Besides the counselors, the nutritionist-cook, and the farmer who cut and stacked the hay in the fields below Quacker Hill, there lived at Manumit a few young men and several young women without discernible job assignments, who were neither summer campers nor staff.

They were just *there,* presumably to be with or around Scott Nearing, then forty-six years old. They were drawn to him by his stern magnetism, sinuous good looks, and revolutionary left-of-socialist gospel. His hair was cropped so close that his fine-shaped head looked almost shaved. In shorts and stripped to the waist, he was seldom without a shovel in his hands. Among that unassigned group was Helen Knothe, who plied a mysterious philosophy called *theosophy* and who not long after that summer married Scott Nearing. Because Scott ate only a salad of raw vegetables with peanuts and olive oil, we too insisted on exactly the same from rough-hewn wood bowls. Our singing sessions were not "Home on the Range" or "Funiculi-Funicula" but rather stirring promises that "The International Soviet" would "be the human race."

I was having my first romance. It was with Scott's son, seventeen-year-old Johnny Nearing. He was short and not conventionally handsome but intellectually precocious, witty, and charming. We dug ditches, pitched hay, swam in the clear icy pool of a dammed-up spring under overhanging tree branches and the moist green smell of ferns, listened to his classical records, and, in the evenings after supper, walked—holding hands—to a spot in the woods, lay on a bed of soft pine needles and leaves, and kissed and counted stars. Johnny said we would have ten children someday. We wanted to sleep out in sleeping bags one night, but I was not permitted to unless an older counselor, Grace, was willing to be chaperon. She was and we did—Johnny on one side, I on the other, and Grace in the middle. It wasn't quite what we had hoped. I took to wearing a pair of Johnny's old faded red basketball shorts he gave me as a token of our "connection." This upset one of the counselors, who tried to persuade me not to wear them, saying it was "unhygienic."

Fragments of socialist-communist doctrine fell around and between these summer camp activities. Without really understanding the issues beyond the rebellion impulse of radical innocence, I took up the slogans "Workers of the world, unite" and "Religion is the opiate of the people." Johnny tried to explain about dialectical materialism. Unable to link it to anything in my own experience, I nodded comprehension, although it wasn't too clear to me. Grace explained about the splinter groups—the Lovestonites and the Trotskyites—who opposed something called the Comintern.

When the summer was over, Johnny was to enter the freshman

class at the University of Wisconsin, then widely acclaimed for its liberal and experimental programs under the directorship of the educator Alexander Meiklejohn, and I was going back to my third year in high school. Possibly recognizing my passage into young adulthood, my mother's nod to sex education was a present of Havelock Ellis's *Sex in Civilization,* inscribed, "To Yvette from Mother—September 2, 1929, New York City." No longer were our frictions about not washing hands or cleaning fingernails or putting things away. I recall my surprise and recoil at what I felt was the vulgarity of her criticism when, walking with her on the street, she told me to "stop swinging your arms like a prostitute—it's attention calling"; or "There's more to think about than what is between your legs." Although I blanked out the fact that she wasn't my "real" mother, I became more profoundly aware of her insecurities, her egotism, her fears, and—perhaps because of them—the dishonesties and misrepresentations that fed my distrust and rebellion.

Johnny and I were writing to each other. Although I made no secret of our friendship, my mother read his letters and decided to break up our relationship. When she went to Wisconsin for a fortnight that winter on a designing job, she invited Johnny for dinner. In his letter to me, he said that she took him to an elegant restaurant and told him that I was so inferior to him he would be wasting his time having anything to do with me. She then sent me a letter saying I had better forget about Johnny because his only interest in me was the same interest that a dog has in a streetcorner hydrant. Despite this betrayal, she would still seduce me back to her with the voice—warm, generous, witty, full of promises—that had made my world safe as a child. I either believed her anew or, when deceived, withstood the hollering that begged me to pacify her.

My mother and her friends were not among those who were wiped out by the stockmarket crash that October; nevertheless, my mother's jobs gradually dwindled. That fall, the summer's Manumit influence and the soft-radical, liberal-intellectual climate at home induced me to go the Young Communist League meetings and join in their engagements of liberation. I persuaded Eleanor Jensen, a school friend, to come with me to the Young Communist League and their missions. We both wore clothes that we thought would make us look proletarian, that is, tough and poor. At the meetings we were instructed to assume false names. I was Joan Roberts, and she was Mildred Brown, names that we often forgot to respond to. I was assigned with a few others to create "a crowd" around a soapbox on the corner of Tenth Avenue and 39th Street, in an area known as Hell's Kitchen, where one of us had to mount the box and make a speech reminding those curious enough to listen how miserable their lives really were, while the other handed out leaflets and copies of *The Daily Worker.*

Closer to home, the fact that the country was in a depression did not yet make itself felt, nor did it occur to me to wonder how my mother was managing financially. Zsuzsi was still serving us the same tasty caraway soup with croutons as the first course at dinner, followed by chicken paprika or stuffed peppers swimming in thick tomato sauce, and still baking almond crescents and latticed apricot squares for the weekends, warning Sue and me, just before leaving for her Sunday afternoons off, not to eat them *all.* My world was still enclosed within the bounds of school, skating, reading, tennis on Central Park's almost-free courts (permits were $2.00 per season), the movies, and, often enough, the theater.

This was the year when at the Stengel's dinner table the radio was turned on to the new program *Amos 'n Andy,* a comedy pair with their entourage of funny characters. We must have had a radio in our house, too, but I can't remember that we ever sat down to actually listen to it then. It was some years later that Fred Allen, Jack Benny, Edgar Bergen's Charley McCarthy, and Bing Crosby came into our lives. Besides the "battle hymn of the workers" type of songs from Manumit, Sue and I knew all the songs in Carl Sandburg's *The American Song Bag,* and we loved to sing. Among the Sunday afternoon guests were usually some who could and would play them on the piano for us. But whether from the radio or from records or wafted in by the atmosphere, we knew all the words to "I Can't Give You Anything but Love, Baby," "You're the Cream in My Coffee," and "Button Up Your Overcoat." We sang along to "He's got eyes of blue, I never cared for eyes of blue, but he's got eyes of blue, so that's my weakness now," rendered in the baby and sexy voice of Helen Kane, who gurgled "boop-boop-a-doop" after each confession. This was also the year the movies became "talkies," banishing from the silent film era those stars whose voices failed to match their roles. And I was reading Axel Munthe's *The Story of San Michele* together with George Eliot's school-assigned *Silas Marner,* which seemed boring by comparison.

Sue and I, with our mother or without her when she was away from New York on a job, continued to be invited for Iroki weekends at Mount Kisco and to the Thursday evenings at the studio on 57th Street, where mingling with the famous in the social, literary, and art world made me hate more and more what I now considered the mediocrity of public high school. Margie Stengel and I began cutting classes and then gradually playing hooky more and more often. We would scramble to the top-level seats of a double-decker bus and ride to its last stop in Washington Square or get off at 42nd Street and Fifth Avenue, where we would enter a Horn & Hardardt cafeteria and, over a cup of coffee, write poetry. Sometimes, when we saved enough of our twenty-five-cent lunch money to pay the cost of admission, we would go to a matinee at a theater on upper Broadway, where we saw first runs or revivals of plays such as *Dracula, The Shanghai Gesture, Charley's Aunt, Madam X,* and *The Trial of Mary Dugan.*

I had just finished reading TD's latest two-volume collection of stories, *A Gallery of Women,* and had started reading *An American Tragedy,* which eight years later he inscribed, "For Yvette, with love." It was the book that brought him to the height of his literary fame and, with *Sister Carrie* and *Jennie Gerhardt,* mirrored that detached, unmoralizing, but compassionate and forebearing acceptance he had of the headlong course of lives moving toward inevitable ends.

Dreiser has been variously described as heavy, brooding, lonely, old-spirited, grim, and humorless, but he wasn't that way with Sue and me. With us, he continued to be an affectionate father who was supportive and encouraging about our youthful discoveries, who liked kidding us, and who was playfully teasing, as in his words for greeting me: "Hello, Sox!" or telling me to go: "Dust," "Beat it," or "So long." He explained that he never said good-bye, being superstitious about its implied finality. One evening, sitting at the dining table in the 57th Street studio when Sue and I were the only dinner guests, we heard the sound of a buzzer. TD seemed not to know where the sound came from. He asked Pearl, the maid, whether someone had arrived. She said no. The buzzer sounded again and again at measured intervals. Sue and I were nonplussed until it turned out that TD was, for the joke of it, pressing with his foot a bell-buzzer hidden under the dining room rug. Leaving the table after dinner, Helen and I and Sue and TD settled on the sofa, chair, and cross-legged on the floor and, at TD's suggestion, made up a story. Helen started, then suddenly stopped at her chosen point, naming the next one to continue until the four of us had helped to weave the tale. We called it "The Story of Hyst" (Helen, Yvette, Sue, and Teddy), and it told of a prince, an enemy magician, a poisoned ring concealed in a tart, a Princess Cerise in danger, and the princess's deliverance. The almost sixty-year-old Dreiser in his bright blue shirt and bow tie seemed entertained and involved in the innocence of this amusement. When the hour grew late, we had to cut our fantasies short. Months later, in a letter to me, he—remembering Cerise—would use her as a model for an imaginary creature sent by the gods to hold him to restraint. Shortly after that evening, we gave him rather good photographs of Sue and me, and he responded with a note of thanks to his "special pets."

At home one Sunday afternoon the living room was humming with the talk and laughter of my mother's open house friends. I was sitting in the middle of our three-cushion sofa listening to what the two men on either side of me were saying. In a little while I saw approaching me with mock measured steps and balancing a cocktail glass in one hand the man with whom my mother was then intimately involved. When he arrived close enough, he made a magniloquently jesting low bow, bent forward toward me, planted a kiss on my forehead, and, straightening up, marched stiffly back to where he came from. We all laughed.

That night after everyone had left and only my mother and I were in the room—I emptying ashtrays and gathering glasses—she began to cry, that cello-deep, heaving crying. I had heard it before—during fights with my father, with Mr. Monahan, with the lovers—and hearing it always frightened me. Now it also surprised me, and I asked solicitously what the matter was. Her tear-wet face turned to me, she replied, "You have your whole life before you. Why must you take my friends away from me?"

I couldn't believe I had heard it right. I stammered, "What do you mean?" and then discovered that the kiss planted on my brow had kindled this scene. I knew I was innocent, and I felt deeply the injustice of this blow. More hurting was the fact that the mother I had wanted as a child was no longer there. In her place was someone who distrusted me and saw me as competition, provoking additional tension between us.

Recognizing in me an impulsive, unanchored, easily influenced young girl who craved acceptance and attention and would attach herself to anyone who offered it, my mother saw this as being not only threatening to herself but also dangerous for me. I was feeling more comfortable at the gatherings of her older friends at our house and at TD's than at school with persons my own age. Among this much older group I felt no challenge; I was not expected to match their contributions or to shine. Exposed to its intellectual-bohemian circle and without always understanding, I picked up and tasted crumbs from their exchanges. This gave me an inflated illusion of superiority over the boys and girls in high school so that I never went to their social or sporting events and never dated. My few school friends came from conventional families, and, as ever, my mother's home was patterned on a different lifestyle. Still it was something of an adventure for me to go to Greenwich Village with its little houses, winding streets with names, painted furniture in oranges and blues, windows draped in gauze, cushions placed on bare floors in large rooms and attics, and restaurants in basements. Although the bloom of bohemia's infancy was a little faded and it was getting harder to pay the cheap rents, the Village still had its own anarchic magic. I could see and I liked its differences from Astoria and from the residences between Central Park and Riverside Drive, with their restraining and secure three-piece living room suites. Nowhere in such places could I experience what I found, for example, at Esther McCoy's apartment on Leroy Street off Bleeker Street. We walked through an alley-like passageway to a little open courtyard that her entrance door fronted. The apartment looked especially "villagey" when we came in from the fading purple light of a winter afternoon: amber warmth from burning logs in a tiny fireplace, paisley throws, colorful pillows, straight up and down kitchen chairs, earth-pink Italian plates, lots and lots of books, an author called Max White who looked like a full white moon, earnest discussion about a Mike Gold article in his magazine *The New Masses.* I listened, I browsed among the books, discovered for the first time *The Ballad of Reading Gaol,* and ate boeuf bourguignon.

One Saturday afternoon, when Sue and I—our coats and scarves already on—were ready to leave our house to go to a matinee performance of *Rose-Marie,* I decided to promote myself to adult status and lit one of my mother's cigarettes. Despite the awful taste and the ensuing string of coughs, I forced myself to smoke it all. It must have taken at least ten minutes, to Sue's justified impatience and annoyance. It was after I lit my second one (most of the time holding it near my mouth rather than smoking it) at the next Thursday party to which we were invited that, standing near a bookcase and pretending to be absorbed so as not to look unengaged, TD came over, slipped a small, folded paper into my hand, and said, "Put this away and read it in private." He then walked past me to talk to someone else. With this gesture, a phase of my life began that I could not have anticipated in my wildest flights of fancy.

3

"Hello Sox": 1930

My immediate response to TD's gesture was a strange mixture of confusion and coolheaded self-awareness. I wasn't carrying a handbag, and I didn't know where to put the note, but I sensed that it needed to be concealed, so I put my cigarette into an ashtray and clutched the little square of paper in my left hand for the rest of the evening until we reached home. Even there in my room I didn't dare read it but placed it between the pages of my Spanish One grammar to read when I got to school.

In the relative privacy and quiet of study hall, I sat down at a far corner table and unfolded the note. It asked me to meet him for tea, alone, on Tuesday at five o'clock in the 57th Street Schrafft's. My glance moved off the paper on to the scratched brown table where the January sun, blazing through the tall windows, made warm stripes over the furrows of initials, crossbones, and hearts. A boy with a pink face and acne shuffled by and slouched into the chair opposite mine. I thought: The most famous and celebrated author in the whole country wants a "date" with me. Except for Johnny Nearing, whom I liked very very much but who was far away in Madison, I had tried dating only once. The boy had taken me up to the tar-paved roof of his apartment building and there, pinned against a sooty chimney stack, I endured a half hour of kissing. With his mouth on and in mine, I stared at the lights across the river along the Jersey shore and thought it all to be inglorious and demeaning but did not have the self-assurance to walk away. Now a famous author was interested in me, would know how to *know* me. The thought was as exciting as it was scary.

Kahlil Gibran's *The Prophet* turned up one day on the coffee table of the Stengels' living room. Margie and I looked over the table of contents and right away turned to Almustafa's revelation "On Love." It was the one that spoke to me not only because I was in that romantic, lyrical stage of wondering what would ever become of me but also because it was relevant to the approaching meeting with TD. The message both emboldened and condoned.

After school on the Friday before the Tuesday I was to meet TD at Schrafft's, Margie and I raked through her older sister Naomi's wardrobe to find something sophisticated looking that I might borrow. We found a grey knit sweater-blouse sprinkled with black embroidered coin dots. We decided I would wear that with one of my own skirts, my black leather jacket, and a wide-brimmed felt hat that tilted over one eye. We decided it all looked very Greta Garbo-ish.

Margie and I had been saving some of our lunch money in a lavender Louis Sherry tin candy box so that someday we might go to a tropical island, where we would drink coconut milk, wear seashells, and write poetry. Occasionally we dipped into this coffer for the price of a matinee. Tuesday being very cold, Margie suggested we take two dollars from the box for a taxi from 91st Street to 57th Street because "your nose always gets so red in the cold. It just wouldn't do for you to arrive looking like that." She said I must arrive ten minutes late and then remark, after a glance at my wristwatch, "Hmm, I understand it's fashionable to be late."

It was five o'clock winter dark when the taxi eased to a stop in front of the brightly lit Schrafft's. I saw it as sparkling. Walking past the candy counters to the back where the tables were, I spotted TD. On reaching him, he waved me to the chair opposite and, with amusement in his eyes and in his smile, greeted me with, "Hello, Sox, how was school today?" This, of course, immediately quashed my intended impression of me as woman of the world or femme fatale. My entrance line had no place to go. Never before had I been entirely alone with TD, and I now saw him as if for the first time. Everything about him was oversized, especially his commanding presence. After choosing cinnamon toast with my tea, I couldn't think of anything more to say and fixed my gaze on the bow tie and bright blue shirt that was his trademark. My ease when in his company *en famille* was now replaced by a mixture of entrancement and apprehension. I was flattered by this famous man's special interest, but although I wanted to be wanted and "understood" spiritually and romantically, I was afraid that he, who was sixteen when my *father* was born, had more in mind when he asked me to meet him alone than to find out how school was.

I glowingly, if shyly, listened to him tell me how lovely I was; how deeply he cared for me, for my poetic mind, youth, freshness; how he would like to help me find and achieve my goals. I pushed from the front to the back of my mind the hovering thought of that "more," though I knew that the very fact of my having come alone gave him license, in a way, to venture in that direction. Curiously, from behind the flushed face, the big head, big scallop of a mouth, big teeth, big fleshy ears, droopy jowls, and uneven eyes appeared a sentimental, dreamy adolescent talking about love and seeming no more profound or sophisticated than I. This made him feel "not old" to me. Just then we were equal except for the riveting, magnetic power he exuded, which eventually would become the support I craved. Whether it was my "father complex" or just the need I had from the day I was born to be wanted and *to belong*, I clung to it. I did not confront myself with the question of the morality of my coming or what Helen and my mother would think and feel if they knew. Yet when afterward he took me to a cheap movie house nearby in whose dark he groped to fondle me, I shrank away, embarrassed by his inelegance, and thought "inglorious" once more. I wanted the romance, the poetry, the admiration, the support, but not the physical fondling—not from him and not yet.

The next time we went to a Thursday gathering at TD's I was listening to Howard Scott explain to me what "technocracy" was—Mr. Scott's solution to the depression, whereby technicians would take over the economy—when TD came over and said he wanted to show me something. Mr. Scott turned to someone else, and I followed TD to his desk, where he asked me to meet him after school on Monday at a little Chinese restaurant on Broadway between 56th and 57th Streets. I went, and for many afternoons in the next several weeks we would meet again over pots of tea at the Chinese restaurant or over warm, dripping butter cakes at Childs' or at the Horn & Hardardt, where TD liked to go for tapioca pudding. As I listened to him wonder about the mystery and fortunes of life and marveled at his detached, nonjudgmental, yet compassionate acceptance of the *fact* of good and evil and weak and strong and as I gratefully responded to his fatherly interest in my young life and aspirations and his confident, cheering encouragement about meeting it, he became intensely, desperately important to me. It was the first time a commanding someone had focused exclusively on me: how did I feel, what did I think, what did I want, where was I going? He became for me a support to lean my back against. He told me that for him I was "youth," "poetry," "gaiety," "understanding," that my warmth aroused his mind and heart and all his sensual desire.

The seventeen-year-old me relished this—all except the pressure he began to apply with increasing frequency to go to bed with him. In a small and far-away corner of my mind, I suspected this possibility loomed larger in his thoughts than my "poetry" and "wisdom." I kept putting the event off with excuses like having to cram for midterm exams or run errands for my mother and "let's wait for spring." But I sensed that if I did not do as he wished, I would lose him, and by now that would have been too crushingly distressing to me.

I suppose that TD's attraction for me was in part related to other tensions in my life. About this time—partly because it was in vogue among teenagers—Sue and I began addressing our mother by her first name. I wasn't getting along with Margaret, as I now called her. She continued to criticize me, entrap me with guile and artful disguises, complain to me and about me among her friends, and shock me by her fabrications and duplicity. Then again, and as suddenly, she would become the temptress, at the same time making me feel I was the cause of her unhappiness. Her jobs were scarcer, and when dispossess notices began to appear in the morning mail, she often took to her bed sick again and borrowed money from her friends.

One morning, waking as usual at seven o'clock but still blank-minded and warm under the bed covers, I suddenly remembered that it was Tuesday, the day I was to meet TD at the 125th Street railroad station of the New York Central after my eleven o'clock Latin exam. It was the day he would take me to Mount Kisco for the "all the way," first-time great event. My concern about the Latin test was pushed sideways by this uneasy thought, which climbed to a level of anxiety not unlike one brought on by a scheduled session with the dentist to have a wisdom tooth pulled. We had arrived at the cliff edge where I could no longer put it off. I would either take a breath, hold it, scrunch my eyes shut, and go ahead or watch him walk away from me. I switched on the light and looked around: my painted orange "skyscraper" bookcase, the "modern" black finished oak desk with the silver stripe edges—a birthday present when I was fourteen—my portable hand-winding victrola, the gold-yellow theatrical gauze curtains fluting down the window and screening the ever-grey courtyard daytime. I mentally stroked the familiar look of my room as if the next time I saw it I and it wouldn't be the same. I felt a weight in my chest, a lump the size of a tennis ball. I couldn't touch it away or brush it off or scratch it. If a doctor asked, "Where?" I could have answered, "midway on the chest and turn inward."

Thinking to make it roll away, I picked up the borrowed copy of *The Prophet,* which I had planned to take along with me, and turned to "On Love" again, starting with the lines "When love beckons to you, follow him though his ways are hard and steep . . . yield to him though the sword hidden among his pinions may wound you." I took the book to the bathroom and propped it against the wall between the washbowl and the medicine chest and, while brushing my teeth, read on: ". . . for even as love crowns you, so shall he crucify you." Then the offer of a choice: either "bleed willingly and joyfully" or "pass out of love's threshing floor, into the seasonless world where you shall laugh but not all of your laughter, and weep but not all of your tears." Confronted by that two-edged blessing—freedom of choice—I realized that things need no longer just "happen" to me and that I could be held accountable for what I did and did not choose.

It being ironing day, Mrs. Chernowitz was already ironing when I went to breakfast. The friendliness of the morning kitchen with its smell of coffee and fresh linen, the taste of my thickly buttered roll with café au lait, and the sound of Mrs. Chernowitz's voice talking to Zsuzsi about her son's violin lessons made me feel as though everything outside my home was dangerous, or at least risky. After eating and just before leaving the house, I went to my mother's room where she was still in bed and told her that I was planning to spend the afternoon with a friend from Manumit who lived in Brooklyn, where we were going skating. I added, "I might not be home til later in the evening in case they ask me to stay for dinner."

"Call and let Zsuzsi know," she said as I kissed her good-bye. At the front door I felt like a fugitive and almost turned around to see if someone were following me.

It was one of those February days after a snowfall with grey-black smudged mounds of slush stacked along the street gutters and single-file paths footed hard down on the sidewalks. There was a faint stirring of spring in the chill, moist air, like a baby bird hunching one wing. I was among the last to leave the examination room and some fifteen minutes late when I ran up the long flight of iron stairs to the elevated platforms of the station. In a heavy tweed beige topcoat, silk paisley muffler crossed on his chest and tucked in, big brimmed hat pinched four sides in the crown into the suggestion of a point that made me think it looked like a cowboy hat, TD stood massive and towering near a ticket window. When he saw me approach he came toward me with his loose-jointed sway of a walk, his clouded expression changing to genial, and said, "I was just thinking maybe you wouldn't come." While explaining my lateness I noticed that he was holding a black leather satchel, like a doctor's bag. It made me uneasy and, after the train pulled in and we boarded and settled in coach seats facing each other, I summoned the courage to ask, "What is that bag for?"

"Oh, just some things we'll need," he said, "a rubber sheet, some Lysol." Visions of accident victims being wheeled to surgery flashed by.

"Oh," I said, and it sounded like the end of a sentence. Then, wanting to recapture the romantic mood the afternoon demanded and wanting to see my crowning—the joyful half of love's world without the partly suppressed laughter—through rose-tinted lenses, I offered to read the piece to TD, who probably didn't need to hear it but who loved to share poetry with me. In love with love, with poetry, and with the lover-father in this celebrated man, I wanted to prove to him that my feeling for him was large enough to brave or dismiss the "crucifixion" warning.

We stepped off the train in Mount Kisco into the wideness of the outdoors past snow-tipped trees and took one of those unmarked suburban taxis that look like private cars for the two-mile drive to Iroki. Its grounds were sheeted in unwrinkled white except for a double line of tire tracks to the main house. The butler, Frank, a light-skinned black man wearing a white jacket, opened the front entrance door, greeted TD, and said he had a log fire going in the sitting room. After taking off our coats, I followed TD there. He seated himself in a rocking chair by the fireplace, pulled me onto his lap, and, not talking, just held me and rocked. I felt like a little child curled up on a firm but soft ampleness, my cheek against the pilous burr of the cloth of his suit lapel that smelled faintly smoky brown. The snow outside in the afternoon light, the firelight inside, and the comforting warmth that touching bodies exude all added poetry and romance.

After a while, he led the way to an upstairs bedroom where he opened the black satchel and took out the rubber sheet, which he spread on the bed. While undressing, my mind lighted for a moment on the image of locker rooms and swimming pools. I lay down on the sheet, hoping this part of the "business" would soon be over with. Then a mountain lowered down on me, propping part of its weight on elbows. Next, the entering, the shoving until, after the puncture of the membrane up there inside me and the short, sharp pain, I heard a long loud wail, "Oh my God. Oh my God. Oh my God." This scared and surprised me. I wondered whether he would ever stop saying that—what could possibly be the matter or so overwhelming? I couldn't imagine—not if this was all there was to it. When the wailing finally stopped and the mountain rolled off of me, I heard TD say, in a crude attempt to be jocular, "You bleed like a little pig." I looked and saw the blood. He led the way to the bathroom, where he took some more things out of the black bag: a douche bag and the bottle of Lysol. After filling the bag with water and measuring out the proportion of the Lysol, he told me to sit on the toilet. Looking like a giant, naked, fat child, he stood in front of me holding the bulging red rubber bag high at arm's length, offered me the nozzle-ending tube, and told me where to put it. Happily relieved that it was over, I laughed up at him as the rinse washed into me, "You look like the Statue of Liberty holding the torch."

Dressing, I now felt frisky as a colt, while TD looked amused, satisfied, even dreamy. He was affectionate as we taxied to the train station and rode back to New York, getting off at Grand Central Station, where he hailed a cab and directed the driver to Lüchow's Restaurant on East 14th Street. We entered the wood-paneled turn-of-the-century dining room through frosted glass-swinging doors and were seated at a corner table. The chandeliers spread gold amber lights whose reflection in the mirrors around the walls looked like dots of jewels glowing back and giving the vast space a festive air. The ghosts of Diamond Jim Brady and Lillie Langtry in velvet and feathers hovered at the tables as did those of mustachioed gentlemen at the bar with their gold watch chains scalloped across their stomachs. Having so recently read *Sister*

Carrie, my imagination easily turned Lüchow's into Fitzgerald & Moy's and TD and me into Hurstwood and Carrie.

Between small bites of the boiled beef with horseradish sauce on my plate, I told him about the "babysitter" my mother had chosen for my sister and me at the Hotel Laclede, who tried to molest me when I was nine. I also told him about Mr. Bodnar's gropings that summer in Milford when I was thirteen—things bottled up and buried that, to my surprise, I now urgently wanted to tell and, after this day's events, felt for the first time that I could. They came bursting out as if someone had pressed a button. TD listened with the unsurprised detachment of one who, from a height, looks down at life and the human condition and nods, as if to say, "I know, I know everything and all the sad things, too, but there you are. That's the way it is."

I got home around eleven. My mother's bedroom door was closed and so was my sister's. No light from the kitchen. Zsuzsi must be in bed. I tiptoed hurriedly to the bathroom to examine my underwear for stains and quickly washed them. I then took a searching look in the mirror, wondering whether my face had changed, whether anyone could tell by looking at me. I was worried about that.

During the next three weeks we would meet in the afternoons whenever TD took two hours from his work and engagements—sometimes for tea; sometimes at a Central Park bench, where I would arrive on roller skates and read to him from some books of poems or listen to him tell me stories about his or other people's lives; and a few times in the Hotel Wellington, conveniently near enough to 57th Street, where, registering under a different name, he would engage a room. I'd be instructed to telephone him for his room number and then take the elevator directly to that floor. It was risky business in 1930, especially as I was underage.

I didn't have to be told that our meetings had to be conducted in secret. I knew that. Nor did it occur to me that I could or should expect any sort of commitment from him. The bed part of it I accepted as something I had to do, like washing my hair or brushing my teeth, if I wanted to be wanted and loved, although despite his assurances I couldn't help feeling that bedding me took precedence over mind and heart.

One day he suggested that we rent by the week a furnished room not far from where we lived. He told me to look for one and gave me ten dollars for rent. Block after block of the brownstone houses in the eighties between Central Park West and Columbus Avenue had rooms to let. Landladies thought I looked too young to be needing a furnished room and, looking me over, said that the vacancy was taken. But times being what they were and money being hard to come by, I finally found a room I was able to rent. It was in the basement with a separate entrance that, as the landlady explained, was one of its desirable features. I was led into a dark brown cavern, and the landlady turned on the forty-watt single bulb in the bridge lamp next to a fat, bottle-green stuffed chair with a napkin-like cloth pinned to its head and arms. A skinny-looking mattress on a studio couch was draped with a faded India-print spread; the window was flanked by limp curtains. A round dining table and two chairs stood at the far end of the room on a carpet sprouting faded flowers. I gave the woman the ten dollars for a week in advance, making some explanation about needing the place for a writing-research project with my uncle. I wasn't very convincing, but she didn't care and gave me the keys. Except for the need and weight of hiding my new activities from home and school, I was too wrapped in my romantic fantasy to look forward or back. With a few stems of real flowers—three daffodils leaning against a fern in a water glass on the table—and TD's book of philosophical poems, the dusky, hollow room came alive for me. We would meet in that basement room on 88th Street for an hour or two of an afternoon whenever TD had the time until he left New York on March 20 for an extended trip to the West to relieve his tormenting bronchitis.

Before leaving, he rented a box at the 52nd Street post office, west of Eighth Avenue, where he planned to send his letters to me. Just before departure, he wrote, "Sweetheart . . . its to say how really dear you are to me and how I wish you were coming along." He tried to answer my doubts that he was more interested in my body than my companionship.

The letters that followed were everything a young romantic could wish for: loving, flattering, encouraging, wistful, supportive, and—framed as they necessarily were, apart from bed—they bound me more largely and closely to him. He called my first letter "exquisite—meditative, thoughtful, poetic, romantic. It is like a still pool at dusk. One wonders at the peace, surety, fullness, beauty."

The bigness of Theodore Dreiser on my still-circumscribed field of vision made school on the Washington Heights hill harder than ever to buckle down to. I confided in Margie, and we continued our too frequent cutting of classes so we could talk about TD and his letters, which kept asking, "When is it you are to be eighteen? But more important—when is it are you to be free." ". . . one of these days you will be free. And then. . . ." I didn't know what I wanted, but it seemed that it wasn't what I had at home and school. In an April letter TD consoled, buoyed, heartened, reassured, cajoled: "Just now I received such a doleful and yet really vital and interesting letter from you. Your so unhappy. You see no future. . . . And no parachute. Excellent. Excellent. At seventeen and a half you are thinking more than most men and women at sixty." At seventeen, the view he opened to me was stirring. He made suggestions for reading, from H. G. Wells to Schopenhauer, and mentioned the range of possibilities open to me. I leaned like thirst to water toward this substitute for a father's "guidance and protection," which mine regretted having to withhold from his "little girl's growing up." I didn't then associate TD with parental guidance. I just believed I was loved and nurtured and romanced. I hadn't heard about a "father complex."

The after-school trips to the post office every other day were charged with swelling expectation. It was a relatively small post office with two writing ledges against its storefront windows and, opposite, grilled wickets next to the section of numbered letter boxes. The "up" or "down" for the rest of my day hinged on whether I saw that thin white stripe of the envelope through the daisy holes of P.O. Box 74. He often enclosed clippings of press interviews with his letters. The "dean of American novelists" discoursed on women, communism, finance, futility, statutes of laws, Prohibition and prohibitions, religion, and what was wrong with everything and how it could be otherwise. "I do not march with any clan," he said. "I see myself as a highly temperamental individual compelled to see life through the various vales of fogs of my own lacks, predilections, yet seeking honestly always to set down that which I imagine I see." He was eager to have me learn to drive a car and sent me twenty-five dollars to take lessons so that we could drive to the sea and the woods. Always he seemed to be planning ahead for both of us.

I acted on his suggestions. The brother of the seamstress who still did the sewing and mending in our dining room would come with a car on prearranged afternoons and give me lessons under some deserted corner of the Queensboro Bridge. I told my mother I had saved up for them out of my lunch money.

Although my mother could no longer cover all our household

expenses, little was cut down or out. We still had Zsuzsi living in, Mrs. Chernowitz on Mondays and Tuesdays for the laundry, and Daisy, the seamstress. For some time Zsuzsi's salary and the apartment rent were owing, and I believe my mother borrowed from certain of her friends.

Before school closed in June, an acquaintance of my mother's found a summer job for me as a mother's helper. The four- and six-year-old boys were bratty and unattractive, and my sleeping quarters in their country house on Lake Mahopac were without privacy. My letter to TD must have been heavy with woe, for his answer on June 11 was a safety net of encouragement, compassion, and support. He would support me emotionally and, if need be, financially as well.

This avowal of support and encouragement contrasted sharply with what I was getting at home from my mother, who whenever she was unable to cope resorted to getting sick or alerting her friends to her impending suicide. With me she had a way of offering the figurative carrot with which she would entrap me when I got near enough. I became increasingly wary and untrusting. I wanted to please her but was also afraid of her, afraid of confronting her, afraid of her hysterical personality. I would certainly not have, at that stage of my adolescent rebellion, confided in her or stayed close. She was then contributing, as a freelance journalist to Hungarian newspapers in Budapest, interviews with those she called "famous intellectuals" and "famous artistic people," among them industrialist Charles Schwab, philanthropist Otto Kahn, actor Franchot Tone, and movie star Joan Crawford. She was not shy or timid, and on hearing of a noted person whose views she shared or whom she might admire or whom it might be advantageous for her to know, she would step right up to him or her and offer an endorsement, a service, a kindness, an invitation. In this manner she often made faithful friends and just as often found herself out of her depth and abandoned. She at thirty-five and I at seventeen were both in pursuit of love, and TD was tugging at my end of the rope with "Its getting hard & boring to be away so long. . . . I would be content to work out in Los Angeles awhile if I could send for you and really bring you out. . . . I think of you so much. . . . I've been actually lonely so often & for you—and am now. . . . if there is anything I can do for you write me. If its in my power, I will."

4

"Dearest Wilding": 1930–31

TD came back in early July of 1930. I met him at noon on a day that was all blue sky with a feather stroke of breeze. In my silk shantung dress, its white coin dots on a deep blue field, billowing skirt, high-heeled pumps, and straw picture hat, I was the picture of "Summer" as seen in a nineteenth-century novel. I thought TD looked back-number spiffy in his light vanilla pants that strained for more room around the stomach, his pointed two-tone buckskin and leather shoes, navy jacket, and printed bow tie. I'd forgotten how big he was until he walked beside me in his loose-jointed way heading for a taxi. Frugal as he was, he didn't stint on taxi rides with me; they afforded the privacy he wanted.

We drove to the Battery, where we got on the Staten Island ferry. As I stood with him at the prow, I felt so alive inside I could have raced downhill—*if* I were on a hill—yet I knew I had to hang back, stay in slower step. Reaching the other side, we took a little train to Princess Bay, where I took off my shoes at the water's edge, and we strolled along an empty beach and sat on a grassy sand hillock, where we watched a skinny black ant trying to carry a load bigger than itself up the mound. We counted ten tries before the ant made it, and TD, wrapped in wonder, asked what was this life struggle, this simple drama in which we all have feature roles. In a nearby bog I gathered some stalks of cattails that suggested dusk with its poetic, hypnotic sadness. Maybe a poem of TD's made me think that way about them. It was a happy reunion afternoon in which we gave, each to the other, the something we found missing while we were separated, even if those somethings were not the same.

Come summer and my mother decided Sue and I should spend the month of August at an adult summer camp named Artemis near Brewster, New York, that had been founded by the Hungarian *New Yorker* artist Julian de Miskey with his Hungarian friend, Francis Kalnay, a writer. It accommodated not more than about twenty people and had few facilities and equipment except for ping pong and pool in the dining hall and two old mares who shared a woodshed. Those who came, mostly artists, writers, photographers, concert musicians, and now and then a doctor or philosopher—predominantly Hungarians—already knew each other or, if not, promptly became acquainted and often amorously involved, for they were dependent on each other for every diversion.

Julian, then in his mid- to late thirties, was "tall, dark, and handsome," with the Slavic feature of almost slanty eyes. He had a sweet, kindly, paternal way with the young such as we but was reputed to be less chivalrous with the score of women who became infatuated with him. His wit and sense of humor were reflected in his many *New Yorker* covers and drawings, but I was more impressed with him as a spiritual thinker, a disciple of Gurdjieff. Julian was not one to set the table laughing, but Francis—whom everyone called "Ferko," with his lean face, slender pointing nose, thin pursed lips, and wiry blond hair—was.

TD came up to visit one day—just for the day—and brought me a copy of *Jennie Gerhardt.* Having him come to visit *me* either raised my status in that funny little dining hall or set minds to question it. As we crossed the little wooden bridge straddling the brook, I asked him one of those questions that can occur to one in the lull after lunch.

"Did you ever have children?"

"Yes," he replied, "two boys."

Surprised, I pursued it. "What were their names?"

He answered without the glint of a smile: "Romulus and Remus."

Roman mythology having so far evaded me, I asked trustingly, "Where do they live? In New York?"

"No," he answered solemnly, "they live with their mother in Italy."

As strongly dependent on TD as I had become, I was still tied a little to the memory of my summer romance a year before with Johnny Nearing, a boy my age whom I could fantasize about marrying some day and having those "ten children." Not being far from Pawling, I rode one day to Manumit on horseback, thinking to make an impressive, unannounced surprise arrival on broad-beamed Maggie. We trotted, walked, sometimes even galloped, but we did not reach Manumit until just before supper. I approached a familiar face and asked, "May I stay the night, and may I shelter my horse and give her feed and water?" I could, but this was another year, and I didn't belong anymore. Johnny said, "How is everything? Nice to see you again." A new girl sat with him after supper on the faded creton-covered sofa in the Mill and listened to Debussy's *Prélude à l'après-midi d'un faune.* I harbored the thought that my mother's dissuading him about me might have achieved its end, and I took comfort in musing on TD.

It was back to school in September, and for my eighteenth birthday on October 12, my mother gave a party again that was attended mainly by her friends. Julian and Ferko came, as did TD and Helen. Helen gave me her own copy of Hardy's *The Woodlanders.* It wasn't new, which made it for me more special. I had a warm fondness for Helen, and I was able to isolate this wholly from my intimacy with TD, which I assumed she did not know about. I did not think anyone knew about it, a secrecy propelled by TD, by my unformed youngness, and by the circumstances. TD had asked me what I would like for a birthday present, and I'd requested the life-size baby doll that I'd seen in the F. A. O. Schwartz toy store, with the enormous price tag of fifteen dollars. The doll was big enough to wear the same size clothes as a real one-year-old. Indulgently, TD said at the time, "Well, all right, go ahead and get it," and gave me the fifteen dollars for it. I named it Patrick, called it Pat, and bought clothes for it in dry goods or department stores. What this might tell about my needs and sophistication at the age of eighteen is pretty obvious.

When the critics and public acclaimed *An American Tragedy* and gave increasing recognition to his other novels, TD became confident of his eminence among American authors. It is said that he was deeply disappointed when the Nobel Prize went to Sinclair Lewis that November because he had expected to win it. I was sitting with him in Childs' some days later. When I tried clumsily to keep the butter from dripping off the hot bun, he denied being disappointed, but I was not convinced. He seemed like a ten-year-old boy no longer expected to cry over a scraped bloody knee, quickly wiping a tear away on his jacket sleeve, hoping no one would notice.

Among my mother's dinner guests one evening in early January 1931 was the author, social and political critic, poet, and lecturer Max Eastman and his Russian wife, Eliena Krylenko. At that time I had only a superficial idea about who he was and what he wrote; I knew that he was a Trotskyite and had been editor of a magazine, *The Masses,* not *The New Masses* that we were all now reading. In his autobiography, *Love and Revolution,* he remembers first meeting me at one of TD's gatherings. If that is so, I don't remember it. I first took notice that evening when he came to our house. Mr. Eastman had shining white hair that made me think of a sunbeam on snow. He had a young, strong face and grey-blue eyes that looked out with scholarly intelligence. He was tall, not thin or fat, and moved with the easy fluid languor of a cat about to settle into the most comfortable available chair or sofa. His clothes were like that too—casual, soft-tweedy in flecked silvery grey, white shirt, silk knit tie not asking for attention, a reddish alpaca sweater vest. I didn't know then that he was forty-eight years old. I only saw that he was strikingly handsome and looked young. Often enough in the course of the evening his words were spiked with wit or humor, making him and us laugh, and when he laughed it was joyous. Eliena seemed older to me. Her short white curls bounced with the turning of her head. Her leathery tan and strong jaw made her look more muscular than feminine—a sturdy outdoor type, I thought, who might dig and lift and fish. She talked with a laughing voice that sounded heartily *glad,* and her expression was mostly jolly.

Leaving the dining room after the guests filed along the hall toward the front living room, I stopped to get something from my room, and Mr. Eastman followed me in. He looked around at my pictures, my books, my desk, asked me what I was reading, what studying, and then, in a sort of drifting along way that diverted its course from suddenness, he hugged me to him and kissed me. I was embarrassed. I didn't know what to say, so I didn't say anything and acted as though nothing had happened. But it had.

Later that night, getting ready to go to bed, I noticed on the floor near my desk an unfamiliar fountain pen. I didn't need to wonder who

Max Eastman, 1931.

it belonged to. The next day I said to my mother, "Mr. Eastman dropped his pen in my room yesterday when he was looking at my books." She was still in bed but quickly picked up the phone to call him about it. She told him she would "send it with Yvette to your apartment later in the day if it's all right." It was.

The rain that afternoon was especially heavy, and I was very damp when I arrived at 39-1/2 Grove Street, pushed the button next to the Eastman name, and was buzzed in. Mr. Eastman was in pajamas and alone when he opened the door to his not very big two-room, kitchen, and bath Village apartment. He invited me in and explained that he was resting in bed because of minor surgery on his inner thigh. Though I don't remember what we talked about, I have not forgotten how it was to be alone in the room with Max Eastman stretched out on his bed. He urged me to take off my wet shoes and stockings. When I did, he rose, peeled off the rest of my clothes, and led me to bed with him. Had I been asked, I might have said "No," if only to establish that I was aware of the prevailing decorum north of Greenwich Village that a "nice girl" doesn't. But as he did not ask, no disapproving censor woke to press the point. Rather, I felt *chosen* and pleased about being liked and wanted. He emanated a clean, eyes-shut passion, a youngness.

Being made love to was no longer the scary Big Thing it had been the first time with TD, and on this particular afternoon it appeared as artless and instinctive as a honeybee zigzagging into summer's blue, lighting for a moment along the way on a berry bush or petal. TD had pulled me into a wider world—away from the conventional path to husband, home, and babies, which is really what I would have liked. Going to bed, having sex—not specifically for its physical pleasures, to which I had not yet awakened—continued to be so easy, a "natural," "no problem" activity if I thought I was cared about and taken as a person rather than as a sex object. But I was never quite sure enough.

The afternoon did not change "Mr. Eastman" to "Max," but I added "dear" to make our communications sound less formal, and so began our friendship. The following winter, when I was no longer in high school but working in short-lived odd jobs, I wrote him in a letter he saved: "You've helped me, Mr. Eastman dear. . . . Think how pleased we both will be when, after solemnly marching down the aisle in cap and gown instead of the white veil, I will rush to Grove Street to unload my B.A.'s, M.A.'s, Ph.D.'s that you inspired. . . . Admire me just a little for wanting so much to earn and hold your admiration. . . ."

There was something else, as he mentions in *Love and Revolution*: "To those days before political lines were drawn too sharply belongs a friendship with Theodore Dreiser which had, by accident, a long, wonderful and momentous consequence in my life." And describing an invitation he accepted from TD:

> I shall never forget another group in which the intimates were Margaret Monahan and her adopted daughter, Yvette Szekely. Yvette was in her late teens, half Hungarian, half French, lithe and dark-haired-dark-eyelashed, and her eyelashes curled upward from eyes sparkling with joyous interest in everything that was said. She was alluring to me in every smile and motion. I learned afterward that she was a dear and very special friend of TD's, but I did not know it then, and wished with unhindered longing that I were young enough to go to school with her.

For the next thirty years we saw each other periodically whenever we were in the same city at the same time and wrote to each other when we weren't, not ever skipping a year. And yes, when time and place permitted, he made love.

Several weeks after I delivered that fountain pen to Grove Street came a note on Hotel Brevoort stationery: "Miss Yvette dear, will you call me up soon? I brought you a green present from Bermuda." It came to me by mail, a nile green cashmere sweater with the message, "When you put this on it will be the most beautiful thing in the world." Here again, Mr. Eastman was an involvement that I thought needed to be concealed but about which I felt blameless. It was TD who unconquerably mattered—held me—on whom I depended. Away on a trip he wrote, seeming too much on the move to reflect as usual on the place and his surroundings. He asked me for a poem: "I like you best living in your fancy."

I could not afford to live totally in my "fancy." And after high school, I enrolled in Payne Business College. It was housed in a building on 42nd Street, where, when he returned, TD would meet me at the lunch hour to sit in the spring sun on a bench in Bryant Park and tell me stories about Hollywood: what *really* happened with the Mack Sennett comedian Fatty Arbuckle and his wild parties. Walking me back to school, we stopped at Woolworth's, where he bought me a pretty ten-cent white bracelet strung with elastic cord, and when he reached home he wrote of our afternoon together that "something warm and comforting enveloped me."

TD was not my only source of instruction at the time. Together with a group of artists, writers, journalists, theater people, and their hangers-on, Max Eastman was one of the founders of a dinner-cocktail club in Greenwich Village called "The Meeting Place," at 86 Bedford Street, above Lee Chumley's restaurant and bar. It was a loft-like space where the intelligentsia could meet for food, drinks, and conversation. My mother went fairly often, and Sue and I sometimes went with her. As at TD's large gatherings, people I saw there fused into one whole. These worldly sophisticates, Rex Stout and critic Ernest Boyd, both with Smith Brothers beards; Lawrence Langner of the Theater Guild; Egmont Arens; and Floyd Dell danced there to "Zwei Herzen im dreiviertel Takt" and "The Bolero" played on the hand-cranked phonograph. They seemed reluctant to bequeath the free love, art, and protest of their Greenwich Village generation to mine, who were just leaving school to enter the jobless world of the Great Depression.

One day a female acquaintance of my mother's suggested I get an after-school job as a waitress with a coffee-pastry shop in Washington Heights. The hours were from 6:00 P.M. to 11:30 P.M., when the shop attracted the before- and after-show crowd from the Loew's movie theater across the street. My attitude toward waitressing was as disdainfully haughty as it had been toward being a mother's helper. I would seat myself at a back table, near the kitchen, and, between arrivals of customers, read *Crime and Punishment,* resenting the interruption when customers entered and serving them with lofty condescension. I need not have worried that waitressing was to be my fate. When I telephoned to say that I could not come in one evening, they were relieved and let me go.

That was the day TD had told me he was going to Iroki in the evening to visit Mame and Rome, his sister and brother, who were staying in his house. Instead of going to work, I yielded to an irrational, adolescent impulse to take a train to Mount Kisco and surprise him. At home, it was assumed that I was headed for the pastry shop. Having only my subway fare, I borrowed a dollar from George, our elevator man. I boarded the train to Mount Kisco at the 125th Street station, and when the conductor asked for my ticket, I told him I lost it but would mail the amount when I got home. I gave him my name and address, and for some reason, he trusted my explanation.

On arrival, I approached a taxi, explaining where I was going and asking the driver not only to take me to Iroki, but also to come back to fetch me in time for the 10:30 train to New York, at which time I would pay him for the round trip. We agreed on the exact hour I would meet him. I had no doubt whatever that TD would give me the money to get back home.

It was a dark, starless night when the driver let me out at the Iroki gate. I walked the long path toward the main house, and when I got near enough, feeling scared and like a burglar, I watched through the windows of the lighted house for TD's face. Instead I saw three figures I had never before seen. The cloud of a small panic moved toward me. If TD wasn't there, how would I get home? I groped my way toward a light in the guest house and, peering in, saw Fabri in his familiar artist's smock cleaning some brushes. He seemed to be alone. I tapped on the window lightly. He turned, walked toward the wrong window, and, seeing nothing, resumed what he was doing. I tapped again, this time a little stronger, and then, seeing me, he opened the door, enormously surprised. I explained feebly that I understood TD was going to be here this evening and that I had come to talk to him about an "assignment" he had given me. "Teddy and Helen left about an hour ago. They drove back to New York," said Fabri.

I now had to confess about the taxi. He gave me three dollars and walked me to the waiting car. On arriving at the train station in New York, I had only fifteen minutes to reach home by the accustomed hour from work and only seventy cents left from the dollar I borrowed from George that I needed to turn in as my supposed tips for the evening. I again approached a taxi, told the driver of the need for haste, and that I didn't have any money. He sort of looked me over and said with some bemusement, "Hop in," then raced to 9 West 91st Street. On getting out, I thanked him and asked whether he would accept the few cigarettes I had left in my pack. It was the only thing I could think of that I could offer, and I wanted to show I was grateful.

"No, that's all right, keep them. You'll need them after breakfast."

When I told TD, he just said, "You kids rush mindlessly to wherever your impulses point." Neither of us recognized the adventure as an expression of my overriding need for him.

By 1931 TD had become almost as famous a crusader for social justice as he was a novelist. Pictures of him and interviews with him appeared in the newspapers wherever he went. Much of that year he was away raising funds for the release from prison of California labor leader Tom Mooney and investigating the conditions of mine workers in Pennsylvania and Kentucky, along with negotiating, in Hollywood, the sale to the movies of *An American Tragedy*. *Dawn,* his autobiography of early youth, was published in May. He wrote in the copy he gave me:

"Yvette
Oasis"
TD

and I read the book with the possessive interest that admits no criticism.

> I was always a "mother child," hanging to her skirts until I was seven or eight years old. . . . It always seemed to me that no one ever wanted me *enough,* unless it was my mother. When not wanted, I preferred to play by myself. . . . I invented certain simple games.- . . . One of these games I can best describe as "train." It consisted of placing half-size cigar boxes in a row, end to end. . . . A spool on a box at one end was the caboose. Smaller-sized cigar boxes, without their lids, made the flat cars. . . . I personally was the engine, cars, conductor, whistle and bell, all in one.

For his sixtieth birthday that August, I constructed a replica of that train using several cigar boxes set end to end and put a small teddy bear in the caboose with this verse I made up to touch on his growing-up references:

At three a groping Teddy I
Who by his mother's skirt would cry:
At ten, defiant Dreiser who'd
Defend that name, 'though black and blue'd;
Fifteen found me less than bold:
A girl's "Oh Theo" and my blood ran cold.
And now, that groping Teddy I
Who's seen the world and still could cry.

In September 1931 TD gave up the 57th Street studio and went to live in the Hotel Ansonia on 73rd Street and Broadway, where he had a round-cornered, sort of semicircle suite. When passing by, I would look up to the fourteenth floor and give his windows a greeting glance. Helen moved to Iroki, and TD was making headlines, for example, from the *Knoxville News Sentinal* (Nov. 9):

DREISER SEEKS HARLAN PROBE BY STATE, U.S.—Calls labor conditions there the worst in the world. . . . Takes bulky evidence to probe demands.

The next day:

DREISER INDICTED WITH GIRL—Charge pair trapped in Hotel room.

The story described the county prosecutor's suspicion about Dreiser's association with a young woman in his party being "more friendly than Kentucky conventions permit." One night, according to the prosecutor, someone knocked on the door of the woman's hotel room, but she was not there. Later she was seen entering Dreiser's room. The "amateur detectives" took toothpicks and laid them standing against Dreiser's door. Hours later the toothpicks had not been disturbed. This trap led to a formal charge of adultery and an indictment by the county's grand jury.

My reaction to this was concern for TD, although I could not very well believe his statement "I'm incapable of committing adultery. . . . I couldn't have. I'm impotent." Nor did I feel I had an exclusive claim on him. Those who knew him smiled and said they didn't know who else in the world would have had the nerve to say it. To me, directly, he waved it all aside as an attempt by the county in Kentucky to divert attention from his probe into the labor conditions of Harlan miners and the persecution of strikers.

TD at this time appeared to me harassed, irritable, short-tempered—trying to cover too many bases. He would designate a time and place for us to meet and at times would not show up. I lost a new job as stock girl at Bonwit Teller when one day at noon, during my forty-five-minute lunch period, I dashed to meet him in front of the 42nd Street public library. He came ten minutes late, and there was something curt and distant about his greeting. As we walked half a block up Fifth Avenue he accused me of "calculated shrewdness," "sly cunning," "ungratefulness," and "going around with other men." He said he had received an anonymous letter telling him that he had not been "the first" in my life, then asked what I had to say for myself.

My surprise moved into a shattering wretchedness. We got into a taxi he abruptly hailed, and while I tried to answer with, "It isn't true," he read his newspaper while whistling "Yankee Doodle." Arriving in front of a brownstone on 48th Street, where he was going to see his publisher, Horace Liveright, he got out and asked in a mocking sort of way, "Where is it that Madam wishes to go?" I got out too and was left standing on the sidewalk as he mounted the steps of a brownstone and disappeared. It was now too late to go back to the job I had, and I could not leave things as they were. I was offended, acutely miserable, and mortally afraid of losing him. Not knowing whether he would emerge in ten minutes or three hours, I waited in the little square yard off the pavement by a basement window. When after what seemed like endless time I saw him come down the steps, he was with a man and he didn't see me. I was desperate. As I took a step forward, I saw TD suddenly stop and heard him ask his companion if he had dropped some change. As they both glanced down, TD saw me rooted where I stood and came toward me. I must have looked the way I felt because he said in a kindly voice, "Don't stand there like that. What will the man I'm with think? Don't do anything foolish. Have breakfast with me tomorrow, darling, and we'll patch things up. Now smile!" At my feet lay the pieces of a broken bottle I had unknowingly kicked, making the sound he mistook for dropped change. We met the next day, and he "patched it up," and our relationship continued, possibly inching toward a different plane. His work schedules and travel made our meetings less frequent.

Periodically there appeared at the Meeting Place a twenty-six-year-old writer-poet who had followed his muse to Greenwich Village, where for a time he was able to sell verses and stories to the Street & Smith pulp magazines. Bill (Willard Edgar) Solenberger accepted my mother's invitation to come and live in our apartment. He looked like a taller Clark Gable and might have qualified as stand-in for Rhett Butler in *Gone with the Wind.* During the six or so weeks he stayed with us—before a friend from the Meeting Place got him free passage on a cargo ship to Cuba—we play-acted the parts of captain-at-the-helm and worshiping sailor, and, I think for the first time, I became sweepingly infatuated, but I never became Bill's engulfing passion. He preferred not to be counted on, and I, wanting to appear sophisticated at a time when it was the thing not to expect commitment and to scoff at sentimentality, pretended it didn't matter. I would find notes left for me in my room:

> G.H.Q.
> Orders of the Day
> Attention: Sailor
> Kindly awaken your commanding officer at 8 o'clock.
> He has an appointment at 9:30
> Will take coffee with crew.
> Signed: WES—Captain

Bill did not replace TD, the illusory father I continued to depend on. He just added to the weight of my burden to conceal.

Around Christmas 1931, I had a brief job as investigator for the Emergency Relief Bureau. In my jacket made of rabbit fur—dignified with the more marketable name "Lapin"—I would enter a Tenth Avenue tenement and gingerly grope my way up three flights of urine-smelling stairs to the kerosene-fumed kitchen of a jobless hod carrier and his sick mother and deliver a two-dollar food voucher to last until Christmas. I was embarrassed to investigate; I wished I weren't wearing the Lapin.

"When did you lose your job, Mr. Smithers? Show me your rent receipts. How much do you owe the grocery store? Can you go and live with your uncle where you were born?"

I felt like the lady from the charities in Elmer Rice's play *Street Scene,* and I thought Mr. Smithers was ashamed to take the two dollars. Something pungent was simmering on the stove. I ran down the stairs out into the waning winter light and smelled the cooking smell that clung to my jacket. After three weeks, the Relief Supervisor, Mrs. McCloskey, called me to her desk just before closing time. "I am sorry to have to let you go but we think that your youthful appearance does not give the clients a feeling of confidence, someone they can discuss their problems with."

My mother, like her intellectual friends, was among the radical elite who although propounding revolution didn't really believe that the International Soviet, in the words of the current song, "will be the human race." I didn't know enough about the small and large differences between the left wing political parties to favor one over the other. Although I believed their causes just, I did not think of myself as being a part of "the working class," as did, say, Johnny Nearing, who left college and went to Russia to work as a simple miner in Magnitogorsk, behind the Ural Mountains.

As the depression deepened, I didn't think so much about a far-distant future as about a near tomorrow. Could I find a job so I could leave home and be free to do anything, see anyone, without having to conceal or lie to my mother about it? I felt only her criticism of me, her draining accusations. We were each living in our own worlds, pulling too far in opposite directions to be close or intimate.

A card from Max Eastman in New Orleans: "Because I was thinking of you there so warmly."

A letter from Bill in Virginia, just back from Cuba: "We'll have a grand talk when I get back to town, Sailor. . . ."

TD sent me one afternoon to visit his sick friend Charles Fort and report back on his condition. Fort was one of the first to write extraterrestrial stories. TD thought he was wonderful and got his very unscientific *The Book of the Damned* published.

I found my way to an address in the Bronx—a shabby looking building. My knock on the apartment door was answered by a little woman in a faded print housedress. When I told her that TD had sent me to see how everything was with them and if there was something he could do, she led me through a short, dark hallway to a little grey living room and from there to a tiny bedroom with only a bed in it. In the bed was a man with sunken cheeks the color of yellow and green. Mr. Fort looked frail. Mrs. Fort hovered about in a humble kind of way, as though I were a cardinal sent by the pope. Fort's message to TD was, "I have three months—then I'll be ready." Three months later he died.

5

New Horizons

Having now, at last, become eighteen years old, I wanted urgently to leave home and be independent. What I really meant by "independent" was not much more than not having to hide what I was doing in my relationship with TD. The strength in the sway of his influence braced me: "When is it you are to be eighteen? But more important—when is it are you to be free. . . . one of these days you will be free. And then. . . ." But freedom demanded that I have a job. TD tried to help by giving me letters of introduction, one of them to George Bye, his agent.

"I will keep you in mind if I know of something," said Mr. Bye. I felt like a bird whose wings are glued down.

My mother had assembled a portfolio of sketches of her designs for lingerie and bade me take them around to the showrooms of underwear manufacturers in the garment district and offer them for sale at five dollars a sketch. The ignominy of this peddling crushed me. Cigar-chewing men in rolled-up shirtsleeves would look at all the sketches and then, as my hopes were teeter-tottering, would say without taking the cigars out of their mouths, "They're very nice but we're not buying now. Come back in a few months." Block after block, building after building, floor after floor.

Sitting at the kitchen table one morning having a coffee and watching Zsuzsi beating a batter for cookies, I was overcome by a towering need to confide my secret about TD to someone other than my school friend, Margie Stengel, the only one who knew. Drawn to risking the danger, I suddenly announced, "Mr. Dreiser is in love with me. We see each other."

The wire beater in Zsuzsi's hand stopped in mid air, dropping pieces of dough. Her very blue eyes opened saucer wide. "Why, he could be your grandfather!" she wailed, not wanting to believe. Her distressed reaction scared me.

"Please, please don't tell. *It has to be a secret!*" I urged. She would not reassure me.

Arriving home one late afternoon some days later, having made the rounds with the portfolio of sketches, I found my mother at the entrance door as I walked in. She stood before me, visibly agitated. In that pressing, accusing, challenging tone that always frightened me, the flush spreading on her chest, she said, "I had a telephone call from someone telling me that you are having an affair with Dreiser!" Her voice rose to an agonized pitch: "Do you deny it?"

I didn't know what to say.

"I'll have him arrested," she cried. "I will put him in jail," she sputtered, raging in anger and heated agitation.

I froze with fear, alarmed that TD would now be gone from me. His support that I so needed, depended on, was in danger of collapsing. She picked up the telephone and called several of her friends. I heard her say that she would call the newspapers and "give them the whole story." She threatened suicide. Answering her urgent call, friends arrived. She was in bed, eyes closed.

Miserable and frightened, I sat in a chair by the living room window like a puppet wearing the scarlet letter to be seen by all and around whom all this excitement was seething. A doctor arrived.

This time I did not think, as I had in childhood, that she would be dead, that I would have to cut off her arm at the elbow to sleep with at night, that Hail Mary's were needed. The humming sounds of "mmmmmm" would be heard, and she would open her eyes. The doctor came out of the bedroom.

"She'll be all right," I heard him say. "You can go in." I sat glued to the chair I was in. I heard the friends try to dissuade her from calling the newspapers.

"You may not care what happens to him about this, but think of what the publicity would do to this young girl. You can't do this to her."

Margaret Szekely Monahan in the 1930s.

In the midst of the hysteria and threats, which, like an unattended pot of milk on a hot range suddenly without warning rises to the very edge and is about to spill over and make a mess, there rose above all my panic the thought that TD would not see me anymore.

The boiling crisis sank to a simmer. My mother did not call the newspapers. She did not "put him in jail." Whether and how she confronted TD is no longer in my memory. She must have, judging from TD's mention of her in his letters to me in the next few years:

"The one thing I want to avoid is argument or complaint from Margaret."

"What about Margaret? Suppose she took it in her head to make a row about you?"

"I've wondered and wondered about Sue and only thoughts of trouble with M[argaret] has kept me from looking her up."

What most astounded and dismayed me was his mistaken belief that by admitting to our liaison I participated in her incrimination of him: "The thing I objected to and do now is your joining with Margaret Monahan to put me on the spot in regard to you. . . . It seems—well I can scarcely say how, more like Margaret than you." With all his suspicions, he continued to offer me support and material help when necessary.

In March the Meeting Place moved from above Lee Chumley's to larger quarters at 3 West 15th Street. I took to stopping by without my mother and sister. Its secretary, Iris Woolcock, lent a sympathetic ear to my desire to move away from home. She offered me part-time work at the club—invitations, mailings, menu postings. I often saw Floyd Dell there with his wife, Bee Marie, having drinks or dinner with Max Eastman and Eliena and Rex and Ruth Stout. It seemed funny that, because of my youth, I was outside that group. It was strange to watch "Mr. Eastman dear" from a polite distance, knowing him as I did. Sometimes when at the cocktail hour the phonograph was playing "Let Me Kiss Your Hand, Madam," he would ask me to dance, and I would imagine myself perfumed with mystery, granting the favor.

Many years later, years that by that time erased the "Mr." prefacing "Eastman," if not the "dear," he showed me a letter Eliena had sent him when he was out of town lecturing:

> Margaret Monahan got hold of me last night and begged me to ask you not to write to Yvette because Yvette was not a worthy girl and

> because she was showing your letters to Dreiser, or at least telling him the contents of your letters to her. I told her to go to hell. I asked how did she know that Yvette was telling Dreiser about your letters, and she said, "I can't tell you, you have to take my word for it." I never thought of asking her how she herself knew what you were writing to Yvette and what there was in the letters. . . . But just now it dawned on me that perhaps you better be a little careful in these virginal matters. . . . Let them get independence first. . . . Leave alone those under protection of mothers, fathers, brothers, sisters . . . especially a jealous step-mother—and still a young one.

When I read this, even so many years later, I remembered my mother opening letters to me from Johnny Nearing and then telling him that I was too inferior to him to waste time on. And later she wrote to my father to warn him about me.

At home my mother appealed to her friends to "talk to Yvette" and arranged for me to go see her friend, Francis Faragoh, managing director of the New Playwrights Theater in New York and noted scenario writer in Hollywood. I had difficulty finding the entrance to 10-1/2 Cornelia Street in the Village because it fronted an alley, not the street. Francis was wearing a bathrobe when he opened the door and said, "I was just about to take a bath." He asked me in and offered tea. The setting did not smack of a session designed to build understanding between me and my mother, and it soon became evident that this small, wiry man with black hair and forceful intensity was not interested in that. Instead he invited me to join him in the bath and said, when I declined, he was as surprised as he was disappointed.

That evening, TD and I met. We went to Horn & Hardardt's, where he ate one of his favorites: tapioca pudding. He noticed that I was wearing a lavender dress and suggested I not wear it again because the color was bad luck. He was out of sorts, complaining that his bronchitis plagued him more than usual and that the demands on him to speak in public on the economy, social injustice, and the political system and to back other causes kept him from getting on with the writing of his novel *The Stoic.* He worried about expenses and hoped the movies would buy *Jennie Gerhardt.* It seemed not the moment to tell him that, determined to leave home, I had looked for and found a furnished room renting for $4.75 per week, but when he said he was thinking of leaving New York for a time to seek the peace to write somewhere out west, I knew I needed to mention it. Trying to make it sound "good," I described it being on the third floor of a brownstone rooming house on 15th Street near Second Avenue. "The window lets in some sunlight and, if you move to its extreme left corner, you can, at a certain angle, see a branch of a tree in the yard of the house next to it."

"Well, go ahead," he said. "I told you I'd help you and I will. I'll send you ten dollars a week, but I don't want any trouble with your mother, Margaret." This was the father—reassuring, supporting.

On an ordinary midweek afternoon, a little scared but more determined, I gathered some but not all of my clothes, my toothbrush, and my doll Pat and left my mother's apartment—my room, my desk, my books in the orange bookcase, the lampshade that glowed a map of North America. Fearing the scene this packing and closing of the front door behind me would bring about, I did it when my mother was not at home. I confided in my sister, who, whether approving or not, accepted my decision. This was important to me. We were friends. I needed to do this so much I couldn't think about what she would have to contend with alone when our mother came home. A week later I received a note from her saying she had meant to come to see me in secret, pretending she would be going to school on a day there was no school, "which doesn't happen to be on Margaret's list of collected knowledge." Instead, she had to stay home and nurse: "Margaret has been vomiting for five days straight, awfully severe, but she is slowly returning to normal. . . . Next week I shall crash all walls to see you. I am suppressing all the vital questions and a burning curiosity until I do. I don't ask how you are getting on. I *know* you're getting on."

In the next six weeks I soared and circled in no particular direction, sometimes like a bird, bumping against an unsuspected window glass. I looked for a job, took free shorthand classes at night school, and met Bill at Stewart's Sheridan Square cafeteria, where, pooling our nickels and dimes, we ate what our change that day could buy. The depression didn't really depress us. As long as we could still scrape together our nickels and dimes for carfare and cafeteria food, we could join the chorus of "Come the Revolution" and quote George Dillon over our cups of coffee:

> Alive in space against his will
> A man may find along his way
> Some loveliness to live for still

* * *

> He clings to something after all,
> Stretched on a flying flowering stone.

And the clean sunny breath of spring with the sprinkled notes from a hurdy-gurdy rolling down the sidewalk and gleefully jumping off key also helped to keep me skyward and aspiring.

Then came a letter from my mother, which was sent to me at the club. She offered love:

> Even though it may seem to be the greatest sacrifice you'll have to make in your life, try and come back to us, at least for a few weeks. My love for you seems to be stronger than all my principles and will power. Stronger than all the disappointment I have had in you.

It implored pity for her past and present sufferings:

> Your life surely will last longer than mine. I've already lived and suffered 37 years. I have gone through agonies often, the like of which you'll never have to know because your personal circumstances are shaped differently. There will be no world war for you to smash your family, for you have no family to speak of. But the people you can call your own, you ought not to let suffer, since you could help it.

She banged on the door of my conscience:

> Since the day you left, I am seriously ill . . . you may find out from Dr. R just how sick I am. I might have to go to the hospital if I do not get well in a day or two for I can hold no food, not even water and have been fed through my veins with salt water solutions to keep me going. I have no money whatever and no one to count on for help of any kind. . . . I am pretty much through. My health, unless a miracle happens, is practically gone.

She offered peace:

> Even if we fail to understand each other in certain things, even though we fight . . . we have no one but each other. It makes no dif-

> ference whatever who's right, who is wrong. It is not a battle, not a race. Just life that is short and filled with sorrow that we cannot do anything about. Save us from the sorrow that is bound to come. Don't wait 'till it is too late. It is too late so soon. . . . There is a letter here from your father, one to you and one to me. I am being blamed for your having no plans, no occupation.

Having often before believed and been deceived, my distrust and fear of her pulled just a little harder than the undeniably considerable strength of my compassion and that "mother" cord. And there was TD helping to pull the other way, as was my free-floating springtime coveting romance. I did not go back—just yet.

I found a temporary job in a small factory mixing dyes for silk scarves and moved to a larger room that was nearer to the club and Stewart's, where I still hung out. The new room had two windows instead of one, and the India-print covered couch-bed was much wider. But lonesomeness crept in: TD was still out west, the job did not last, and Bill's lack of money exiled him to the family home in Pennsylvania. Teas at the club lost their savor with so many people going off to the country or the Cape for the summer. Max Eastman was leaving for Europe, Palestine, and what was then called the Near East. His note to me said, "Miss Yvette dear, all I was going to say, I guess, was that I am rushing for the boat—literally—and I can't play anymore. Au revoir, sweet and wise child."

Lying on my ample couch-bed one morning atop a rubber hot water bottle to relieve menstrual cramps, I heard a knock at the door. I opened it, and there stood my mother. That scared feeling pushed up in my middle and with it the flight impulse. It didn't surprise me that she had found out where I lived; it wasn't hard to do. I invited her in. Surprisingly calm, she came to offer terms:

"Either you come back home to live or you go back to your father in Budapest."

Without a skill, without a job, without money, and with the realization that I neither could nor wanted to depend on TD's ten-dollar subsidies indefinitely, I replied, "All right, I'll go back to my father." My answer must have given her soothing relief because we went to lunch and talked quietly about Sue and me going to Camp Artemis until she settled plans with my father. At the end of that week I moved my few possessions back to 91st Street and some days later went to Artemis to wait for her to arrange my return to Budapest to live with my father, his wife, and his nine-year-old son. I hastened to write and tell TD.

At about ten o'clock on the morning of July 7, 1932, the taxi carrying me, my mother, my typewriter, a suitcase, and my doll Pat rolled to a stop at the departures entrance of the Cunard pier. I was booked for one-way passage on the *SS Berengaria* bound for Cherbourg. I was a little uneasy about not having a passport in my own name. Since it had not expired, my mother sent me on *her* American passport, issued to Margaret Monahan that included her two minor children, with the fourteen-year-old me staring out from the group photo. I had in my handbag train tickets from Cherbourg to Paris to Budapest and thirty-five dollars. There was the clang and rattle of commotion under the canopied pier; departing passengers milled with friends and family until the final call for visitors to leave the ship, among whom was my mother.

Suddenly I felt widely, enormously alone—horizon and shore line erased.

6

Home as Found 1932–33

At the end of the thirty-six-hour train ride from Paris to Budapest on the Orient Express, I step down onto the station platform and recognize the slightly plump youngish face of the man with the cane, limping toward me. His dark, hardly creased linen suit still managed, in this July noonday, to look elegant. He, at forty-four, and I, at nineteen, have become strangers—shy of each other even as I remember the silk-thread smile and the cold moist skin with his greeting kiss.

In the taxi to his home, we make polite conversation about my trip before he tells me that the day after tomorrow I will be going to stay with his mother and sister while he and his family—Anny and nine-year-old Tomi—will be away on a two-week vacation in the Austrian Alps. I remember the cold, stern, unsmiling grandmother in black taffeta. The taxi finds its way to 51 Avenue of the Italian Trees in Buda and stops in front of a white mansion. The marble stairway leads us to the middle floor, where my father's ring is answered by a maid. I see Anny coming toward us—tall, slim, dark-blonde with expressive light blue eyes and wearing a silk dress. She looks the same to me as when I was seven and she washed my neck and ears, and as that summer when I was fourteen and she took Sue and me to Custom Tailors to be fitted for blue pleated skirts. She seemed ever—and still—at the unshifting age of those "in charge."

She said to my father in the high, surprised, somewhat indicting tone, "Dinner has been waiting—what took so long?" He answered in a low, even voice.

Anny accepted me in their home as if she were discharging an ethical obligation that, given a choice, she would rather have done without. If at the time I had had the maturity or generosity to see it from her point of view—the rankling position of having her husband's nineteen-year-old daughter by a former relationship come to live with them—I might not have felt so victimized. But Anny was as accomplished in victimizing as she was captivating. She could not tolerate my being alone with my father—our talking, getting to know each other. Invariably she would call me away and assign some trivial chore: "Would you please come and get the mud off these brown shoes of Tomi's?" Then again, she could be seductive, seeming to enjoy taking me to tailors and dressmakers for new clothes and even persuading my father to agree to the expense of removing the hair on my legs by electrolysis in a cosmetic salon. She was as inventive and spellbinding when telling a story or sharing an experience as she was quick to quarrel and seemed to me to be ever doing the latter, especially with my father and especially about me.

The sudden change from my recent stray, undirected, unharnessed life in New York to the limits now imposed on me in my father's household—dictated partly by its social conventions, its decorum—was hard to adjust to. I wrote and told TD that resignation had taken the place of what I fancied was once my joi de vivre. Although I felt that I had been squeezed into a pinching girdle, I at the same time saw a wry humor in being required to get my father's approval of any young man who asked me out dancing ("What is his background?" "Who is his family?" "Do we know them?"). Then I had to honor the midnight curfew he set for me and find him sitting up until I got home.

Although I didn't learn to sing in my golden cage, I learned to make the best of it, and for the rest of what was left of summer, I saw and did the things the season offered, feeling always that something was missing—largely TD. Even though the lovemaking was not possible or missed, the romantic bond held tenaciously; the magnet still pulled in both directions. Nostalgia crept into his next letter after I sent him a lacquered letter opener decorated with Hungarian peasant designs for his August 27 birthday—his sixty-first.

"You paint an interesting picture of your life over there. . . . It sounds so far away. Do you like it better than New York—(57th St, the Ansonia, Central Park, the little Chinese restaurant at Broadway & 57th St)?" All the special trysting places—all remembered. "Dearie—as you row on the Danube blow me a few loving thoughts. They will be so welcome." There followed a short note about a literary newspaper, *The American Spectator,* that he and George Jean Nathan, Ernest Boyd, James Branch Cabell, and Eugene O'Neill were launching.

* * *

August 21, 1932: Cablegram: ESTABLISH IDENTITY AMERICAN CONSULATE SEND PASSPORT IMMEDIATELY FRITZ AND I MARRIED WILL COME SOON LOVE MOTHER. I vaguely remembered a big, blond, and good-natured German who sold ginger ale bottles and was not very intellectual. Sue followed up the news with this report:

> Fritz fills two yawning gaps in the household. . . . Our house was always singular for its morbidity rising from Zsuzsi's aching corns and hanging from the wreaths in December windows. . . . there is a bit of humor and warmth now. . . . As for Margaret, the presence of Fritz makes less change than one would expect . . . she still won't stand for being happy . . . she lies abed 15 days out of every month, cannot retain food and needs an injection every day before she does anything so that she may be able to stand on her legs. . . . The doctor sent her to a specialist who found nothing organically wrong . . . it was all nervous agitation. . . . She has had several patents she hoped to sell and, with the money, get to Europe.

Two weeks later from Sue: "Our European trip has pretty much withered away." The contracts for Margaret's patents for which she was going to get fifteen hundred dollars and large royalties on signing "bounced back and forth . . . then, the prospective buyers changed their minds. The money was to have been the magic wand that would untie the ropes that bound her."

After the cable announcing her marriage to Fritz, my mother now wrote me, "I did not write, I hope, that I *actually* married him" and asked me to "straighten it out" with my father. "Explain that I *was to* marry him, then thought it over. . . . He was petty and brutal," and he did not share her interests. "I don't think there will be another man I would ever consider marrying." By mid-December she gave up the 91st Street apartment and, putting furniture and household things into storage, moved with Sue to a residential hotel where they had a two-room suite but often not enough money for food. Zsuzsi went back to Hungary to stay with her brother.

I told TD, to which he answered, "Your letter about Sue just received. I'll do my best to get in touch with her, but the one thing I want to avoid is argument with or complaint from Margaret. The only thing I can think of is to send some neutral third party to give Sue a little money for her personal use."

I longed to get closer to my father, to like him and to be liked by him. In this desire lived an almost unconscious expectation that if I succeeded, it might last longer than TD's paternalness, if for no other reason than that he was *really* my father. And I needed one. Not only did Anny make having a closer relationship difficult, but Margaret, although sending me loving letters and American cigarettes, at the same time wrote to my father to beware of me because I was capable of causing him and his family no end of trouble and sorrow. I did manage some afternoons to join him in his study and browse among his beautiful books, being sensitive to his refinement and learning and proud of the entry I found among the volumes of reference:

> Székely, Artúr, Economist, born 1887 in Kisber. Completed study of law in Budapest, Berlin and Paris; Secretary of the Budapest Chamber of Commerce and Industry; Director of Hungary's Inter-Commerce Bureau. Chief Works: "The History of Materialism," "The Law of Economics & the Edicts in Time of War," "The Politics of Hungary's Commercial Contracts."

Penetrating his cool restraint was a challenge. During one such afternoon, the sun printing a pattern on the floor, he in his lounge chair with a cigar, I sitting nearby, he asked me if I spoke French and whether I was familiar with the French poets—Baudelaire, Rimbaud, Verlaine, Éluard. I had to admit my limitation to La Fontaine's "La Cigale et la fourmi," which was assigned by my ninth-grade French teacher who also chose me to recite Victor Hugo's "Après la battaille" at a school assembly. Since his student days at the Sorbonne in Paris, my father had become somewhat of a Francophile, loving the language and the literature. To "keep up," he engaged a French professor who came to the house once a week for conversation.

"My French is not as learned as yours," I told him, "but is adequate for reading and simple talking." He chose not to test this. Rising from his chair, he took down from among his books a slender volume of French love poems, *Toi et moi,* by Paul Geraldy, and said while presenting it to me, "I think you will enjoy these."

As I turned some pages, he walked to his desk and removed a letter from one of its drawers. Handing it to me, he seemed both discomfited and at ease. "Your mother, the one who gave birth to you, asked me to give you this."

Surprised and a little scared, I looked at the neat, even handwriting in purple ink on the square, linen-finish lavender envelope addressed to Mademoiselle Yvette Szekely. I did not want to open it just then, nor, I thought, would my father expect or want me to. He must have felt some obligation to tell me something about her. More genial and relaxed than I was used to seeing him, he told me my mother was a French-Swiss girl he once knew and loved who came from Geneva to spend a year in Budapest. Her name then was Marthe Meylan, but since her marriage it has been Marthe Vautravers. She lives with her husband in Geneva. For all these nineteen years my father has been writing to her secretly, keeping her informed of where and how I was, sending her pictures of me at various stages of growing up since babyhood. As immensely curious as I now was, I didn't feel familiar enough with him to ask for more than he volunteered to tell me. It was like the passing of a platter of bite-sized tea sandwiches that after two or three offerings are not passed again. The way he said she was "very nice" led me to think that he harbored a tender memory of her, especially when he went back to the same drawer of his desk and gave me two small photographs of her that had been taken when he first knew her—when she was my age. They showed a very pretty young woman in what looked to be a long dark velvet dress with a lace collar, one picture in profile, the other looking straight out with a broad, happy smile.

Here, alone with my father and another mother, the afternoon light beginning to deepen into shadows, I felt for a moment a little like a feature player in a stage drama. When later in the privacy of my room I looked at the picture again—searchingly—I thought I saw a resemblance in the eyes, nose, and mouth. It pleased me that she was pretty and looked joyful. Hesitant, yet with a deliberateness, I opened the letter addressed to me. The easy flowing handwriting was so neat, so even, letters not flourishingly large nor closely scrunched, that I pictured the writer as one who was composed, assured. Written in French, the letter reads in translation:

> Yvette, cherie!! tender object of my most intimate thoughts, my greatest care, my cruel sorrow, my heavy secret, will I find you again??? Do you want my love? Will you deign to come and draw from the bottomless reserve of tenderest feelings that for twenty years I have nurtured for you? Would you try to come to me? Will

Marthe Meylan, Yvette Szekely's birth mother, as she looked when Artúr Székely first met her in Budapest in 1911.

> you give me the ultimate joy of holding you in my arms??? Be good—don't say no. For twenty years I have lived but for that day. If, later, the future must separate us for always, you will carry with you the thought of having given me the greatest happiness of my life. I believe I deserve it. You will judge for yourself after having heard me. Only you perhaps will be able to understand the nameless sacrifice I imposed on myself.
>
> Write to me sweet loved one. Tell me that you forgive me. I place here the expressions of my piteous emotions, my heart, my tears. Having broken through their barrier today, I send you that tumultuous flood of feelings that was pressed in my heart.
>
> I kiss you much more than a million times. I am all yours! Call me "Marraine."

I stepped aside a little from this flood's path. Max's comment, after I quoted it in one of my letters to him, was

> She sounds like a character in one of those old-fashioned novels where they talk in paragraphs. The inappropriateness of that letter to your character and your cool clear eyes as I see you reading it is complete and perfect. She surely can't have all these feelings, can she? Mothers are a queer species and I don't know. But she's French, and I guess when she gets through with that you'll find she lives largely and somewhat coolly in her head.

TD read it differently:

> You know, at first when I saw these two pictures of your mother, I thought they were you, made up to look a little older & more severe—some Hungarian hair stunt. And I laughed. But after I read your mothers letter I studied her face. Alike! Your almost the image of her. And her letter sounds like you. You two must have a lot in common. Better go see her.

They were both right. Her letters that followed were considerably calmer. Possibly from emotional necessity, I read into them not only a common appreciation of nature and aesthetics but also an uncritical adoration for me that I now imagined could come only from one's *real* mother. Eager to confirm this, I rained forth somewhat of a spray myself with questions like "Are you happy?" "What kind of a man is your husband?" "What does he do?" "Does he know I am your child?" "Why didn't you have other children?" "How old are you?"

I was to learn the answers but not just yet.

Summer having ended, I attended the University of Budapest, gave private lessons in English, and read all the Tauchnitz and Albatross paperback editions I could find of Maugham, Joyce, Huxley, Hemingway, and Dos Passos. Despite reports of the ratio of unemployed to employed in New York now being one out of three, spelling dim prospects for supporting myself, my sights were set on returning to New York before the end of 1933. Encouragement came from both TD and Helen. He told me not to consider my future dark and that he would help me. "I feel that with your gifts you will not need or want help long. And that is not said in order to lessen your needs in connection with me. What I do will be done gladly—and you need not worry as to that. . . ." Helen wrote me of "a big plan" she had for Iroki that would ease TD's financial burden of its maintenance. "He must always be free from that in order to be free in his creative mood." Her idea: to take "a few people—our kind" as paying guests.

> No money would be made, just expenses, and all those guests would naturally be people not antagonistic to TD's temperament—maybe advanced writers fairly successful who would ordinarily take summer places only this year would be economizing. My ultimate aim is to establish a retreat for a period for really sincere and talented people, maybe in the field of letters, science, and art. Of course TD's spirit is back of it all. No one interested in the material side of the life of TD will qualify because that had never been a part of what he and I based our relationship on. After Iroki is really launched there will always be room for young aspiring people—a study room and board I hope, certain hours for work and play etc. You are welcome to come for intervals or longer if you wish, with your father's consent. . . . If you decide to come to America TD says that he can give you part time work anyway to start you off—and you may stay with us for a while—as long as it works out

> agreeably. But he says that you would have to have the written consent of your father and real mother. He doesn't want any plots and schemes from Margaret or any trouble with her whatsoever.

Helen went on to say that their scheme of life from here on was going to be a communal one with everyone contributing to the making of it; no one would be maintained at the expense of anyone else. "But anything you do in this connection, I want the request to come from your father. I am not worrying about Margaret maligning anyone . . . she can only interpret other people by her own motives."

When I wrote to my sister about this possibility for me if and when I returned, her answer was fraught with warnings. "There could be all sorts of action on Margaret's part, action that simple minds like ours cannot foretell," and "you would be giving Margaret the most fertile grounds for making the air teem with stories . . . you would have to face people on the basis of 'what have they heard about me.'"

Letters from Margaret, wanting me back as soon as I wanted to come, reassuring me that she had changed a lot since we parted: "I too grew up somewhat and I am certain you'll like me as an adult, taking things less tragically and ever so much more calmly." She wrote that although jobs and money were scarce, there was hope. "I am trying hard to land a job for you with the Federated Press." Meanwhile, she was trying to get a job for herself in Washington, D.C., with the National Recovery Administration and had sold three articles to the *World Telegram.* She was also laying great store on one of her inventions that she named "The Fantom Grip," on which she had obtained a patent. A Saks Fifth Avenue advertisement in the *New Yorker* described it as "a new and brilliantly simple device, a one-piece garter tip that can't possibly make a lump under your sleekest frock. We were so impressed that we had special foundation garments made with Fantom Grip stocking supporters."

My Swiss mother, who had kept my relationship to her a strictly guarded secret from her husband and family, invited me to come to Geneva in May and stay at least through the summer, asking that I not make too many plans for beyond. "Lay your cares aside, think only of the happiness of being reunited . . . all will fall into place." She wrote of her plans for where I would live: "I will try to find the environment I want to see you in: not far from my house, pastoral setting with garden, near center of town, young companions. . . ." She was signing her letters to me with her initials, M.V.

Later, it was agreed that I would go to Geneva, making my departure help toward smoothing the disharmony between Anny and my father that my living with them occasioned or at least accentuated. Anny would write me,

> Not to seem conceited, but I dare state that perhaps I am indeed the one in whom you can confide, to whom you can write and tell everything for the very reason that you don't stand close to me. I can be objective while humanly understanding, and I like to help. For instance, I now have the feeling that you're a little scared of returning to America and that maybe it would be better to listen to me and choose the good old boring but secure Budapest life.

The leaves turned green again along the Avenue of the Italian Trees, and afternoon tea was moved to the terrace, where one could almost swallow the yellow of warm Spring. The cable car railway on the hill opposite now carried picnickers instead of skiers. Sunday mornings, my father, in buckskin shorts and loden jacket, would set out with Anny and me for a not-too-strenuous hike in the hills, timed to arrive after two hours at a noted garden-restaurant. If not exactly Edwardian, the picture resembled a kind of Old World gentility that screened the present and muted its rumblings. Preparing to leave for Geneva later in the month, I felt the time arrive to draw a curtain closed on the golden cage in which I hadn't learned to sing.

A porter hoisted my baggage onto the train bound for Geneva. Anny, my father, and I stood on the platform near the steps I would mount, waiting for the "all aboard" signal, thinking about what other parting statements to make. We would not miss each other, and yet, having lived together for a year, we were loosely basted to each other with a spider's thread.

The closer the time approached arrival in Geneva, the more jittery I felt. How must I meet a mother I had never seen? A mother who never saw *me* after I was born? It was just past noon and sunny when the train slowed past the station sign GENEVE and then came to a halt. Travelers in my compartment were gathering their belongings. I was in no hurry. From my window seat that offered me cover, I looked out at the people who had come to meet the arrivals. Which one was my mother? How would I know her?

Porters came on board for baggage. Slowly I made my way along the corridor to the nearest getting-off steps and down to the platform, where I stood and scanned its length. I felt apart from the human race, apart from the men and women who milled about, greeting dismounting passengers. My eyes selected, then discarded, this too short one, that too fat one. I fastened upon a woman in a navy blue suit and a white straw hat who was pacing up and down, looking. After she passed me a few times, I suddenly had a sure feeling that I was the one she was looking for. The next time she approached I sought eye contact with her. She came toward me with an unsure questioning look. "Are you Yvette?" When I nodded yes, she clasped me to her and, overcharged with emotion, this perfect stranger poured out an excess of endearments, a tide of released feelings that had long been suppressed. Having just come from a year of snow-capped propriety and restraint, I hung back from this disconcerting demonstration.

As she was leading the way to Le Buffet, the station restaurant-café, I took a critical note of what I presumed to be a provincial view of elegance—rings, chatelaine, a touch of frill—or was it just being French? Passing up the sidewalk terrace, she chose an inside corner table and ordered lunch that would keep us there long enough for me to hear what she seemed to have a pressing need to tell me. I had the impression that she felt an urgency about it. In the course of our next five months together, she would be filling in a detail here and there when something touched her memory or I asked questions. But now, between bites of food and sips of wine, she sounded a little dramatic with a tinge of self-pity, and there entered also flecks of guilt suggestive of a confession and its quest for pardon. She did indeed sound "like a character in one of those old-fashioned novels"—not like me, as Max said.

She began by describing the home in Le Sentier where she was born and grew up—a town nestled along the Jura Mountains by the Lac de Joux. It was the locale of Switzerland's great watchmaking centers, where her grandparents, Charles August Meylan and Julie Duvanel, came from a generation of watchmakers.

As she unfolded her story, I could not yet bear in mind that this stranger was my mother. I looked for a physical resemblance between us. Seeing her nose, I recognized mine—a slightly more humble version. We had the same brown eyes, but her rounder face with its pleasant look of acceptance and her engaging sweet smile more strikingly resembled the mother of Queen Elizabeth II as she looked then. If one knew how we were related, one could find a likeness.

Without feeling an association or identification with the story she told, I felt a spark of interest that fanned my curiosity as might an absorbing novella from which I was far removed. My listening to it was sort of aloof, almost condescending. Because I didn't know what to call this mother, I avoided calling her anything. Weeks, months later, if I wanted her attention when she was not in the same room with me or in close earshot, I would go to where she was. On all counts, hers and mine, I could not call her "Mother," and perhaps because we knew that that is who she was it didn't seem quite well put to call her by her first name. Nor would "Madame Vautravers," with the formality and distance such a term of address evoked, have measured up with her admiration of my bare back as I dressed and her remark of pleasure: "To think I made that!"

But to go back to Le Buffet and that corner table where I was to hear, in part, how all this came about.

When the youngest of Charles Meylan's five sons, Jules-César Meylan, and his wife, Josephine Vananti, gave birth to a daughter they named Marthe-Ida and two years later a son, Gaston, they were to become my unwitting grandparents. They were a reserved, a frugal, an industrious, and, for that, a prospering Swiss family, self-contained and devoted to one another. Marthe grew up in the valley, skating the three miles to school on winter's frozen lake, the mountains in the distance thickly green and purple and tipped with snow. After secondary school, she attended a junior college for the learning of the domestic sciences, a training then expected of young women for their presumed future roles as wives and mothers.

At nineteen, after returning home from a short stay with a cousin in Paris, Marthe's flights of fancy scaled over and beyond the Jura Mountains, envisioning herself on the French stage in the role of Marguerite Gautier. When a visiting friend of the family, a Mme. Darcy, now living in Budapest, talked about its liveliness and bright lights and suggested that Marthe might be interested in accepting a position as French companion to the two young children of a Hungarian count and countess, she eagerly applauded this prospect. The parents gave their consent on Mme. Darcy's assurance that she would watch over and befriend Marthe. The first two months in Budapest in the home of the count and countess were not only disappointing but also untenable when, among other slights, the portions doled onto her plate at the dinner table became appallingly scant. She left and went to share an apartment and expenses with a young French woman, Nadine Aubert, a little older than she, with whom she had earlier become acquainted. With help from her family and some money she was able to earn by giving French lessons, she could manage to stay on in Budapest—the big city, the "Queen of the Danube."

Nadine, who was more sophisticated and had a lover, invited Marthe one day to join them and a friend for dinner and a concert. It was then that Marthe met twenty-three-year-old Artúr Székely, a young economist and doctor of law, who seemed to her sublimely handsome and worldly and with whom in a matter of weeks she became wholeheartedly enamored. Nadine and her lover teased them about being so old fashioned and correct, but after a time they began a love affair. Marthe considered herself engaged and was happy and trusting about the relation. Artúr was not quite ready for marriage. He wanted to delay it even after she became pregnant, but meanwhile, being honorable and complying with the convention of that time, he wrote the expected letter to her father asking for her "hand." In mid October, eight days after I was born in a private clinic, Artúr took his child to a wet nurse who boarded infants and small children outside the city. It was Artúr's plan that Marthe go home to her parents and that they would marry in June. They visited their baby just twice before Marthe left Budapest to return to Switzerland, never having revealed to her parents the birth of her child. Not knowing, Marthe's parents did not look with favor on their beloved only daughter's intent to marry a foreigner, and Marthe had a hard time persuading her father to give his consent, if not his blessing.

For the next several months the trousseau was being readied—seamstresses embroidering initials on bed linen and towels and lingerie—and Marthe, in secret behind locked doors, was knitting baby things. When all was ready and the trunk lid lowered, there came a letter from Artúr that said he was in love with two women—one of them she, the other someone in Budapest whom he planned to marry if

Marthe would release him from his commitment to her. If she were willing, he was prepared to keep the now seven-month-old baby and adopt her legally, changing her name from Meylan—as entered on the birth certificate—to Székely. In that event, the law required that the mother sign an affidavit declaring that she abandoned the child.

It was at this point in her story—the facing of agonizing choices—that I thought back to the extravagant plea in her first letter to me: "tender object of my greatest care, my most intimate thoughts . . . my cruel sorrow . . . my heavy secret . . . my nameless sacrifice . . . you will judge for yourself after having heard me . . . tell me that you forgive me." Watching the movement of her wrist with its tinkling bracelet and hearing the raising and lowering of her voice, I thought she might better have realized her girlhood fantasy about being an actress.

Crushed by the letter and heartsick, Marthe made her painful decision to sign the affidavit. She justified it by reasoning that, compared with the alternative, it would be in the child's best interest to be legitimized and given the advantages Artúr's social and financial position could provide. She chose never to tell her parents or anyone else. Given the social and moral climate of that time and place, she would have been considered disgraced in the eyes of family, friends, and society.

Marthe accepted Artúr's proposal that they meet in Paris, where he and his bride were to be on their honeymoon. She wanted, besides, to see the woman who would have her child. They met at a prearranged café, where behind nerve-stretching tension, Marthe signed the papers.

The event sent her into such despair that, by accident or by reason of her state of mind, she walked into an oncoming streetcar. After her marriage two years later to Edouard Vautravers, who loved and pampered her and indulged her slightest wish, she was to discover that as a result of the accident she could never again become pregnant. Marthe was happy in her marriage except for being obsessed by the memory of her child. She would have recurring dreams about a little girl, who when approached and almost within touch, would disappear. Unable to tell anyone, especially not her husband, she carried the burden alone. She had an arrangement with Artúr whereby he would send a card with "Greetings," this being the cue to a letter awaiting her at General Delivery in the main post office. There she would find pictures of the child in her progressive growing stages and news about her. Marthe fantasized that in the years to come her secret child could spend her summers and school holidays with her. These hopes were shattered when Artúr wrote to tell her that his marriage was the greatest mistake of his life: his wife, whom he divorced, had gone to America taking his two children with her.

Here the voice of this stranger, my newly begotten mother, intoned enough drama and level of stress as to make me want to "turn the page," curious to hear what happened next while my connection to it felt unreal. But it was time to leave that corner table in Le Buffet. I would hear more in the course of the summer. Paying the check and slipping on her gloves, she ended by telling me that she explained my expected visit to her husband and to the family with whom I was to board by telling them that an old acquaintance from Budapest was sending his daughter to Geneva to study and had asked that she watch over her. From the weekly allowance from her husband for household expenses, Marthe was able, by various economies, to secretly set aside enough money to pay for my living arrangements and board in the home of M. and Mme. Monachon, who had a daughter my age and lived in a house with a spacious garden within walking distance of the lakeshore. They also had two other students as live-in boarders. My instant new mother and I would be together for afternoon walks, on weekend visits to her home, and for excursions.

Having told all this to TD in my letters to him, I received a reply, in which he said he was interested, but "do not believe all of your real mothers story. It has odd gaps and vague psychology spots." And again in a later letter, he asked how I got along with my "long lost mother. Somehow I cannot quite swallow all of her smooth story, but if you really like her and she helps you mentally or emotionally in any little way I can be glad that you found her."

Nineteen-year-old Mady Monachon was tall and blond and had deep brown eyes and a wide smile that invited gladness from the beholder. She and I became close friends and each other's confidantes, although, of course, I could not reveal my relationship to the woman we both referred to as "Madame Vautravers." My room, which was next to Mady's, was small and square with a big balcony overlooking the garden. The one window framed the pointy steeple of a church and, behind it, the peak of Mont Blanc, which looked from this far distance sometimes white, sometimes like the smoke of one's breath in cold air. The room had patterned wallpaper, a narrow bed, a table, and an armoire. I propped my doll, Pat, on the bed next to Mady's doll, Nelly, and tacked on the wall above the table—which I used as a desk—a picture each of my father, TD, and Max. I felt the homely comfort of a home and of belonging and of having everybody fond of me.

When I was not in school or an observer at the League of Nations, this mother would call for me, and we would spend some hours together in one of the parks or on the terrace of a café or along the lake promenade, sometimes taking the boat to Evian or to Coppet to see the museum-house of Mme. de Stael. In the course of the time we spent together, I gradually became aware of her serene commonsense wisdom coupled with a contagiously happy way of looking at life and accepting it. We formed a close and curious friendship. While feeling no constraint about talking to her, as I might to a girlfriend, I blissfully basked in the corona of her secret mother love for me. She adored me, and I reveled in it.

After meeting him and after an occasional weekend in their home, Edouard Vautravers enfolded me in a paternal affection, innocently enough calling me "la fille de la famille." Their house, looking like an illustration for the letter H in a child's alphabet book, sat on about three acres in a pastoral area on the route de Cointrin, where besides a vegetable and flower garden and an orchard they kept two riding horses, some sheep, chickens, barn cats, and their English setter, Jessy. They named the place "Le Poirier."

I was invited to stay there for a few weeks in August, during part of which time their other houseguests included my unsuspecting seventy-six-year-old grandmother and two young cousins, fifteen-year-old Georgette and ten-year-old Pierre-César, children of my equally unmindful uncle. We rode the horses and petted the sheep and fed the chickens and picked the fruit and flowers and had teas in the garden and picnics in the mountain woods—all the summer things. My grandmother reminded me of a jovial brown teapot—a little round, a little squat. Leaning her arthritic weight on a cane, she had a wit and comic humor that could send a young group of us into seizures of laughter.

One afternoon when we were gathered under a shade tree and had just finished tea, my mother asked me to walk up the road with her a bit on the pretext of having something to show me. As we sauntered off, arm in arm, heads together as when telling and hearing a confidence, she said, "Just before we came to the garden my mother called me aside and asked me, 'How old is Yvette?' When I told her, she asked, 'When were you in Budapest?' and then she just looked at me and nodded and said nothing more."

It was a happy time, those months in Geneva, as if their blue-skyness were bottled into a single unhurried day that could wait to let an insect with shiny wings pass by. It seemed that I was content in a way I had never been before—swathed in warmth, love, and humor. My mother dared hope that I might stay, get married, raise a family, and live near her—happily ever after. However that may have been, and despite the flower-bordered sanctuary of the Monachon and Vautravers gardens, a centripetal force tugged at me to go back to TD, back to New York. With all its uncertainty, much less the expectation of a welcoming band with bids for my indistinct services, I felt I needed the broader space.

Although she half expected and half hoped it and held out inducements, I did not want to go back to live with my mother Margaret. To circumvent the possibility of having from necessity to do that, I wrote to Margie to ask her mother if I might go to stay with them in Rockville Center for just long enough to find my bearings and set my course. When they agreed, I could give my father an address to which he could send a monthly allowance, its modest amount dictated by the limitations imposed by the Hungarian government on money sent out of the country. At the end of September 1933, he bought my ship passage from Le Havre to New York and sent me the money for railroad fare. His several letters in those last weeks were so weighted with detailed instructions that I must have asked was there no sentiment, no feeling, to which he replied: ". . . vis à vis personal feelings, they don't lend themselves to paper—but you can be especially certain that I too very much regret you will once more cross the ocean and God knows when we'll meet again. Take care." He asked me to convey his warm greetings to Marthe and to thank her for him for everything she did and would do for me.

After I left Geneva for Paris, Marthe wrote that since my departure she had suffered "cruelly" from the ensuing void. She was glad she had had the courage to come to the station, where her eyes had followed me until I became a speck in the distance on the moving train as it gathered speed. After that, she had gone into town and bought a new hat.

7

New Deals: 1933–38

It was an anxious crossing on the *SS Manhattan,* sailing from love and shelter into a chancy, fenceless world. On arrival in New York harbor there was the same clang of commotion under the canopied pier as when I left more than a year ago—this time with arriving passengers being greeted by friends and family and lovers.

As I walked down the gangplank, I suddenly felt very small, very alone, unsure. Finding my way through the noisy turbulence to a telephone, I called the number I knew by heart. TD's voice answered. A sense of relief mixed with apprehension grazed me. Hearing me all of a sudden here in New York took him, I think, by surprise. He suggested I check into a hotel then called Manhattan Towers at 76th Street and Broadway, three blocks from the Ansonia, where he had permanent quarters. After that I could "come up and say hello" to him.

When I appeared at his suite after not having seen him for a year and a half, his bigness, the way his eyes latched into mine, how his mouth curled into an amused half smile over the big teeth when he greeted me with, "Hello, Sox," he was again familiar and yet new and strange enough to make me feel shy and in awe of that impenetrable detachment he emanated, as if nothing could touch him. He asked me about my plans, and I told him about the possibility of going to Rockville Center to stay for the time being with Margie's family. Had he *not* approved, that would have given me the strength of his support, the feeling that he was concerned enough about me to take a position, but he only said, in that joshing, kidding way, "Tra la, off to the perilous backwoods to convert the heathens. But don't worry, you'll always land on all fours." I wasn't so sure about that—I was treading where I couldn't touch bottom and sort of hoped he would toss out an inflated rubber ring, that is, offer an alternative. I thought of his encouragement to come back, how he had said he would help out until I got a start. "As bad as things are here I dont think you make any mistake when you return. . . . As for looking after you for the time being, if you choose to come I can do something for you and will." His telephone rang. Turning to me before answering, he said, "Call me tomorrow—we'll go for dinner."

I visited my mother Margaret, whom I, with my sister Sue's help, had prepared for my not coming to live with them. She now accepted this and seemed pleased to see me. She was being assistant secretary for the Foreign Press Correspondents Association.

For the next three months I lived in Rockville Center with Margie's family on a tree-lined street of suburban homes with front lawns and back yards. Prodded by the need to earn money, we conceived the idea of starting a private kindergarten in the large basement room that had a door leading out to the yard. We were buttressed by the assumed knowledge Margie had gathered from having attended the Ethical Culture's "Normal School" for the study of teaching preschool children. The Evemar Kindergarten began and ended with six children. Margie's authoritative knowledge in the field was not exactly charged with exuberance, but we set out optimistically enough with a not unusual curriculum of games, stories, crayons, eleven o'clock milk and peanut butter, and back yard jumping around for fresh air. After some weeks this began to pall, and we dreaded the nine o'clock doorbell. We ran out of fresh ideas to keep the tots at least busy, if not enthused. The enterprise gradually and irredeemably wound down like an unattended hand-cranked gramophone and then stopped—three months after its inception.

But before that there would be my occasional trips to New York from afternoon to next morning when I would see and be with TD. In between these visits he would send playful notes with information about his comings and goings.

After we discontinued the school, I moved back to New York, where, in a brownstone rooming house on 83rd Street near Riverside

Drive—near enough to TD—I rented a furnished room for five dollars a week that was large and square enough to permit supplementing the bed, chair, and table in it with a desk and bookcases I fashioned by painting and stacking orange crates from the A & P and an old rocking chair I found and painted canary yellow for TD to sit in when he visited. I was getting thirty-five dollars a month from my father (to share with Sue), and I was to earn six dollars a week for typing, editing, taking dictation, and writing for TD. My typical list of "to do's" ran as follows:

Write introduction to "Mahatma Gandhi: The Magic Man"
Make six copies of "Communism in America"
Edit movie script for "Sister Carrie"
Write study of Samuel Butler's life
Write introduction to "The Way of All Flesh"
Take dictation and type
Buy baked beans, milk, bread
Go to library

On those occasions when TD came to my room in lieu of my going to the Ansonia to discuss work or take dictation, he would seat himself in the yellow rocker, where he spent little nuggets of time-out from his desk and its demands—rocking, brooding, and—like his Sister Carrie—dreaming. Although my father was sending letters of concern and well-wishes with his monthly help, it was still TD who was my giant father figure, whose displeasure I feared, whose affection I coveted, and on whose illusory upholding pillar I leaned even though I was ever apprehensive that some small thing, or something imagined by him, would elicit such beet-colored jealous rage as might make him go away from me forever. I never lost my awe of him or those little spottings of fear, nor did his literary stature get smaller in my eyes as I stayed blind to what critics called his "lumbering" style.

As the depression wore on, Franklin Delano Roosevelt's New Deal sprouted more and more initials—NRA, CWA, WPA, CCC, NYA, ERB—and those my age who were not exactly in a position to be architects of their future applied for the jobs with the initials. Somehow I was made aware that the ERB (Emergency Relief Bureau) was hiring young college graduates for the job of Social Investigator at the unbelievably high salary of $27.50 per week. I applied, was credited with the equivalent of the educational requirement, and was accepted. I continued my work for TD on a more sporadic schedule. After some years, the ERB job assumed permanence and, with it, security under civil service for those who took and passed the examination. But in that May of 1934, reveling in my newfound affluence, I first moved quickly to a ten dollars per week room on a higher floor in the same brownstone and soon after down to Washington Square into the Holly Hotel, with the yellow rocking chair for TD tied onto the back of the taxi. After that, I found my very first unfurnished apartment, a tiny room facing a school playground on Sullivan Street.

Before signing the lease, I needed to know whether TD would like it, would approve. I left him a note asking him to look at it. When he did, he answered that it was about the smallest thirty-three dollars worth he ever saw, considering that I got a room with all service at the Holly for forty dollars. "Of course you'd make it charming with a few blunt pencils etc. So, if it will really make you happy, take it."

On becoming TD's publishers that September, Simon and Schuster gave a big cocktail party on October 28, 1934, at Iroki. Margie and I were among the couple of hundred guests who received an invitation. In mine was a note from TD: "Here is $\$4^{00}$. That will get you two out here. We will see that you get back. Love." Drinking, eating, talking, the celebrating celebrities mingled, sniffing that touch of sparkling snap in the afternoon's late October air. I had met many of them before at the 57th Street Thursdays. Being always the youngest in such a group, I sensed I was regarded somewhat like a friendly curious pup weaving in and out between their heels, some of them bending to give a sort of absent-minded pat on the head.

My relationship with Helen Dreiser was a mutually friendly but guarded one. My great liking for her was canopied by the hovering cloud of my necessarily concealed liaison with TD. For her part, she seemed to try—sometimes succeeding, sometimes not—to suppress her shadow of uncertainty about it. When I was in Budapest, she wrote to say she hoped things were better for me. There was a shade of admonition, if not reprimand: "Controlling the muscles of the body does not mean the body is less beautiful."

Two weeks after I got the ERB job, Helen sent me a somewhat tight little typewritten note, wishing me well and responding to the previously talked about possibility of my renting the little log cabin at Iroki for weekends and vacations. She said she would be glad to have me rent it "as long as things are pleasant," but she did not want "any contact whatsoever with Margaret . . . I have been bothered a great deal in the past by the meddlings of other people in my affairs, and Margaret played a part in this."

With regard to Helen and me as it concerned him, TD was loath to brook problems. When they were both in California and I was staying in the cabin, he told me to send my letters to him in long business envelopes with the address typed and to mail them from New York instead of from Mount Kisco. "Helen lives in the idea I must live for her alone but it cant be done." "I have told her repeatedly that I cannot & will not live an exclusive life with her."

My life also in some indistinct, undefinable way was not lived exclusively for him, and so his exaggerated jealousies and often unfounded accusations had a tinge of truth. I was attracted and attractive to younger men, while I not only believed but strove to persuade him that he was the chief person in my life. He could not accept, undiluted, he said, my declarations of love and devotion; he had to think that I cared for others. "Naturally you would conceal knowledge of the others so as not to hurt me." He had gone to see the movie *Escape Me Never,* based on Margaret Kennedy's *The Constant Nymph,* and said that in many ways Gemma reminded him of me. "But after all—as Gemma said of her artist-god—I would not change you. You are as you are. And if I value your friendship and your diluted affection . . . I try to understand and endure as you understand and endure."

But he was not consistently so forgiving. One late afternoon when he was visiting me, I answered the telephone and could not suppress my delight on hearing it was Bill, "Captain" of that long-ago magical short-lived spring, whom I had not heard from in at least three years. TD drew his conclusions: "you cannot expect me to rejoice in the spectacle of myself as a secondary figure, serving as a stop-gap in the absence of your real love or first choice." "Lets call it a day." But we didn't. I somehow withstood the force of these storms that would abate after a while and return to the familiar SEE YOU WEDNESDAY NIGHT YOUR ROOM SIX THIRTY LOVE telegrams.

Helen rented me the log cabin at Iroki for the summers of 1934 and 1935. I shared it and the twenty-five dollars per month rent with Marion Neumeister, a girl I made friends with when she stood behind me in the line of applicants for the ERB job. On Fridays after work we took the train to Mount Kisco, stopped to buy groceries, and arranged with a Greek handyman-caretaker whose English was minimal to drive us to and from the train station. During daylight hours we did our summering mostly around and under the trees by the little cabin. On those sun-warm shining mornings, fern-green and smelling of grass, the *Eine kleine Nachtmusik* spinning indoors on our portable hand-wound phonograph would reach out and encircle us where we sat on orange crates having breakfast at the tree stump–supported table top. We cooked on an old two-burner oil stove whose worn-thin wicks when lighted would flicker for a minute, die, and have to be relighted—match after match. Inside, where the shuttered, odd-shaped windows kept the room cool-dark, oil lamp and candles and the bright yellow-red flames from the burning log in the fireplace—which didn't draw too well—furnished the light by night. There being no plumbing, we washed the dishes and ourselves with water we carried in pails from an outside faucet at the Big House, which was rented for the summer and whose tenants were not too happy about this arrangement. There were weekends when we invited a group of colleagues from the office, twenties-young, unattached, now roasting frankfurters, now singing interchangeably "There was a union maid who never was afraid" and Cole Porter's "You're the Top." Boy met girl, girl met boy, and sometimes along the way they married—among them Marion.

At the end of the summer of 1934, I moved again, away from the tiny apartment smelling of still-new paint on Sullivan Street that a friend dubbed my "chest of drawers," to another slightly larger one, a basement apartment on Perry Street, where daylight was underexposed but a wood-burning fireplace and TD's rocker made it cheerful and warm, a place he loved to come to. Later he would write, "You know I think so much of that little Perry Street basement. . . . You may find lighter, airier quarters but whether with more real charm, I doubt."

The winter of 1935, around the end of February, TD left the Ansonia to stay in the Mount Kisco house, coming to New York periodically on some business or errand when he would alert me with a note or telegram, "Necessary to see you tomorrow evening if possible be there." He came to Perry Street to sit in his chair by the fire, seeking love and understanding yet not quite trusting what I gave to be undivided, exclusive. When in May he left for some months in Los Angeles and I went to live in the cabin, he lamented, "some how I can only think of you as living with other persons—and betimes writing me. . . . If you love me so intensely, why the fascination that other temperaments have for you." But for each misgiving, each accusation, there came assurances of his caring: "You have to be taken as is . . . after all, Yvette-Gemma, I love your spirit, your approach to life, your kindness, your understanding . . . you're like sunshine and flowers."

When we were together, although making love was rarely excluded, I no longer felt, as I had at first, that that was his primary reason for wanting me. Rather, it now seemed that he craved affection, companionship, and understanding.

That winter TD was mostly depressed, confused, burdened by appeals from various Communist-sponsored platforms to speak against fascism and related dangers. At a time when news of Germany's persecution of Jews became known throughout the world, TD was confronted by the Communist magazine *The New Masses,* asking for an explanation and contradiction of his antisemitic views. It prominently featured his statement that he had no hatred for the Jew and had nothing to do with Hitler or fascism. "I emphatically repudiate any inference in my writing that will be interpreted as counter to this."

When he got to California he was again and still burdened with legal and financial troubles and alternating physical distresses—his eyes, an infected toe, stomach cramps—the while writing about a theory of philosophy based on science. He was sharing the home of his friend, George Douglas, and was not amused by the people around him. He was lonely. "Some essential thing is wrong," he wrote me. He kept proffering the possibility of my going out there to visit, to be near him, to help out, until he wired "VISIT IMPOSSIBLE COMPLICATIONS." He worried a lot about money, was afraid about spending it, and was concerned about the price of things. He said he would try not to make so much of his dark thoughts. "Just to make you feel better, I'm not so blue (today). Tomorrow? You see *every day* I have my five to nine A.M. horrors. I never get a break. They never take a holiday."

During the summer of 1935, Chris, the Greek caretaker, was giving me driving lessons. That those lessons were more in Greek than in English demands no small credit for my passing the road test in Katonah. For seventy-five dollars I bought from a Mount Kisco garageman a second-hand maroon-red convertible roadster, twenty dollars down and five dollars per week on the balance. Having given up the Perry Street basement, I had to think about another place to live for the winter. TD suggested the Ansonia, where, he said, I could get a large room and bath for fifty dollars per month, including the otherwise added expenses of laundry, telephone, utilities. He offered to contribute ten dollars a month toward the rent to make it affordable for me.

The end of the summer I moved into room 10-161. It didn't have much daylight, but I had gotten used to that on Perry Street. With its wall-to-wall carpeting, lots of electric outlets, a big old-fashioned bathroom, and huge closets, it felt wonderfully luxurious. With the insistent offer of a too artistic friend who wound bright multicolored yarn around the frames of lampshades and covered the couch-bed with a lively royal-blue spread, we stripped the room of its monochromatic hotel beige-brown. Books, pictures, flowers, and TD's yellow rocker completed the transformation. TD said he was moved by it: "To me its as good as any island in the South Seas or a peak in the Alps or the Andes—or streets or restaurants in Paris or Moscow. . . . a place to go to and be in. . . . You could set up a lovely livable world in a hall or a barn."

Earlier in 1935, there appeared on the front page of the *Halifax Mail* a picture of a very young man gazing earnestly out of the column, captioned "Takes Bride." The lead in the article read, "Word has been received from New York of the marriage on January 24 of Kenneth S. Clark, Superintendent of the Canadian Press Bureau in that city, and son of Rev. Dr. and Mrs. J. S. Clark of Halifax, and Mrs. Margaret K. Monahan, the marriage being performed in the presence of the bride's daughter, Miss Suzanne Szekely."

Ken, a thirty-five-year-old widower, and his six-year-old son, Cornelius, with my mother, Margaret, and sister, Sue, moved to an apartment in the West Nineties near Riverside Drive. Not having cooking facilities in my hotel room, I arranged to have my dinners with them for a small contribution.

While getting to know him, I, along with others, became charmstruck by Ken. He was six feet tall and rounder in a cherubic way than that newspaper picture of a youth used for his marriage announcement. The horizontal lines on his high forehead would lift and lower with bemusement or brooding above his wide-set blue-grey eyes. With his full lips and with thick, short-cropped porridge-brown hair capping his neatly rounded head, he looked like a younger Winston Churchill, a

Ken Clark.

young Orson Welles. Everybody liked him. He was winsome and engaging, and he exuded a sort of bending-over tenderness that was almost womanly and mingled with a kind of clean innocence.

But it was not Ken's charm that consumed me so much as thoughts of TD. One of the better things connected with my civil service job was a one-month yearly vacation that, by some astute juggling with weekends, could be stretched to five weeks. Within a day after returning to New York after a holiday in the Canadian Laurentians with Sue and another friend, I was to be driving back with TD in his car to a prearranged several days together in Vermont at one of those simple guest houses on the banks of a rushing river. In the only snapshot of him that I took myself, he is sitting in one of those Adirondack chairs on a grassy

Theodore Dreiser and Yvette Szekely on a vacation trip to Vermont, 1936.

lawn reading a newspaper, a white plastic rabbit with ears erect by his feet. He was in a relaxed, genial mood—actually singing as I drove him around the countryside—singing this little snatch of a song in an unexpectedly small high voice:

> There are men who love now and then
> But they vanish when
> they hear wedding bells ringing—
> But you must agree
> That between you and me
> It's forever or never.
> For me.

He and his song were so touchingly sweet and old fashioned to me, as though I had taken a step backward into the nineteenth century. For breakfast in Brattleboro he surprised me again by ordering pork chops and mashed potatoes, a thing I thought to be just as improper as I once thought making love in the daytime was.

Often when I fell into a mood of being sick of my job, wanting to make a change, TD tried to help me with suggestions and letters "To Whom It May Concern," affirming his consideration of my services and judgment to be valuable. Once, referring to my "always looking for some entrance to the stage," he even suggested that I go to see an actor called Davenport who ran a free theater. Actors were not paid, but a voluntary collection was taken to cover minimal expenses. Of course, for me to consider this as a stepping stone to my "opening night" was out of the question as was his "tip" about a French perfume concern offering fifty dollars a week for a bilingual receptionist to greet incoming buyers. "If you . . . went down looking your smartest you might pick it up," he said.

Despite our continued relation, other parts of my life intruded. A year and a half after their marriage, the climate between my Margaret-mother and Ken—who were far apart temperamentally and in their way of looking at things—fluctuated between storm and lull, each aggravating the other the while he and I became sharply conscious of each other. I was drawn to his sensitive, reckless, amusing self, attracted by his grace, by the way he laughed comfortably out of affection, by a slow-curved empathy that arched an enfolding tenderness. For his part, he perceived me, he said, as "a quiet green young moon in the background." In one of her overemotive seizures, Margaret helped Ken lose his job as head of the New York bureau of the Canadian press when she telephoned his boss in Canada to ask him to discipline Ken for drinking. Their large gloomy apartment was now full of debts and fears: Margaret without work as a designer but trying at home to perfect her invention of a hand weaving loom, Ken trying to write short stories in hopes of selling, and Sue out of work. I became the mainstay, supplementing Ken's occasional earnings from short-lived temporary work writing publicity for the March of Dimes and for Franklin Delano Roosevelt's presidential election campaign. When I asked TD if he would meet and talk to Ken, he said he would be pleased to and would suggest what he could. After they met, he wrote me to say that he liked Clark very much. But he thought him too depressed to impress himself on anyone in a position to help him.

Things eventually improved for Margaret and Ken when he got a job as a feature writer on the *Toronto Star* in Canada, and Margaret, having perfected and patented her weaving invention, was featured in the *New York World Telegram:* "Exiled Writer-Inventor Devises a Loomless Weaver That Outdoes Art of Navajos." She gave up their apartment to join Ken in Toronto, and Sue came to live with me in a two-and-one-half-room apartment we found on East 17th Street.

Occasionally I saw TD in fresh surroundings. On a summery June day in 1937 TD came to spend a day and a night with me on Fire Island, where I was spending some ten days along with Sue and Cornelius. It was there that the shaking news of Stalin's Moscow trials and purges of the old and trusted Bolsheviks and their "confessions" reached us. TD did not want to believe the confessions, but he did want to continue to believe in Russia as a utopian social ideal.

TD was also now heavily into his scientific-philosophical investigations. He was gathering materials for a long treatise that attempted to explain the phenomena of life scientifically, a work that he never completed. After some weeks at the Marine Biological Laboratory in Cold Spring Harbor, Long Island, from where he wrote me that the meals were "fierce" and the scientific people talked too much science, TD rented a studio apartment in that country-like row of houses on West 11th Street, then known as the Rhinelander Gardens, with front porches and grassy, leafy front yards. He had a large room with a fireplace and windows from floor to ceiling that opened like doors onto a tier-like balcony. It was there that he taught me to roll newspapers to serve as logs. He loved to come to our little 17th Street flat, often announcing that he would have dinner with us there. When asked for his preference, he would insist on "something simple, nothing much, I'm not so hungry. Just a steak smothered with onions, some potatoes, some peas, maybe a pudding." Sue was doing occasional typing for him when he was in the process of writing about protons and electrons and discrediting Alexis Carrell's *Man the Unknown.*

In June 1938 at the request of the American League for Peace and Democracy and the League of American Writers, TD left suddenly for Paris to attend an International Convention for peace. His July 14 letter to me from aboard the *SS Normandie* was a lightsome, airy message. All he had to do was "to go and say I represented them and that I believed in peace. That seemed easy so, since I needed a lot of peace just then, I decided to do it." In a later letter, he wrote about Paris, his disappointment in it, and the French—"I'm not happy away from America"—and the fact that he missed working in New York.

He came back to New York in August and for the next three months stayed at the George Washington Hotel near 23rd Street. Because of my friendship with Ken, he was wonderfully helpful then in trying to get publishers and editors to take an interest in Ken's short stories and his outline for a novel, arranging contacts with Arnold Gingrich of *Esquire,* who published one of Ken's stories, and referring him to his own agent, William Lengel. He even offered to find a publisher for a collection of the stories and to write an introduction to them, which he subsequently did. But TD was restless, unhappy, and more than ever bothered by his bronchitis. He left New York in late November to live permanently in California.

8

Final Years: 1939–45

Except for TD's abiding, if often disengaged, attachment to Helen, whatever romances and love affairs he had with other women were something that he never let me know about, nor did I expect him to. The bond between us and my visceral dependence on him held fast. It wasn't until years after his death, reading biographies of him, that I learned of the other women he loved at the same time. They too must have thought they were the only one, as perhaps did he when he was loving them.

World news became more and more gruesome with the horrors of total destruction of cities in the Spanish Civil War, Hitler's murderous march across Europe, and the concentration camps in Germany. And my mother Margaret, too, was warring with me. Whatever foreboding menaced her, she felt that only I was to blame. Her tirades were angry, combative, loud. TD referred to my "at-wits-end letters" as being "fascinating documents" and my situation "almost unbelievable—outrageous." About himself, he gave a picture of pressured busyness, being "caught up with too many things," agents, movie companies, propositions, and—compared with New York—"the absence of real intellectuals—and the stir that goes with them. . . . people of temperamental value to talk to." He spoke of his morning depressions and of being lonely: "And I miss seeing you, your little apartment and Sue. . . . So often I wish you were at hand, just to talk and, better, bathe in your temperament, for you are rest giving. I feel better for being with you. . . . I never forget you anymore than a tree forgets sunlight."

With that recurring restlessness and boredom with my regular salaried job and the need for something in my life that I didn't seem to have, I played with the idea of going to Los Angeles to explore the chances of something nearer to TD. If not to stay, at least to take my month's vacation there. Hadn't TD written so often that he wished I were there, or nearer, and about the favorable prospects? ". . . often I feel that you might do better out here than in N.Y. . . . I believe that you & I might do an occasional film together which would sell." He seemed less encouraging when he thought I might actually come, pointing to possible difficulties, his heavy schedule, his uncertainty of the likelihood of an adequately paying job for me there, but ending by saying that if it didn't look too troublesome for me "and everyone," he was willing to send me one hundred dollars toward expenses for the trip.

He had given me permission to use the upper cabin on the Mount Kisco estate, because the big house was now rented and on the market for sale. He asked me a little nostalgically how it was up there. "It must be charming at Kisco now. . . . The summers are always lovely. But where does loveliness reside? Not in one's surroundings alone unless they harmonize with one's wishes and dreams."

A co-worker friend from my office, Aurelia Salba, joined me for the vacation trip to Hollywood, where we rented a Model T Ford and found a little efficiency apartment. TD invited me to his house on North Hayworth Avenue, where he lived with Helen in what seemed like a smallish duplex. It had a sort of garden-yard attached. TD was sitting in a wicker chair, a light noon breeze catching his thin white hair. He laughed as I approached and made some jocular, teasing greeting. Helen joined us at lunch—just the three of us—doing whatever she was doing with that same devotion to Teddy and forcing a giggle or two to assure him that we were all enjoying ourselves. She was warm and friendly toward me. As usual, when with them both, I was constrained and a bit shy, feeling as though I were wearing a school uniform. All passed smoothly enough, like polite visiting.

After that initial meeting, it was TD who often came to call at the little rented flat I was in. His letter followed soon after I got back to New York, hoping the trip had been interesting and "The little song you taught me runs in my head." He sent along a formal letter of permission for me "to take possession until further notice of the little frame cabin on the hill" at Iroki. The main house and fifteen acres had just been sold. I used it for many weekends the following summer with several of my friends.

TD despaired of the world situation, seething over social conditions in America and everywhere in the world except in his idealized paradisiacal view of Soviet Russia. He despised England and especially blamed British, French, and American industrialists, "the money Lords," for building up and financing nazism in Germany. Instead of a novel, he wrote a book he called *America Is Worth Saving* that was aimed at keeping America from joining the Allies in the war to stop Hitler. Although presenting himself as undismayed by the Stalin-Hitler nonaggression pact, therein seeing safety for Russia, he was shaken a few months later when Hitler started bombing her. Then TD was all for America joining the Allies. He came to New York at the beginning of March to address the American Council on Soviet Relations. He called me late one night from the Commodore Hotel, asking me to come over. Carried away as he was by his conviction that the Soviet Union was the only country to have solved the problem of economic injustice, he complained of Communists using him and his name for propaganda purposes, not always with his consent.

My mind flashed back to his counsel to me ten years before: "But you are going to live in a period of enormous social changes here in the U.S.A. . . . Bother the communists over here. Turn your face to gay, thrilling instruction." When I told him I felt older, more sober, less hopeful, he agreed that I was "a little more sober" but that it added "enormously to your charm," making me "sweeter and more lovable" than in my "playful, restless amorous youth." Two weeks later came a letter explaining that he had to rush off to Newark, Philadelphia, and Washington. He enclosed a copy of his tribute on the death of Sherwood Anderson. I was struck by TD's use of so many quotes from the Bible, his religious allusions to "poetic prayer," "happiness that passeth all understanding," "Christ's dictum . . . the rain falleth on the just and unjust," and "Take no thought of your life, what ye shall eat, or what ye shall drink, not yet for your body, what ye shall put on. Is not life more than meat and body more than raiment?"

When on December 7 the Japanese attacked Pearl Harbor, the

Communist *Daily Worker* asked him for a statement. TD urged all Americans to form a united front to serve the government toward the destruction of the enemy and win the war. But his fanatical rage against "the titled and money'd class of England" did not lessen.

Even before Pearl Harbor, "pro-Allies" America was on an almost-war footing. Now everyone was in some capacity involved in and with the war effort. I wanted to join the WAVES and applied as well for a job with the Red Cross. Neither of these materialized, although TD told me that the assistant director of the Red Cross in Washington wanted to consider me and that he, TD, had sent an honest and, he hoped, helpful letter because he felt I was just the person for the job. It did not occur to me that a recommendation from the Communist-loving Dreiser may possibly have provided a reason for my not being chosen.

Ken, back in New York, was now working as a feature writer and columnist on the new afternoon newspaper *PM,* founded by Ralph Ingersoll. He was separated from and living apart from Margaret. Their conflicts, her recurring hysterical behavior, and their insecurity worked to cement rather than separate Ken and me. My withdrawal from Margaret since before I went to Budapest to live with my father was such that I felt blameless. My fear of her came to be paralyzing, and inevitably our ever-thinning tie snapped apart. I did not see her again until twenty-five years later. Margaret refused to give Ken a divorce, not quite believing the separation to be irreversible. They maintained a peaceable connection and association, he making a financial contribution and visiting often enough at the Village apartment she rented. He kept just enough of his salary to live apart in the small unfurnished room with fireplace and bathroom that I found for him, where the rent was only twenty dollars a month. On the same street a block apart I was sharing the apartment of a co-worker friend whose husband was in the army overseas.

We were all eager for the war to end, TD writing to tell me that it weighed on him heavily, as did "the mystery, misery and futility of life." In May 1944 he came to New York, having been invited by the American Academy of Arts and Letters to receive its award on May 19. He told me he would be arriving May 14, but I did not see him until June 2, when he came at 10:30 in the morning to the shared apartment I lived in. He stayed for only an hour. He said he would call again two days later, on June 4, but he didn't. On June 15 came his letter from Portland, Oregon, saying he was there with Helen whose mother was very ill. He did not make mention of the fact that he had married Helen on June 13.

He did feel that I would probably marry Ken. "You'll never know how sorry I was not to be able to get down there since I wished so much to be with you. . . . We've been attached so long! . . . I wish now deeply that you weren't going to get married yet I know you cant waste more of your life on me. So I can only wish that you were to be near me always. . . . Your such a precious portion of my hurried & troubled life." Ken and I, in fact, never married. The complex story of our relation, which ended a decade later with his death in 1954, ran parallel to and then beyond my relationship with TD.

TD told me that his sister Mame had died while he was in New York. It brought back to me a long-ago rain-drenched day when I was driving him, in *his* car to Astoria to "see Mame." As we were crossing the Brooklyn Bridge, the car skidded on the wet road and, whirling to a sudden sharp right turn, headed straight toward the barrier beyond which it would have plunged into the river below. Before the car stopped, TD, with what seemed like resigned acceptance, turned toward me and said, "Well, so long." I wondered what affinity he might have felt when, in a letter to me two months after his sister's death, he had the impulse to add a postscript that had no connection with his preceding thoughts: "The last words of Mame to me just before she died were 'Not all the people of the [world] in combination and thought can make a single blade of grass. Yet God can carpet the fields!'" If mentioning this signaled a shared belief, I could not quite reconcile it with the three-page typed photostat copy of "Theodore Dreiser's letter applying for membership in the Communist Party," which he sent the following year. Its attached message to me read: "Yvette dear: Here's another document for you to throw in the waste-basket." The "document" didn't sound at all like him. It wasn't the way he wrote; it was more like a propaganda proclamation composed on a party-controlled typewriter. Although he was not prepared to toe that line, he *did* apply and join, calling it "The Logic of My Life," thereby underlining what then seemed to me a contradiction to his having taken communion on Good Friday that year. To him, it was not a contradiction but rather an affirmation that communism embraced Christ's teachings.

By February 1945 Ken and I were expecting a child. For two

months my joy and despair lived together. I envisioned the baby that was in me as a little boy looking just like Ken. But the times made it impossible. It was a period long before rich and famous actresses broke the barriers to single parenthood, a time when I would have been dismissed from my civil service job with its steady, if modest, income, a time when there was no immediate hope of Ken's getting a divorce, a time when we didn't really have a roof to stand a crib under. Abortion was the only answer. After an interview and examination at the office of the Park Avenue doctor I was referred to, it was arranged for the procedure to take place on a forthcoming evening with an anesthetist also attending. On our way there in the Lexington Avenue subway, the lights in the car Ken and I were riding in dimmed from bright to faint as if to shield from view my dumbstricken despondence.

Curiously enough, TD's wistful response to this, after our sixteen years of attachment, not only surprised me but found me sharing it with him: "I wish I were the one whose infant were on the way," he wrote. "I'd like to see what we'd make of it, how much true pleasure and comfort we would be able to see or experience in having it together! Lord! Lord! this world! and what wishes & sorrows it presents us with."

Two days before that Christmas he was writing me: "dont forget me. I so much like . . . to feel that you still care. . . . think of me."

A few days later he died.

Afterword

The fancied knothole, in that illusory fence through which I watched TD's funeral, gradually widened to include scenes of my life until then: a sixteen-and-a-half-year-old coltish, romantic teenager enticed by the needful attention paid her by this fifty-seven-year-old famous author. She tells her youthful diary: "A letter from TD!! I am exultant when I hear from him. I love him as I will never love again. There is no one I would rather be with right now than with him. A word of his determines my state of mind." But for the chance event of our meeting and my being too unformed in the beginning to have a principle or tradition to guide me, my life without TD might have been quite different. I could not then recognize the lure nestling behind his flattery or resist the magnet of his celebrity.

Presumably I grew up. TD perhaps realized it when he referred to "the fascinating type of woman you've grown to be. . . . My mind was full of your new charm that plainly had come through more world experience." If I learned something along this spiritual, physical, psychological journey it was by slow absorption rather than by sudden enlightenment.

I came to realize that if I had never known TD, I might have gone to college, married, had children. He pushed me at that malleable age out of what might have been a conventional life into an often choppy sea that cast me on to uncharted shores where the choices I made were ruled by emotion rather than by reason. In part, at least, I thought that my quest toward being taken as a person rather than as a sex object was impeded by TD's influence.

When later I moved beyond the boundaries of our early relationship, and TD as well was undergoing changes in his life, including his permanent move to California, I saw him less, and the relationship continued on a different plane. More of my life lay ahead, yet his shadow and care followed me and continued to give me the abiding illusion of a supporting presence that, until the end, I leaned on. Perhaps these lines written to him after the death of Franklin Delano Roosevelt sum it up best:

> Whatever philosophy I have been able to arm myself with, I have learned from you—and in those moments when I feel lost and defenceless, I have but to think of you and your strength and your courage and your complete acceptance of the wonders and phenomenon of life, which in spite of your acceptance, you continue to probe and seek answers to with almost childlike candor.

On a more lighthearted note, the jingle I sent him in the early forties expressed another part of our relationship:

> I wished to say 'hello' TD
> As by this ballad you can see—
> Come soon your drooping lass to save
> Ere she dances to the grave.

It would appear that he too needed me, saying that I was such a precious part of his hurried and troubled life, giving him kindness, understanding, love, a shining spirit, and the knowledge that he never spent a single unhappy hour with me. If he also said this to the many other women who loved him, helped in his work, and bedded with him, I think he meant it each time, and we each believed it. His letters to me unfold that part of the design in his work and life perhaps not seen by many of his critics and his biographers: his capacity for love was co-mixed with tenderness, humor, and romance, as well as self-interest.

Today my memory of TD remains loving and wistful, if no longer needful. He spoke for both of us when he wrote: "I could never think of wholly giving you up, or feel that you were wholly willing to give me up. And so, we have gone on,—month after month, year after year."

And in memory, after death.

The Letters
1929–45

Chapter 2: Enter TD:1929–30

THEODORE DREISER

200 West 57th Street
New York City,
April 11, 1929.

Miss Yvette Monahan,
Warwick Hotel,
St. Louis, Missouri.
My dear Yvette,

I am so sorry to hear of your illness and want you to get well right away, because the sooner you get back to New York the sooner you will find an Easter present that was left for you. And furthermore, don't you ever think of telling me that you wish I were in the same city where you are, for if you do I might actually come.

Tell your mother to hurry up and bring you and Sue back and one of these days I will take you all to the country.

Yours,
T.D.
Theodore Dreiser

* * *

For Yvette

THEODORE DREISER

Feb. 5—1930

Dear Suzanne
Dear Yvette

Or I'll make it sweet Suzanne and Yvette. Which of you thought to send me the two photos? Or, did you think it out together? Anyhow it was a lovely thought and I am so pleased,—even proud. Its so comforting to have my especial pets here with me and I'm thinking of "<u>framing</u>" you together and then <u>hanging</u> you (that sounds a bit rough, doesn't it?) in my room where I can see you on waking and on retiring—keep an eye on you, as it were. Your my Babes in Joyland. I like to think of you both as young and strong and happy. And I want you to think of me as one who wants you to be that way. Always I look forward to seeing you both with so much pleasure and would like to be with you both more—so much more, if only I could.

Love. And thanks. I'll do some thing for you both as soon as I can think of some nice thing to do.

T. D.

200 West 57th St

* * *

Chapter 3: *"Hello, Sox": 1930*

[March 1930]

Sweetheart:

This is the real note for you. And its to say how really dear you are to me and how I wish you were coming along. You talk of having no intellectual companionship with me—only body. Is that how good your memory is. What about all the serious things we have discussed & the hours of poetry. But there is intellectual & poetic understanding on both sides & that is why I am missing you now. Will you miss me. Love—Love and write me now to Tucson, Arizona—
General Delivery.

* * *

Santa Rita Hotel
M. Edward Olson, Manager
Tucson, Ariz.

[March 1930]

Yvette Dearest:

Only now I received your first note addressed me here. It is exquisite—meditative, thoughtful, poetic, romantic. It is like a still pool at dusk. One wonders at the peace, surety, fullness, beauty. And that you should be attending a high school! And making grades!! I never wonder that you smile ironically. You will need to, much in this world. And arm yourself with fortitude. You are a poet, darling—born to write. And since you are a poet—very likely to suffer keenly. But your strength and gayety should help. I hope they may. Such a note as this of yours is the same as a pale fresh flower in a vase. Its beauty like a perfume dwells in mind amidst many other things. It rears faintly, sweetly, helpfully. I think of you dancing to me on a street corner—your eyes smiling whatever your thoughts are. No wonder when I suggest the commonplaces of experience—their necessity among the bold economics of life—you smile. You should. I wish I might keep you fresh in the vase unharmed. Truly I wish I might.

T. D

Shall I add love to admiration?
Do you need that?

* * *

Chapter 4: "Dearest Wilding": 1930–31

Santa Rita Hotel
M. Edward Olson, Manager
Tucson, Ariz.

April 3rd [1930]

Dearest: Yesterday afternoon I walked miles out in the mesa here. All beyond the city is mesa—hundreds of thousands of acres perhaps, surrounded by mountains, peopled with cacti, mesquite, chapparal—and except for the cacti, low bushes all. But with such smooth, dry, firm, warm brown earth in between so that you may walk as among the very young trees of a young orchard. And the sky over head with now & then a single white sailing cloud! And the changing colors of the mountains! And the cool pure wind! No taint of any city—which you smell as you return, as though it were a hot odorous animal. And the lone birds seeking lone prey,—here an owl, there a sand shrike. Perhaps in places cattle browsing, the rough shaggy herds of the mesas, that must make their own way as best they can—find food & water or die. And here & there in a hummock of brown earth in the sun I lay & thought and thought and baked. What is life? What man? Life is so unmindful of him. He is built with a few powers & then pitted, as in an arena, against so many others. But here the drama is so simple. Search for food. Guard yourself or be food for something else. A few ants. A few flies. I lie where there is no single fly but presently, should I throw a crumb of food of any kind on the ground here is one and there two and there ten and twenty. And from where? Over what distance? By what marvellous sense of smell? or what? Among many things I thought of you, meditating on life—dreaming of what to do about it, how to proceed? What the end—for you?—and loved you for what you are. I wished you were lying with me. That we could look & dream over all these things together. At dusk—under a new moon I walked back—miles. In one lone cabin a half mile distant a radio was singing "Sighing for the Carolines." It was as clear at half a mile as in a room. Our great land! Our far flung people! And all seeing & hearing if not knowing the same things at once.

T.

* * *

Santa Rita Hotel
M. Edward Olson, Manager
Tucson, Ariz.

April 3rd 1930

Dearest:

Just now I received such a doleful and yet really vital and interesting letter from you. Your so unhappy. You see no future or—you are falling all unprepared into one from the great height—youth. And no parachute. Excellent. Excellent. At seventeen and a half you are thinking more than most men and women at sixty. You have weltschmerz[1]—that most upbuilding disease that can attack youth. You really feel so bad that your going to do something about it, by George! Excellent, baby. I can think of nothing more healthful and encouraging. It even inspires me at three and a half times your age. . . . .But what is going to please you most is that you are going to get somewhere. You have youth, brains, health, and looks. Kids at your age are—where they have real brains—always dispairing as to their future. But you are going to live in a period of enormous social changes here in the U.S.A. People are going to read. A heavy percentage are going to weary of numbskullery and fol-de-rol and sigh for worlds to conquer. There are going to be vital changes in government. If you want to be in on things—read first chemistry, physics, bio-chemistry and all phases of science. And then sociology. It would pay you to read law—and pay well. A law course would be invaluable in your case. Also a course in philosophy. But read now—and at once. Will Durants Story of Philosophy. And if youve never read it H. G. Wells—Outline of History (which reminds me that I owe him a letter). Get Schopenhauers The World as Will and Idea and read that. If you want to go to college perhaps that can be arranged. If you were to study science enough you could become a technical assistant at good wages & learn besides. Dont forget too, that the movies are going to provide an enormous field for educational ideas. People are going into Hollywood pretty soon who are going to construct social and scientific documents in film form—things that are going to teach & change the world enormously. Bother the communists over here. Turn your face to gay, thrilling instruction—the conquest of more & more amazing natural facts. Just now I have a bid to go to Hollywood (Warner Brothers) for some such work. If so I may give you a lift. But I am not going to leave New York. Not permanently. And should I go for awhile I'll send for you because I feel you can be of help to me—and to yourself. And even should I go—I'll be back before I go—and arrange some things with you. Will you come? Will Margaret have sense enough to let you. You see how interested I get on the mental side. But there'll be moments—too, when you'll want me to "Hold me." Well, I will.

Its still marvellous here. No rain. No clouds yet. All sunshine. They say it rains but I havent seen any. And I'm feeling better. No coughing at night at all. And none in the day to speak of. I still wish you were here. It would be fun strolling around with you here. And how.

Write me. Cheer up. Eat an apple every day. Get to bed by noon. And blow me a few kisses and a few hot thoughts. No hot thoughts—no great ideas. I gotta have moments.

T

1. *Weltschmerz:* melancholia, of a youthfully romantic sort.

* * *

BRIGHT ANGEL CAMP
Fred Harvey
Grand Canyon National Park
Arizona

April 12—1930

Well Tease:

At last a really sweet letter—the one on the roof—in the chair. And all the worries settled—keys, X (the main trouble) and my wandering letters. But meanwhile all I have had is pin pricks concerning them—little jabs. Worse—if I write you a really sensuous letter I get called down. And if I indulge in descriptive scenes—the mental side of all I see—well anybody can do that. You remind me of the story of the father & son who started to drive the donkey to market and who trying to please everyone pleased no one. I mean you bring to mind the fable—since I appear to be in the roles of both father & son. Worse I am holding out a well buttered peice of bread to a person who is starving! God! What shall I write?

That I love you & wish most of all that I could invite you, pay your way and take you along with me through all this? Oh, no. Only Cerise[1] can do that. Its commonplace, routine, the expected—the necessary. And if I say there's never a night that I turn in alone that I dont wish I had Yvette to hold close to me. Oh, no. Vulgar! Fleshly. The lower side of life: the brutal side of nature. And if I say you have a beautiful mind & write lovely poetic letters, I'm kidding—worse doing it for a sly purpose—trying to put something over on you. In short I'm a total loss. As a love I'm a bale of straw. Just the same this last letter from you is close & sweet. May I say Madame—that I love you for that?

The Total Loss

1. The princess in the story that Dreiser, Helen, Yvette, and Sue made up one evening in Dreiser's 57th Street apartment (see p. 39).

* * *

FRANCISCAN
Albuquerque, New Mexico

April 14—1930

Dearest:

Seated in my gold-plated chair in this what looks to be an 18 story Biltmore but is only a nine story and much less pretentious affair I am thinking of (—well, anyhow, Cerise told me to say this)—you. She also said that I was to write a description of the country through which we passed—from Phoenix north to Grande Canyon—and Grande Canyon to here. She said if I stuck to scenery it would keep me off of or away from much more earthy or material matters. You know. And, as you see, so far, I'm doing pretty good. . . . . But then of course there you are. And here am I who should be walking miles and lying in the sun here and there in order to give the KO to bronchitis still sitting at this table and thinking of you. Cerise objects. She may not let me send this—if she catches me. Just now she's out and I'm safe. And alone like this I can express my mind. And my mind is just this: your too compelling and delicious[1] for me not to write you this way when I get a chance. (God its terrible to have another woman watch over this way and never give you a chance to breathe, aint it. Dont you think so?) Anyways, Baby here I am talking to you all unseen. And now that I got the chance—oh, sweetum—say, Are you the candy? You are? And would I like to see you this minute!?! Would hi! Its just high noon and the sun is blazing outside, but if I had you, here I'd stay. Theres a big comfy wicker chair right behind me. And in the corner a wide double bed. And in the distance tall blue mountains. You could lie in my arms and I'd play with my sweet—hold her close—and then maybe—well, you know. Put—put—pudup. We gotta have moments. Only since I've been out here not one. Wait & see. But since I left Tucson (no word of this to anyone do you hear!) I've been driving a car. These mountains and side runs were too attractive to bother with busses or trains so I leased one for a month. Its a roadster & I have been driving all by my lone. (I see you believing that. But I dont care. Believe it or not as you will.) But practicing. I wouldn't have endangered another—not even you at first. So when I get back. Incidentally heres that 25^{00} and you can take 15^{00} of it and take those lessons. . . . . Only what I was going to say was that afterwards (evil thoughts these, dont you think) we could run out in one of these strange moving deserts. The colored rocks—the barren sand patches! (Cerise stuff) the cloudless sky, the actual indian villages, the distant spirals of sand that a romping wind makes—a honey colored funnel of sand dancing like a genii away and away over a level plain. And cattle red and brown and black. And lone bushes or scrub palms. Ah! The splendor of barrenness in great requiescent silence and inutility. I love it. The inutile. You would. You could sit close. Or drive. And I would. Being alone—free of the watchful Cerise—we could talk—or just be still. Tonight then I could take you in my arms and hold you to me. And tomorrow would be another day. Savvy? (Thats Mexican for "understand").

When is it you are to be eighteen?

But more important—when is it are you to be free.

Signed—not by
permission but most
slyly—she's out.
T.

Are you my sweetheart now? Like it?

1. Dreiser here drew an arrow, pointing it toward "delicious" from below.

* * *

FRANCISCAN
Albuquerque, New Mexico

April 19—1930

Yvette Babe:

Two letters addressed to Grand Canyon reached me today. Both appear to have been mailed by you on the 14th. Allowing for their going to Grand Canyon & back here, it took about 3 days for them to get here. The reason is that they come in a straight line to here and the Canyon. If they have to be re-entrained as they do in certain instances it takes longer. I'm not leaving here just yet so I'm expecting a letter or so more. Anyhow, even if I go any mail that comes is fairly promptly forwarded. And besides—on leaving I'll wire your P.O. Box where to address me.

I like the little picture ever so much—it's so gay, but I wish you'd have five or six snaps made & let me see them. I do so want a real girlie-girlie picture of you—the kind of picture I see when you come swinging toward me.

And the love call in this brown paper letter is darling. And dont I wish I could be with you or better still have you here with me. Such hours! I'd like you to see all that I see. And then at night—a little tired—we could cuddle up together and I'd hold my baby and we'd do all the sweet thrilling things we could with our strength and desire. It would be so delicious to kiss and pet your whole body—to have you open yourself to me—over and over. I can feel your breasts and your soft shapely thighs now—and your body pressed against mine. It makes me heavy and almost a little dizzy with desire. I want you so much that way, just as I want to talk to you about so many things that are in mind. Think with me about these things and when you want me much, this way, write me of it.

Albuquerque isnt as charming as Tucson or Phoenix although about as large as Tucson. It hasnt the romantic flavor some how of the desert south which is there. Its a lively little place—the largest in N.M. & many say the healthiest. It may be. Personally I dont feel quite as good as I did in Tucson. There are no cacti here—and no palms,—but many indians & Indian towns or pueblos. But Mexicans are not nearly so common & some color is lost that way. Today—Saturday—at 1:10 I am leaving for Santa Fé for a day or two—(its only 60 miles away)—then returning here. Its now five of 12 so I'll be leaving in an hour. Wisht youse were coming along. I'm going on the bus. In regard to the $\$1^{\underline{80}}$ for a telegram—I sent you $\$25^{\underline{00}}$ some time ago. I suppose you got that and I'll send you some more when I hear whether you recieved it & what you did with it. I would send you some photos from here but they're not so interesting. Santa Fe may prove more picturesque.

Are you learning to drive. When I get back we can do that—play in the woods—since there'll be a car. But I wish you were here with me now.

T

* * *

Santa Rita Hotel
M. Edward Olson, Manager
Tucson, Ariz.

April 30—[1930]

Yvette: Another cloudless day here. Last night I slept in one of these rooms here whose outer wall is replaced by a screen. You lie in your bed and sleep as though you were out in the open. And the air! And the stars! Lying and half dreaming I thought of but one person & how she would love it. I know how you love the open spaces. I wanted you near me just to look & feel the cool pure air. And in New Mexico one night last week I could not make the town I was bound for Hot Springs. So at 7^00^ in the open desert I ran my car into the bushes—behind a hummock of sand—cleared away the gravel & rock with a spade—dug up the earth a little to soften it & taking two blankets rolled up in them & went to sleep. But the night air! The distant sounds—foxes or wolves—or what—I dont know. At nearly dawn the last 1/8th of a thin yellow moon—a mere yellow feather arose. An hour later the whole desert was flooded with a pale shell-like pink & silver. The mountains! The enormous sea of sand & low bushes. I sat up & gazed until the sun peeped over the eastern edge of the desert. Then to sleep again. But you—do you think I did not wish you were there. We could have shared the two blankets, and overcoat & sweater and an old rug which I didnt even use. We could have rolled close & kept warm. . . . But one of these days you will be free. And then. . .

Do you love me—a little

T.

* * *

El Paso,
May13—1930

Yvette Sweet: El Paso tonight. Did 620 miles from San Angelo Texas to here—and leaving early in A.M. for Phoenix Yuma & Los Angeles. Should be there by 17th or 18 and hope to find a letter from you. Its hot and I'm tired of driving & staying out here. I wont mind Los Angeles if it leads to anything definite because then I can return fairly quickly to New York & will. I wont mind if nothing happens either because then I shall return East & we shall see each other again. Its getting hard & boring to be away so long. I wouldnt have undertaken this trip except for the movie prospect. But since it came up & there was a chance to let Helen see her mother[1] again I decided to go through with it. But now I wish I were back in N.Y. Or, and believe it or not—as you will—I would be content to work out in Los Angeles awhile if I could send for you and really bring you out. I find thinking of you & not being able to get hold of you—take you in my arms too trying. I think of you so much. You know how—and the talks we have. Despite the difference in years we have so much in common & I like to share so many thoughts with you. When you write me angry or critical notes I get very much out of sorts but when you write me some thing tender the situation changes at once. I feel so much better. And then I wish, wish. But I have the comfort of feeling that when I do get back we will have our happiness together again. I've been actually lonely so often & for you—and am now. And you—me? Write & tell me how you are & say a few sweet things—so hard for you to me. And if there is anything I can do for you write me. If its in my power, I will.

Love from
T

Address Gen. Del. Los Angeles until further notice—by wire.

1. Helen Richardson's mother lived in Portland, Oregon.

* * *

BEacon 7141 Roosevelt Hotel
West Park and Salmon Sts.
Portland, Oregon

June 11—1930

Baby Sweet: I got your letter from Mahopac last night. It sounds rough but <u>it</u> <u>is</u> reality—the reality that confronts not all—by a long shot—but millions & millions of beginners. And worse than that even. Your young. You want to be happy. So do I. So does everybody. But life wont let any of us get away with very much. Just the same your my sweet (in part anyhow)—and I want you to be as happy as possible. I told you once that if you left home & took a room I'd finance you to the help yourself point. I meant it. Even now—if your staying at home I'll help you. I'll be there very soon and we can talk things over. You need change to look around with so here's twenty-more. But I'd like to know what you do with it. A part will go for a fountain pen I suppose—unless you got that out of the other $\$15^{\underline{00}}$. I wish I could train you into secretarial work but your pretty young & you dont know stenography or typewriting & perhaps dont wish to know. If you did though I could use you & that would keep you near me. If that doesnt interest you I'll give you some money when I get there and you try your hand at jobs. Its good for you—even one-week jobs because you get a line on life. And you should. Meantime don't think I don't sympathize. I know all about it. I've been there. If you dont want to do anything but just study & play for the next year or so I can fix that. I say that so easily because I know that presently with your restless & beautiful mind your going to do some thing. And it will be worth-while. Meantime I'd like to keep you close to me. I want to baby you so. You dont know: I wish I could take you up naked now and rock you and feel your warm sensuous mouth against mine. When we are together—your legs and arms about me I am lost in a warm regretless, rewarding dream. It seems—it is—a central, pivotal heaven—from which one (I) takes flight into a cold void & to which I return to be warmed & healed. You have youth, poetry of thought, poetry of mood, poetry of form. Embrace me wholly in your thoughts richly—sensually—beautifully—as I do you. Are you my baby—now? Really?

T.

Here is my route for the next week anyhow.
Spokane, Washington — $13^{\underline{th}}$
Livingstone, Montana $14^{\underline{th}}$
Bismark, N. Dakota — $16^{\underline{th}}$
Minneapolis, Minn — $18^{\underline{th}}$
Chicago,— — — — $20^{\underline{th}}$

All letters & telegrams to General Delivery each place. I'll be a little late—but not much.

* * *

Feb. 5—1931

Dearest Wilding
I am carrying with me a sense of newness if not strangeness. It seems to me you grow wiser & stronger while retaining that gay freshness I love so much. That last morning. The pattering of your feet behind me on Thursday afternoon. Just you, with your letters and your laugh. I am not going into what I am doing. It is not fascinating enough—(the people), and I am moving from place to place. The simplest way is to address me c/o Arthur Pell,[1] 61 W. 48th Street. Put the addressed letter sealed & stamped in a separate envelope & mail it to be forwarded. It will come to the nearest point wired him. Write me what you think of change,—and a poem. I like you best living in your fancy.

Love & all from T
T[2]

The next check will cover everything for several weeks.

1. Arthur Pell was the treasurer at Boni & Liveright, Dreiser's publisher.
2. Dreiser here drew an arrow, pointing it toward the final "T" from below.

* * *

Tuesday
[New York, March 1931]

Yvette Sweet
Today was a lovely day with you. To see you standing just outside that door—framed by it—from where I stood—and looking—the crowd for decoration. Something warm and comforting enveloped me.

And the talk in the park. Naturalness, understanding—no foolish irritating inhibitions—just wine like life sparkling through the channels of a strong, fair mind.

And so much health to take life with. Everything before you—all the years. I gained by the very pressure of your young body—the touch of your head or hand.

I think of you as youth, warmth sensitivity—tenderness—generousness and so I care and love—much. And why not?

T

* * *

Chapter 6: Home as Found: 1932–33

Mt. Kisco—NY.
Sept. 15 1932

Dear Yvette:

The long letter written about the time of my birthday[1] came just now. But before it—really in time for my birthday, came the gay paper cutter which I like very much. It harmonizes with some slavic ash trays & other thing out of Russia & Czecho-Slovakia—a highly colored pottery pencil holder for one. You paint an interesting picture of your life over there—your father, grandmother, the home and your rowing on the Danube. It sounds so far away. Do you like it better than New York—(57th St, the Ansonia, Central Park, the little Chinese restaurant at Broadway & 57th St)?

I like your analysis of us. It is very near correct. You are so wise & resourceful & yet always you pretend to be so simple. But regardless of whatever things that I often think you should never even tolerate as thoughts, let alone do—I not only care for you but miss you. My thoughts run back to so many things—your vivacity of spirit, your energy of body, your interest in people—your natural kindliness if not your sympathy. I never forget the time I first met you, the softness of your voice, the reticence, the something of smartness that took my fancy. But so fast—so fast the stream of life runs by—so many things have happened since then. And now you are so far away. But really I treasure what has been almost as much as what may be. Because what was I have. But what may be may still not be. It is in the land of dreams.

It is very beautiful here now. If you were really free & could work with me here unannoyed you would like it. The stone walled lawn before the house (a new thing) is very lovely. And a large circle—the centre of a turn around for cars, is filled with brilliant cannas. There is a full moon now & at night it makes a German fairy place of the house—a sort of Hansel & Gretel realm. (Rapunzel! Rapunzel! Let down your hair.) "An so she let down her hair & by it he drew himself up."

I write in the big stone room. It is not so easy this book—but I work on, sometimes destroying all that I do not in one day but five & yet go on. If you were here I would teach you lots of practical things. Working would make up for the later idler moments. But the practical would have to be to carry all the other & make it palatable & durable. We think of so much & have capacity for so little.

Just now I look out of one of the big arched windows in this room & see the first fall tree—all afire with red & yellow & brown-green. So comes & goes another fall.

Dearie—as you row on the Danube blow me a few loving thoughts. They will be so welcome.

T.D

1. Dreiser's birthday was on August 27.

* * *

The AMERICAN SPECTATOR[1]
A Literary Newspaper
Edited by
George Jean Nathan * Ernest Boyd * Theodore Dreiser * James Branch Cabell * Eugene O'Neill
Published by
Ray Long & Richard R. Smith, Inc.
12 East 41st Street, New York City

[September 1932]

This is a thing that may interest you. It is to be a monthly at first—10 cents. Later a weekly. At first it will pay only 1 cent a word,—later 5 cents. No article can be over 2500 words. None shorter than 500. Personalities from all over the world will be writing for it & will be on sale every where—Vienna, Budapest, Rome, Constantinople. If you think of any important critic or writer whose thoughts might be worth while—ironic or poetic name him or her. If you do a Hungarian etching yourself let me see it. Maybe I can get it in. The paper isnt out yet but will be. I'll send you a copy of the 1st issue.

D

1. *The American Spectator,* a literary newspaper started by George Jean Nathan and Ernest Boyd in 1932. Dreiser was one of the principal editors.

* * *

Dont mail letters to 1860 Broadway.
Miss Light[1] isn't there now. Monday—October 10—1932
Her new address is 2931 Davidson Ave.
N.Y.

Yvette Dear:

What are cannas. Oh, theyre big red flowers on tall strong stalks with long fairly wide green leaves all about. You've seen plenty. They make marvelous Pompeian red spots in any garden. This bed is 30 feet in diameter.

Your letter of Sept 30— comes Oct. 10— and it says in one place "Write me in time for my birthday, Oct 12." Well that gives me two days to get it to you. Please page Earl and Goth—or Mr. Lindbergh.[2]

You know, at first when I saw these two pictures of your mother, I thought they were you, made up to look a little older & more severe—some Hungarian hair stunt. And I laughed. But after I read your mothers letter I studied her face. Alike! Your almost the image of her. And her letter sounds like you. You two must have a lot in common. Better go see her. You might find an ideal companion. Needless to say I like her face because she looks like you. But dont tie up with her & settle in Geneva. Better persuade her to come on back with you.

Oh, yes. Happy Birthday

I forgot.

Its turned warm again here. Today, Monday, and yesterday were like soft June days. And tonight theres a marvelous three quarter moon in the sky. I just went outside to enjoy the silvery feel of it and to think how it looked over Budapest. As for caring for you—no—a year wont make any difference. You'll always be the kidding, laughing, exploring Yvette to me, running here & there like a young pup, just to be running. I wish you might never change. And wish it much in spite of all change.

The American Spectator is coming along fine. Lots of interesting articles for it. And lots of comment all over America. The first issue wont be out before Oct 20— but I'll send you one.

Yes—you may keep that letter

Remember the Budapest restaurant on the East side? It failed. Also another quite good good one accross the street—Rudolphs. You Hungarians aren't very patriotic. But often, evenings when I'm in New York I wish you were there to go along to some such place. Remember The Stork in 58th St.?

Well, what else is there to say. I'll write you regularly. You dont need to pick any daisies to find out. You'll always be the candy kid to me. But do learn stenography & typewriting. This typewritten letter of yours has mistakes. You loafer. But love. And I'll throw in a few xxxs for good measure. And I wont sign this D. but—well now lets see. "Double-D____? (That sounds a little rough) Well, then—affectionately.

Saint Theodore, the Nubian"

What kind of a shrine should I have anyhow? Can you think?

1. Evelyn Light, Dreiser's secretary at this time.

2. Charles Lindbergh, American aviator who made the first solo nonstop transatlantic flight in 1927.

* * *

Friday—After Thanksgiving
[November 1932]

Yvette Sweet: You'll think I'm long on silence. I've been to the west coast—San Francisco & Los Angeles. Went to speak for Mooney[1] & to cross-examine a new witness—Paul Callicotte who went to the Oregonian in Portland, saying that he carried the bag that carried the bomb that killed 12 people at the preparedness parade in San Francisco in 1916. Also that the two men he carried it for was neither Mooney nor Billings.[2] I cross examined him privately in the Mark Hopkins Hotel in San Francisco before eight friends in order to satisfy myself that he was telling the truth. I decided that he was. Then I cross-examined him before 18,000 people in the Civic Auditorium in S.F. for 2 hours. He came through in fine form. Very convincing. Then I saw the District Attorney, as well as a judge who may retry him & then departed for Los Angeles to help raise some money for the communists there. We raised $1600. The labor of doing so consisted of sitting around in two very gay parties looking very pontifical while a lot of young enthusiasts told each other that it was their duty to contribute. Sam Ornitz[3] bagged the money for the local cause. I put away about eleven high balls and felt as though I had done nobly by my country. High balls have a way of doing that.

. . . By the way Miss Light mailed you copies of the 1st & 2nd issue of The

American Spectator. It sold 60,000 copies the 1st issue. And this second looks to go 80,000 or 90,000.

. . . Next I enjoyed that factory picture—all those ambitious Hungarians anxious to come over here & lead loose immoral lives. A fine comment on what America stands for. . . . . As for me as a monument? I like the picture. My ample lap full of girls and you paying me visits. My future looks better than I had hoped.

What news of your mother? Any. I meant to show those two pictures of your mother to her, but I forgot. Now she wants to see them. So if possible, I wish you'd send them back. For all her sharp words I think Helen likes you. You ought to write her a little letter.

Are you really all set for a year? It seems a long time. And I hope you don't work yourself into any routine frame of mind. Your too brisk & gay for that. Rather I wish you'd write an article entitled The Hungarian Yen for America—or the European Yen For America. You could use that letter almost as you wrote it—or I could incorporate it in a slightly longer article. Want to try?

It's Friday night & I may go out to Mt. Kisco. Helen & I came down Wednesday for Thanksgiving. The weather here just now is perfect—like early October—warm & bright. I'm going without an overcoat. I wish you were here. We'd go over to Hungarian place or maybe—instead I'd take you to 146 East 61. It's almost as charming at the old Stork. Not quite. . . .

Do you miss me. Remember when you were working for the Charity Relief? And afterwards that cloth-hand printing concern? The poor working girl? And her lack of diversions! I can see your playful ironic grin—even now? I write again in a few days.

Love from T.D.

On a German movie introduction the other night I saw "dialogue by Hans Szekely." Any relation?

1. Tom Mooney, labor leader who was convicted in 1916 for bombing the Preparedness Day parade in San Francisco that Dreiser mentions.

2. Warren Billings, labor leader who was convicted with Mooney for the 1916 bombing.

3. Samuel Ornitz, novelist and social activist.

* * *

Be sure you get the full value in Pengos[1]—if thats what they are

N.Y. Dec 24—1932

Dearest Yvette:

This encloses ten in American money or its equivalent in Hungarian—(I'm going to try to buy Hungarian currency with it unless I find you can get more Hungarian money for it over there than I can get here) and you are to spend it for what you would have spent it for assuming that it had arrived in time. I have been so busy. And worst of all sick a part of the time. Will tell you more about that if I ever see you again—which I wonder—will I. B-P is so far away. A letter takes so long. And when I think (sometimes) how long it takes one to get there it tends to discourage communication—but not permanently as you see.

Here by us as the Germans say its been a cold fall—really ever since Sept. 15th. Bitter patches mixed in with relaxing days (one or two) after which it froze up again. But what between helping edit The Spectator, writing on my novel,[2] planning a new moving picture & so on the days have passed without my fretting too much.

What do you mean by saying send me The Spectator. Every issue beginning with no. 1 has gone to you. Do you mean to say that not one has arrived. Then its disappearing in the P.O. and all I can do is to try again. I'll have Miss Light send them all in one bundle. Tell me is your mother still here. Helen met Fabri[3] & she says he told her that she was. Yet you wrote me that she had married and was abroad. Has that blown up or was it just a report?

Somehow my dear this Xmas lacks kick for me. I'm not in any particular trouble nor do I lack contacts but as interesting as some of them are I find myself relying on work & reading to pass the time & think on better days. Iroki is all right. The house & all connected with it is in good condition but for me it lacks the old vivacity that went with it about two years ago. Do you remember the Sunday Fabri was working on the little cabin and you & Kay Sayre[4] had the wrestling match? And the time we were having trying to put up the tent! Sense & nonsense. But charm. Crazy gaiety such as still is in your letters mostly but not here. And yet quite a few people are coming out tomorrow. Bill Woodward[5] & his wife, Feuchtwanger, the German novelist. Hubert Davis the painter & his wife, the Lengels,[6] a Southern girlfriend of Helens. But mentally I shall be alone. It's in the cards for me. It's too bad, but so it is. And so it will be I fear unless someone like you comes along to break the monotony. . . . . Just the same your letters are bright spots. They amuse & cheer me—for because however you feel mentally you glow with romance & thought. And these are the lamps of life. Write me. And a swell new year for you.

Love from T.D

1. The pengö was a unit of currency that was introduced in Hungary in 1926.

2. Dreiser was working on either *The Stoic* or *The Bulwark.*

3. Ralph Fabri, a Hungarian painter who had helped Dreiser with the plans for Iroki.

4. Kathryn Sayre was Dreiser's research assistant at the time.

5. William E. Woodward, editor, banker, writer. Woodward hired Helen Richardson as his secretary when she first came to New York.

6. William C. Lengel, who first came to New York in 1910. Trained as a lawyer, Lengel took a job as Dreiser's private secretary at the Butterick publishing firm. This began a lifelong relationship between the two men.

* * *

March 12—1933 [New York]

Yvette Dear:

I'm a long time writing, as you say. But if you knew how crowded are the moments here just now you wouldnt blame me. I'm still involved in the movie idea but this bank holiday business[1] here and the fact that not any of the banks all over the United States seem to be more than 30% solvent as against a necessary 100% shows what we may be up against. There may not be money for a large experimental moving picture idea. . . . . Glad you sent me The Hungarian Yen. It's good. I cut off the 1st paragraph, changed the past tense to the present (I am walking along the Danube) and sent it to Nathan & Boyd. They immediately agreed with me that it was ok for the Spectator. I believe it is going in at once. I am signing it Yvette Szekely, as I address you that way now & it sounds so Hungarian. You'll get 1 cent a word. It reads so interestingly. You must write more things because I know with practice you can sell them.

As for September, Ok with me. I think I will have things for you to do. . . . . It's been a bad winter here—lots of cold days, snow, bitter winds. Just now for one week here at Mt. Kisco, it's really been bitter cold. The cold doesn't affect this house any. The rooms in both houses are always warm. But to walk around the place means health and strength—if roughing it ever really means that.

Helen is ok. She looks very good. I've wondered and wondered about Sue, and only thoughts of trouble with M[2] has kept me from looking her up. But its a wonder Sue wouldnt write me once in a while. As bad as things are here I dont think you make any mistake when you return. By temperament you are American & maybe this great change will bring better opourtunities than have been. You can afford to try it.

Just this morning Yvette the air is a little warmer. And its bright. Two robins, a small family of crows, some wrens & at least 1 blue bird—I saw it—(meaning a pair as usual) have arrived. The blue bird was nosing around the little guest house. I hope it means warmer weather.

Life is so strange. Its such a show—gay & bleak by turns. But plainly not getting anywhere unless a play can be said to get somewhere. And I think of all the corpuscles & atoms that it takes to keep this show going. And if death is really the end, what a fantastic, almost unbelievable series of experiences.

Love from
T

1. On March 5, President Franklin D. Roosevelt declared a nationwide bank holiday and placed an embargo on the exportation of gold to help stabilize a faltering banking system.

2. Yvette and Sue's mother, Margaret.

* * *

Easter Sunday, April 16
1933

Dearest:

Just got your letter of April 3. And only yesterday received the May issue of The Spectator which contains your article. Because of space limitations they cut it some more as they do most everything at the last minute—Boyd and Nathan. But there you are. It isnt as good as when I finished with it, but it opens the door to something else by you.

I see you worry about making your living in America but I dont think you need to worry so. Things are bad here certainly but somehow those who have share not a little with those who haven't. And dont forget America was bursting with wealth when this thing happened. It has been taking off excess fat constantly, and has been slowly but surely descending to the idea that work if hard is necessary. And it hasn't even reached the place yet where it can stop kidding itself, or blowing, or telling itself how good it is. It doesn't want to deal with Russia and it does want to save the capitalistic system, trusts, banks, rich men and all, so why worry. Personally, you know I will do things for you & besides you know that you have genuine ability and resourcefulness. It shows in everything you do. Another thing living—if prices dont rise again is much cheaper—certainly 1/2 less—maybe. And I notice that people still get jobs, write books, paint, sing. Good things on the stage, in the movies, in the shops do well. We only need to drop to careful, economic living and the country will be allright for quite a while. So there. You can get a new dress for a quarter, a new hat for 15 cents, shoes for 20 and stockings for a nickel & your all set for a night club. So what?

Margaret has a job apparently. I received the enclosed letters from the foreign press correspondents and was inclined to go until I saw M______s name as assistant Secretary. Then I decided best not for I never can tell what her real motives are. But—she has a job. She always lands on her feet and always will. But please, when you come, if you are going to reestablish close relations leave me out. I'm in no mood to be further annoyed by her kind of plotting.

It is spring here—at last. Rainy, but green. Up at Kisco the pussy willows and crocuses and Jack in-the-pulpits are all up and doing. The chorus of frogs in the pool for a few days was maddening. Now for a week it has ceased and the "knee-deeps" are having their day or rather night and a long full night at that. I think of you so much, just now. It may be that you are thinking of me but for days I've had an urge to write you. So here it is. And dont worry about the money due from the Spectator. If they haven't already sent the check I'll get it & spend it for you. If they have, send it back and Ill do the same. You'd do as much for me, wouldn't you. And anyhow cheer up, sweet. You'll like New York again, and you'll get along. Love—from

TD

* * *

April 27—1933

Dear Yvette:

Who should walk in on me the other day but Iris Woolcock.[1] She was Secretary of the Meeting Place once and you did some work for her. And so a long and engaging revelation concerning you—your affairs, your hitch-hiking to Phila with that young fellow Margaret took in, Margaret's attack on her because she helped you move—and advised you so to do. But I recall your protests to me in regard to your lack of interest in that youth—and your reiterated assurance that Margaret blamed no one but me. And while you were going with others you still—evidently to do what?—aid her or yourself—"confessed" to having had relations with me. And admitting as I do that I never really believed you, still your protests of innocence & fairness & this & that look odd in this light. But dont think I am angry—or holier than thou. Merely to show you how things do come to light and how they caution important and faith or belief of dubious import at any time—anywhere. And you see how this exclusive devotion of yours looks at this writing. And how much I feel that it ought to be rewarded.

1. Iris Woolcock, painter and secretary of the Meeting Place in Greenwich Village.

* * *

Hotel Ansonia
Broadway—at 73 Street
New York City

July 5 [1933]

Dear Yvette:

The letter I wrote you covered my real criticism of and objection to your conduct. I do not mind your playing with and loving whom you please. You will do it anyhow. The thing I objected to and do now is your joining with Margaret Monahan to put me on the spot in regard to you when at the very same time you were doing as Miss Woolcock indicated. It seems—well I can scarcely say how, more like Margaret than you. And I thought you were different—too downright decent to share in an attack based on nothing—or one of the nicest things in me, my affection & admiration for you. It has made an impression which I cannot overcome—causes me to suspect any development or turn whether one ever occurs or not.

At the same time as a temperament and an artist I really admire you intensely and from a writing point of view will help you all I can. This last little article you enclosed strikes me as very wise and amusing and I feel that Boyd & Nathan will think so. Incidently I like the two drawings. They are perfectly delightful and I want to keep them. If you return to America as I think you will, you will find no trouble I am sure in breaking into the New Yorker, Vanity Fair and other clever publications & making enough to live on. Also I feel that you are destined to write clever comedies or movies or both which will make you a great deal of money. You should not consider your future dark but bright, since you are gifted.

As for looking after you for the time being, if you choose to come I can do something for you and will. But I feel that with your gifts you will not need or want help long. And that is not said in order to lessen your needs in connection with me. What I do will be done gladly—and you need not worry as to that but you have the skill which brings success I am sure. You should write skits in playlet form. The New Yorker, The Spectator, Vanity Fair & all clever publications like them. Tell me how much you think you will need when you get here. Perhaps you should stay in Europe for a little while & submit clever things about the life there to our American publications. They are interested in Europe now—not political but social Europe.

I read your letter to Helen & was interested but do not believe all of your real mothers story. It has odd gaps and vague psychology spots. However write me your plans & what you need. My delight in your ability somehow balances my criticisms of your conduct toward me—or I choose to let it. One is in one scale and one in the other. But you should not repay good with evil—ever.

T.D

* * *

Dear Yvette:

The little rocking chair with teddybear at ease in it is on my desk. The properly folded hdkf is in my grey summer coat pocket. The record of <u>For Answer</u>[1] is here at Mt. Kisco. To re-witness your general cleverness and skill and to hear your voice reciting For Answer was moving of course. It brought back the very nicest side of you—your gay, aware and tolerant personality. I wished that you were here so that you might share this weekend in Mt. Kisco. Naturally I care for you—or for the temperament which is the best of you and most of all want you to make a great deal of it. You should and will.

What are you doing these days? Writing? or reading? or working at something? And how do you get along with your long lost mother. Somehow I cannot quite swallow all of her smooth story, but if you really like her and she helps you mentally or emotionally in any little way I can be glad that you found her.

Everything goes about the same with me. I write—(short stories, sketches, editorials, or my novel). I listen to all sorts of peoples woes, by mail and sometimes in person. I see lots of people, confer about the Spectator and fight all my various battles as best I may. And the days go by. Just now on this sheet of paper—(it is $9^{\underline{30}}$ P.M. and I am in the big stone room at Mt. Kisco)—some queer little spec of a fly—less than a pin-head for size began a saraband—something like a figure 8—repeated & repeated & repeated until at last I thought—shall I kill it or not? It was delaying this letter. But I decided—no. Such a little time it has to spin, perhaps a day or so at most. This night might see it ended. And is my saraband so much better? My figure 8. I shook it off the paper and proceeded as you see.

The incident points my mood these days. I go on and on—inexplicable impulse to be doing something guiding me. One of billions of flies. And yet—so I question—is the entire universe doing more. Perhaps it is cutting figure 8^{s} and betimes repeating itself—rebegetting itself in all its endless forms—and trying to forget that it has been doing so for so long. . . . . . And yet I am not unhappy. Sarabands are not so bad if you can only avoid thinking too much—or perhaps (and this much better) caring too much.

I feel grateful to you for all the little remembrances and particularly for the record of your voice. It was sweet. And—as you intended it to be—quite moving. Write & tell me about your plans.

T.D

I am living mostly at the Ansonia & you may address me there. I think it would be better.

Sunday, Aug 20—1933

One week from my birthday.[2]
What is birthday in Hungarian?

1. Yvette had made a record of one of Dreiser's poems, *For Answer*, as a birthday present.

2. August 27.

* * *

Chapter 7: New Deals: 1933–38

Thursday [November 1933]

Fairest Genevieve
I judge the school is a huge success. So wholly engaging. No time for a word. And this is Thursday. Friday P.M. I am off to Washington D.C. with Sherwood Anderson on a Spectator stunt. Back Monday. How about Monday night? Or Tuesday night? Anyhow, how about word of some kind—even a single word such as—well here are four. Love, ... Bunk . . . . . Bologny . . Rats! And here are three two word phrases. Dust: you! Beat it! . . . Back, ham! Postage from Rockville Center to N.Y. is 3 cents. Ah, Romance. Divine Love.

As You Desire Me

* * *

Saturday [January 1934]

Dearie:

Enclosed is 5$\underline{^{00}}$. I'm up at Mt. Kisco. Brought up George Douglas[1] who left today. Mail to—or leave at Ansonia—those writings. I'll suggest you & Margie[2] or you & Sue coming out here. I'd like to see you finish that bath room. I have a load of work to do but hope to be down Tuesday. If I'm coming I'll phone or wire you. Give my love to Sue.

T.

You two should live together.

1. George Douglas, Australian-born journalist and critic who encouraged Dreiser in his scientific and philosophical studies in the 1930s.

2. Yvette's friend Margie Stengel.

* * *

I
R
O
K
I

Simon and Schuster, on the occasion of becoming the publishers of Theodore Dreiser, request the pleasure of your attendance at Mr. Dreiser's home, Iroki, The Old Road, Mt. Kisco, on Sunday afternoon, October 28th, after three o'clock.

R. S. V. P.
Simon and Schuster, Inc.,
386 Fourth Avenue,
New York, N. Y.

THEODORE DREISER

Yvette:

Here is 4^{00}. That will get you two out there. We will see that you get back. Love

T.D

* * *

Monday [1935]

Yvette Dear:

You said you would not write or complain. But you did write & you didnt complain. I'm sorry that I could not see you this last week. We're trying to rent this place. It has to have certain work done—repainting, repairing etc. I've been sick & very so with bronchitis. I cant tell you how much—coughing all Saturday & Sunday nights as in the old days. Severe chest pains. I'm going to have to see a doctor and get some remedy. I thought I was over that for good. Today I feel like h____. But maybe tomorrow I'll feel better. When this place is rented Helen may leave for a while. And while I have to work I'll be freer than I am now. That last visit was charming—quarreling but winding up differently. It seems to me you grow more in force & charm as time moves on—nothing lost and a lot gained. I hope to be in some day in the middle of the week—perhaps Thursday—but if not bear with me. This week end I have to be on the place. But if so next Monday or Tuesday I'll see you. Its queer. I have disturbing resentful feelings at times. But they appear to pass & I find myself thinking of better days in the past & in the future. How to make a pattern or harmony of so many conflicting emotions and conflicting intents. I wish so much that I could.

T.D

* * *

Tuesday March 19 [1935]

Yvette Dear:

Dont let the letter worry you. I wish you would let me see it. Beside H is going to be here after May 1 I think. May be not that long. If you want the cabin take it. As for me I'm feeling some better just now, and if I keep on should soon be in good shape again. Perhaps in a week or so I could come down there & stay all night. But I wouldnt want any guests. If you think that is all right let me know. Plenty of early to bed and freedom from an endless chain of requests demands have quieted my nerves. I'm not as savage as I was because I'm not under the strain that I was. Let me know as to my coming down—either some weekday night or Friday or Saturday. And dont worry about writing here. Use one of those City of N.Y. envelopes if you can get one—or a long one like the one enclosed & typewrite the address. H might open the mail—but not a long envelope I'm sure. And let me see her letter or a copy. I know she'd prefer you to another in the cabin. Its just me that bothers her.

Love
T.D

* * *

Dear Yvette:

I found a letter forwarded from N.Y.—The Paris Hotel—when I got here & your second from Mt. Kisco arrived this morning. Poetic letters full of emotion but some how I can only think of you as living with other persons—and betimes writing me. And the Paris hotel! You see I know of that. And not only of it but of the region. And from the newspapers. Also from people who have lived there. Its very free—no questions asked. So! . . . . But after all such is your temperament. I've always known it. And nothing will stop you from satisfying your desires. And why not. You live but once. But you realize too, that full knowledge of that—makes a <u>little</u> difference in the value of the declarations. I try not to let it—for I've known how you were doing this long time. But—And so— I find that I have to look on you as one looks on a man friend. Take his mind and his temperamental impact on one for what it is to one—the measure of its intellectual and emotional appeal and let it rest at that. And I can do that just as you can.

It was a long hard run accross the country. Decided to take the car & made it in eight days. If I had wanted to drive at night could have cut it to five easily. But I dont like night driving.

So here I am—232 So. Westmoreland. It's a charming Los Angeles house. I have a living room, a bedroom & a work room. George Douglas and a woman house-keeper are my sole companions. I am getting a stenographer who will come in & take dictation and do typing. Meantime I will read, write or dictate. Later Helen will come out and take a small apartment. Then I suppose I will live there—a part of the time anyhow. I have the feeling though that if you really wished you could do this work and make things go better than they are going now. But now that you are finding yourself I doubt if you would feel like making the sacrifices that would be involved & I'm getting to the place where I feel queer about even talking about it. Two people who have a lot in common but find it difficult to arrange team work.

So you see I'm not very happy & I have a big job and somehow not just the setting. The sun is out. All the same tropic trees & flowers are around but I find myself oppressed by the lack of a sensual and yet effectively productive atmosphere. Love & work! If only they could be truly combined. If only.

T.D

Los Angeles. Thurs. May 16—'35

* * *

232 So. Westmoreland Ave.
L.A.

Thursday, May 23rd [1935]

Dear Yvette:

No, I am not thrusting true love back at you. Nor could I at any one. In your case it would mean a great deal. But the nature of true love is what? Today I cant go on with this because I have working appointments. But you can carry on the thought. I will write more in a day or so. . . . . You say from June 1st on address me care of Iroki—house 3 etc. But Helen has not gone yet. And her last letter indicates that she may be there. If so I cant write you there & not until she has gone. Youd better let me write you care of the Hotel Paris or somewhere else, until she is gone. And please let me know when she really is gone. That is important. And then I'll write.

Yes, I'd like to have you come out. As from the beginning your temperament—the mixture of poetry and desire holds me. It activates & refreshes as true poetry & desire ever do. If Helen is here I shall have to arrange a vacation—some California trip. If you were fully equipped to do my kind of work, I could take you in here since I have to hire another at 20^{00} a week. Living is cheaper here. Very good rooms (and I'm not exaggerating) can be had for 3^{00} a week. Apartments—nice ones for \$$20^{00}$. Food is not high. Helen would rage but she'd get over it since it would involve constructive work as well as the affection and intimacy. If my finances are better around July 1 I may be able to help you. Climatically it's fascinating here. The city is so different, too. Write me about this address matter.

T.D

Very soon I shall take a P.O. Box. For if Helen comes here your letters will have to go to the box.

* * *

June 3rd 1935

Dear Yvette

Yesterday afternoon I sat in a garden where roses climbed a wall to the sun and a pink marble bowl sunk in dark green grass reflected some leaves of a eucalyptus towering high above. The table was of clear glass and about it sat besides Douglas & myself two physicists—members of the California Institute of Technology. And explaining research methods. These related to neutrons and dueterons, and cosmic rays and space-time. But as I looked at the roses in the sun, the forms of the leaves reflected in the crystal water, the rich green grass & felt the warmth & the light soft air, I could not help thinking suppose I knew all—or at least more about grass, light, roses, leaves or the shadows of them in clear water would my enjoyment of life be greater—or less. Incidentally, seeing them so I felt as though the scene was not a setting for analysis or research but rather one for lovely sensuous enjoyment in which human beauty & human love would add to the beauty and where analysis would not detract from it. It made me very sad and very lonely. And so am I today—24 hours later.

T.D

I will answer your latest letter when I am not so blue.

* * *

June 4—1935

Dear Yvette:

Your last letter reads not a little like a carefully worked out indictment. And certainly you have covered all the points. And to them there is no answer to be made except this. That they are not new. The only partially new thing is that you are getting tired of them. But unless Helen & I should part I do not see how I can make a different arrangement. If as I have said before you were a full fledged secretary I would employ you as that and pay you $25[00]. If you had been prepared to do secretarial work when you came back & particularly when Miss Light left I would have put you on for I was stuck for a good secretary & still am. Not only that, but for me you would make an exceptional one because you have all the literary and mental qualifications. In a way of course the work is beneath you & perhaps too technical & routine. Yet you really cannot charge me with insincerity. I could have put you long ago as you know.

Out here just now the situation is as described. As I understand now though Helen after she arrives here is going to live by herself for awhile. She wants to try some work of her own. At present I am living with Douglas but if you were here and working either for me or someone else we could spend much of the time together. As it is George & I are hard on the philosophy book & making not a little progress.[1]

Girls here with brains such as yours get in the reading departments of the movies. As a rule they begin as stenographers but are soon advising as to movies. Besides there is a real field here for the intellectual & artist who can advise these people. They are as thick as mud, and centered mentally on the blonde beauties without brains. But they need women with brains as well and there are few of your type & temperament out here. I do honestly believe if you breezed around out here a little you'd connect and get in on that phase of the work. I put an adv. in the Times here & got 91 replies. I saw fifteen. All the others were obviously impossible. Out of the 15 I finally got one sober plodding woman of 38 who will do, for the present anyhow. She's not quick or clever. Knows nothing of books or articles or novel composition but I have to use her. So you see how they run. Lots of those who answered were scenario copyists—but by God! Hence Im giving this tip for what it is worth.

As for love—I know that you care for me just as I am drawn to you. And I find happiness in being with you. But I've proved that I'm not the only one and so I know that you can do without me even as this last letter of yours indicates. And I am not blaming you. All I wish for both of us is that love were as it is dreamed to be. But since it isn't— As for me now—with my work and my years I could settle down. But I would not expect the same of you or any girl. Life is not like that.

Wait until after July 1st & I'll know better what to say & do.

Love
T.D

1. In the 1930s Dreiser collected scientific and philosophical notes for a book that would synthesize his thinking on the nature of human existence. He never completed what he referred to as "The Formula Called Man," but a selection of its chapters, fragments, and notes were published as *Notes on Life* (1974), edited by Marguerite Tjader and John J. McAleer.

* * *

Thursday. [1935]

Yvette Dear:

You ask me not to be ill or rather not to talk about it—not to make so much of dark thoughts. Well, I'll try to. However, I notice that when any dark thoughts assail you they get the front page, column <u>One</u>. Perhaps mine do too. But I cant write different from (or is it to) what I feel.

And as for Love (Tell me do you love me?) Please define Love for me. I know how it works in your case, but just the same I'd like your definition. When I get that—just what you think Love is and how it works—I'll answer. I may even give you two definitions of Love. And one of passion.

Just to make you feel better I'm not so blue (today). Tomorrow? You see every day I have my five to nine a.m. horrors. I never get a break. They never take a holiday. Actually I consider myself an iron man to have stood it since 16—and not crashed. But I muddle through and by 10 or 11—(usually) I'm a better man. It reminds me of the sun in winter—in L.A. it breaks through anywhere from 11 to 1. 25 black birds in the back yard here. Two mocking birds and two wood pidgeons. The two mocking birds are unwelcome to the Blackies but I notice it takes 10 Blackies to do up 1 mocking bird. They're game. And wont be chased. So in spite of 25 Blackies two mockers are walking defiantly around. I cant help admiring their nerve.

But for all my mental gadding—theres pages & pages of work for me. So——

As for the Ansonia—try the big room for awhile or the little. You can always wheedle a change out of them there. And please see that no mail is lying there for me. If you search you will find some. They're the only ones that hold up mail on me.

Love
TD

You recieved my check of course.

* * *

Monday, June 11 [1935]

Yvette Dear:

This is three of a Monday afternoon & I am down in the dining room working at a long black table that has a black polished top that is nearly as good as mirror. Hot dry sunlight outside. Some black birds bathing in a small bound pool in which one goldfish and about it ivy, small sword palms and blue flags. Still—except for distant cars. A tall, lone Eucaplytus towering over the house and incessantly dropping hard pink blade like leaves that have already rotted from green to pink. And mocking birds. And two ring doves. And a humming bird. And an occasional yellow cockatoo like creature whose name I do not know. And silence. George is at the office—the Examiner. Its chief Editorial writer. Mrs. Douglas is in San Francisco attending to real estate. Hers. One girl Halley is script reader & book finder at Columbia. The other girl Dorothea is in college—still and winding up Examiner. My table is covered with ms & books. Upstairs a stout forty year old typist who is slightly lame & walks with a cane types away on my stuff. No one will return until $5^{\underline{30}}$. Then George. And my friend Calvin Bridges,[1] a friend of his—a professor of Indian (Hindoo) literature arrive & we will dine. And at midnight—after a long confab—to bed. . . . . . But so it goes day after day. I rise at $7^{\underline{45}}$ or 8, have coffee & toast at nine and then to this. Now & then I sit out in the sun. Its becoming regular now—the sunshine. Or I walk around a long flower & tree & grass lined block—for the sun. Or at noon go to a nearby restaurant for whatever I may want.

Science. Philosophy. Ideas for stories. Endless arguments at night with George.

But sometimes the work palls. I wish some one would ring up or I could. I wish for instance that you were upstairs and doing my work. Interlude. I have the car here. It is in the garage. I drive it very well now & occasionally take George & ride out to the beach—15 miles—and sit there—often in the car looking at the Pacific. Its cool at night. Sometimes clear—sometimes foggy. On the clear night I like to stare at the black sea. If I could fix things my way now—sell a book or close some deal—I would telegraph you the means & have you close up & come on. As it is—what I do is to pay in crazy obligations each month four or five times what it would cost to have you here. It is to avoid suffering on the part of my relatives & lawsuits on the part of those who once cared for me. But I am hoping at that for a sudden change. And it may come. Betimes I sit here just as I say & read & work,—or stop & look at the grass, sun, & think how different it might be. How very tame the complications of life can sometimes make one.

TD

1. Calvin Bridges, a scientist Dreiser met at the Woods Hole research center in 1928. Bridges was a professor at California Institute of Technology.

* * *

Tuesday—June 25 [1935]

Yvette Dear:

Here it is Tuesday again. I expected some word from you after the account of Mr. Gredeer[1] but no word. In so far as I know you are still lying naked in the next field and rather intrigued than not, I judge, by the thought of some healthy Gredlerish male coming on you unawares and taking you by storm. And perhaps so taken. (The Secret Archives of a Pagan. You might peice them together some day from bits here & there.)

During the last week I've been under a strain. George has been sick & a little disturbed over something. Helen is in Portland and I have to go up tomorrow to straighten out some property troubles there. Then she is coming down. She still talks of finding a place for herself but has asked if she can come here for a few days—three or four. Yet she may not. All will be all right if you typewrite the envelopes and mail them in New York. I'll let you know about coming as soon as I definitely know what she is planning.

Since you wrote me, I have had a letter from Margie telling me of her work. She must have secured my address from you, and possibly she has been up there. Anyhow she is not happy in what she is doing and indicates that she is much more efficient. If she has become a good stenographer and less temperamental I would like her for she has real understanding and can work out from instructions almost any difficult problem. Her speed in gathering data at times was remarkable. Out here the stenographers are a joke. One did not know how to spell Philadelphia. A second, Ceaser was a town somewhere. The one I have now wanted to know if Southampton is in England. But you cant keep changing every week. And they all come loaded with recommendations. Two of them insisted that what they thought I wanted was a good looking girl with an apartment of her own. When I insisted that I needed a real secretary they left. Both of them said most men dont want that kind. But how are you & Margie getting along these days.

To peice out expenses here I did an article called Overland[2] & sold it to Esquire. It should be in one of the summer numbers. And just now I've finished a second on Mark Twain[3]—whether there were mentally two or one. It is also so, and goes off today. Tomorrow I'll go back to my Philosophy Book—the Formula Called Man.

You know I think I am incurably miserable. Except when deeply employed or when close to someone who is mentally and emotionally in accord with me, I brood so. To be sure I like George & when he is well & comes home at five we make a fair evening of it. The rest of the family is meaningless to me—and almost to him.

But why the silence? Are you so busy up there that there is no time for a note. You have no more to do than I have—scarcely as much. And I have such bad mornings. I swear I'm not myself until eleven or noon. Today no one is here and I work & work.

Love,

T.D

Is the little cabin just above you rented? And who is in it?
There are camps up in the mountains here where two weeks could be spent in a strange, colorful different mountain world.

1. Dreiser rented the large house at Iroki to a Mr. Gredeer, who wrote Dreiser to report that Yvette had been sunbathing in the adjacent field.

2. "Overland Journey," *Esquire* 4(September 1935):24, 97.

3. "Mark the Double Twain," *English Journal* 24(October 1935):615–27.

* * *

Saturday, July 6—1935[1]

Yvette Dear:

Please dont get so excited. Have just wired you and now am writing. I wrote you from Portland. I had to go up there last week because Helen was stuck with the car—valve trouble—holding her there days and sick in the bargain. She claimed she couldnt make it—that is drive down here alone with Nick & her bags and asked me to help her. So I went up and only late last night got here. Tomorrow or Monday (she is resting up today), she is going out to find a place of her own. But I can see from the way she talks and how she feels that I will not be able to leave here & go somewhere else at once. She has a proposition in connection with some movie script which may take here and if so she will get into the movie field. If so she will be on her own. But for just now I find she is looking to me for some introductions, and these it will be good business for me to give her. Under the circumstances I don't see how the visit is to work out between now and the next two weeks and accordingly I have just wired you. But this does not mean that positively I am not to see you before long since there are negotiations looking to the production of the Hedgerow Theatre version of An American Tragedy in New York—as well as in London, in which case I will have to come back there. Incidentally the Liveright suit comes up in October and as I have to go on the stand, I'll be there and see you.

But all this is apart from your excitement over Margie's desire to work for me again. I thought she never would wish to, seeing that I did not agree with her attitude toward the work and myself. Now however she tells of her experience and of course I know that she has the ability to do the work—especially the kind of philosophic work with all its research that I am engaged on now. All along I've been wondering when I would find one person who could be of real help to me and then comes this letter from her. Of course I cannot pay her much—not just at present anyhow but she would certainly save me time & money if she worked steadily for me and in the long run I could make it up to her. Margie has never been in love with me and has frankly said so. But her reasons for wanting to work for me is that I do the only kind of work that gives her any mental satisfaction,—that all other work of this kind is Boring and that she is willing to work hard and do all the things that will further my work. In the face of the fact that here I can get no one worth a sou you can imagine how I feel about this. I have not answered her last letter which has been here for several days but will tomorrow. Whatever Helen feels or does not feel in this instance does not matter since it is the work I have to do that I am considering. Whether I will be able to let her come soon is another question. I am considering ways and means and want to hear from New York—from the Shuberts,[2] Jasper Deeter[3] and my literary agents first.

As for us I have not changed in any way. I feel just as I did before. I know that as you say you can have a good time there if you don't come and I also know that whatever else you do or whoever else you go with you still care for me—otherwise you would not bother. And if I could arrange for your being here now I would. As it is for the time being I can do nothing. As soon as I see my way clear I will let you know.

Now please don't do anything or say anything to Margie that will cause her to feel dubious about this or to dissuade her from coming for you know she has the mind & the temperament suitable for my work. And do not write her and discuss this or us with her since it is not necessary. You represent yourself to me. And Margie is herself. And, if she is willing to come I do not want her to feel that there is a mixup here or that I am consulting you as to her qualifications or her right to work for me if she wishes to. I need the kind of help she can give me and you should be willing for her to give it to me and keep your own counsel.

And this is not lecturing you—it's plain sense and wholly fair.

Love
T.D.

The Western Union has just called back to say that my message can only be sent to you by mail after it gets there. So I'll air mail this instead.

1. On the first page of the letter, written near the top left parallel to the long side, is "Keep the Tibbett ms & please call at the P.O."

2. Milton Shubert was preparing to produce a translation of Erwin Piscator and Lina Goldschmidt's German adaptation of *An American Tragedy* with the Group Theater in New York.

3. Jasper Deeter, founder of the Hedgerow Theater near Philadelphia. Deeter had recently produced Piscator and Goldschmidt's version of *An American Tragedy*.

* * *

Wed. July 17—35

Yvette Dear:

You are wrong about the handwriting not being mine. I was doing stunts as I sometimes am when it comes to addressing. I'll be more careful in the future. And you can mail what you wish here providing you typewrite the envelope. Helen is not here enough at present to present any real difficulty. And, as a rule when she is I am here working. When the mail man comes sometimes I answer the door—sometimes Miss Tisdall—my secretary. But wherever I am Miss Tisdall gets it and puts it on my desk.

It's very hot here—96 or 97 outside now. But I don't mind the heat. When I'm in it I perspire and feel lively enough. It is when it is damp & gray that I suffer most.

I wonder if you will do a peice of work for me. I will gladly pay you what you think is fair. You recall that French Dramatization of An American Tragedy, by Georges Jamin and Jean Servais. You read it I believe & thought it exceedingly good. So do others. I need to have it done into English. Wont you do it for me. If it is ever produced anywhere—here or England or wherever in English and I can get your version used it will carry your name as translator. If you can & will—I'll send it on to you registered and you can work on it. I want three copies for myself. If you want to keep one you must make four. Let me know by return mail.

Work, work, work. Here at my table again. And just a little cynical. But at that it is better than nothing perhaps. For someday, of course there will be no table and no me.

As ever

T.D

A Eucalytus leaf from the garden. It just fell from the tree.

* * *

[1935]

Los Angeles, Calif.

Dear Yvette

Loving made easy! The do it for you and do it first school of enticement. Office and vacation chambers Mt. Kisco, N.Y. Branch office & reception chambers on Manhattan Island to be arranged. Classes in kindness, forethought, patience, forgiveness, courtesy and humility and ideal service each week-day from nine to five. Private classes in lust, charm, magnetism, hypnotism, et cetera from 8$^{\underline{30}}$ to 3 A.M. Applications considered in the order of their reception. Student body limited as to numbers. Qualification blank furnished in application. Front face view & twelve artistic poses (photos, required with each application). Address with self addressed envelope and \$10$^{\underline{00}}$ application fee. Yvette Szekely. Iroki, Mt. K.[1]

MUCH LOVE from <u>TD</u>.

1. Dreiser wrote, parallel to the long edge of the letter, "As you see Ive worked out this marvellous proposition in adv. form. Your fortune is made."

* * *

July 27—'35

Yvette Dear:

That is a lovely fresco of Riveras[1] which came yesterday from you. Beautiful. And I liked the gay little pictures made about the cabin. Very summery. If you are as joyful as those pictures you are very joyful. As for myself I've been through a seige. My eye—which got worse but just now appears to be better. An ingrowing toe nail which suddenly threatened blood poisoning and was very painful—(better now) and a perfect storm of argumentative letters and telegrams from the Shuberts and their agents anxious to do the Piscator–Hedgerow Theatre version of An American Tragedy, but not very anxious to make reasonable terms. To this minute I do not know whether I am to be called to New York or not.

And so here I am reading, having notes copied, writing out scraps of observation. But so it goes day after day and resting betimes. I think of you—only at present you seem very far away: probably because your mind is elsewhere just now. But maybe it will return. Helen is busy with some movie schemes of her own. Douglas is departing on a vacation of his own. I am sincerely working.

By the way I registered the French version of the play[2] to you at Kisco. Hope you can find time to do. I hear now that there are two more dramatic versions, both unauthorized. One in Vienna. One in Russia. I am hoping to obtain copies.

It is hot, but cloudless. The goldfish in the pool stay near the bottom. A fig tree is heavy with ripening figs for which the birds are waiting. When the spirit is secretly troubled as mine so often is—silence and isolation tend to calm it. Just now silence & isolation help most.

T.D

Regards to Sue & your friend. So glad you got the raise.

1. Diego Rivera, the Mexican painter.
2. A French adaptation of *An American Tragedy* was done by Georges Jamin and Jean Servais.

* * *

Thursday—Aug 1—[1935]

Yvette:

Please, honey, dont write me cross or angry letters. This has been a hard year for me. I have listed only a few things. I will not outline any more. All that was really against me in New York was climate. You knew I was sick. Since I have been here there have been additional things. Do not forget that when I went to Portland I wrote at once. But because it did not reach you at once there was a storm of complaints. But I was travelling and writing was not easy. Since then I have written as before, a letter for each one I get from you. Somehow I am physically tired. I sleep as a rule from 9 to 7[30] or 8. Then, as I say, I work from 9 to 5. I have secretarial troubles—plenty. My eyes. Almost all right now. An inflamed toe. Endless trouble about the play in New York and in addition financial troubles. But thats all. As these things clear up I will be alright again. I'll come back to New York & you will get your wish to be with me alone. It is mine. But I am sombre for all of these reasons—and maybe just a period of psychic depression. But dont scold. You are the last one to do that. And your natural spirit is priceless—poetic and altogether lovely. I'll write regularly.

T.D

* * *

Aug. 8th—Thurs [1935]

It is very hot. So hot that I wish for evening. Two letters came. One containing a picture initialed "no letter." Another containing five pictures and making me out better than I am. So I mixed the two—mentally—and found it a tasteless drink. Thus I decided to leave myself as I looked at two differing moments.

It does look as though you were prospering. A better car. Driving to work. Unquestionably entertaining freely. Your pictures look happy. I wish I could maintain such ebullience. Not that you or anyone does—but I wish I could.

No, I am not through with my job but one day I will be. A great deal of reading goes with it. Heavy reading which I have to assort and assemble into comments on or answers to definite problems.[1] It is slow work. Yet of all the things I have done it is the most gripping. Even though I fail to put it right it is still all wonderful to me.

As for the life around me—well except for my lungs (bronchitis) I could work anywhere. Here the heat drives it away most of the time.

I still need a secretary. And how much. One of these days—maybe—I will find the right person.

My toe. At last it is well. My eyes. It has been decided that the glare here is partly responsible—& now—outside—I wear smoked glasses (that is in the daytime & the sun). But my legal troubles! And my financial! My God.

Sometimes—maybe—it is best to be repressed and defeated.

Maybe. I work here with the thought that work should solve my material ills. The others? Some of them I know are incurable.

Love
T.D

No one makes any snaps here. The picture in this article—as posy as it looks was snapped over a back fence or through a window & without my knowledge. The article came as a complete surprise—and first over the radio! I think George Douglas had something to do with it but he says not. It sounds like him—part of it.

1. Dreiser is referring here to "The Formula Called Man."

* * *

Address
232 So. Westmoreland

4922 Rosewood Ave.
Los Angeles.
Aug 15—'35

Yvette Dear:

Please note the new address. But dont send mail here yet. Continue to send it to 232 So. Westmoreland, and I will have it forwarded from there in a new envelope. Helen is here with me. She grew suddenly very desolate & I compromised on this. But one day she saw one of your gray envelope letters—properly typed and all—and mailed in New York. But she recognized it and raged. I settled that by warning her not to bother in any way since this relationship was not to be disturbed. She dropped the matter, but not without telling me that a constant visitor of yours at Kisco—one whom you slept with there nights and regularly was a young Jew—the same one I judge as rang the bell in Perry Street. I allowed for rage & so forth, but not for the description. And Helen does not lie. She asserts what she knows. I know that. Curiously though—just before I wrote that "diluted" letter some one else who is at Mt. Kisco and whom you know by sight anyhow wrote and asked me if you had a brother—that she or he—(you will have to guess whether male or female) saw a young man about the cabin with you quite frequently. So you see. I have nothing to say. Your emotions and necessities are your own. But when you write me vehemently of love and devotion I cannot accept it undiluted. I have to think that you care for others. Naturally you would conceal knowledge of the others so as not to hurt me. Wont that explain the last letter?

The other night—for the first time—I saw "Escape Me Never."[1] I truly liked it very much,—thought it beautiful. And in many ways Gemma—or whatever her name was reminded of you—your spirit and wisdom and gift of feeling and romance. Also your sly cleverness. But after all—as Gemma said of her artist-god—I would not change you. You are as you are. And if I value your friendship and your diluted affection I will have to make the best of it. I cannot help liking you. You have genius of mind and skill at living. You are kind & forgiving and understanding and ready to help all who need help. I cannot change or make you into anything and do not wish to. I try to understand & endure as you understand and endure. In real life I fancy Gemma was not better than yourself if as good.

I'm sorry about the Perry street room. I liked it so much—until—and still like it in a way—because I know that another place wherever it may be will not be any more sacred. Certainly I will come to see you when I get back—but dont you think you should do the picking? I notice that whatever you choose and wherever you are you create a loveliness especial & peculiar to you. And it is soothing to me.

But, ah, Yvette—I am really lonely. I cannot tell you why? Some essential thing is wrong. I know that I am liked well enough. A to-do is made. Here & there a girl will frantically seek me out—and many men. But just the same— In your little rooms though I have been happy. And for the most part in your presence this almost crushing despair has fled. I wish it would go forever.

T.D

1. *Escape Me Never* (1935), a film that featured an itinerant waif named Gemma, was based on a novel by Margaret Kennedy.

* * *

Saturday, Aug 24—[1935]

Yvette Dear:

You are mistaken as to any cruel intentions. There were none. I was in a kidding mood. But my humor must have overshot the mark. My second letter on the paper you sent me must have proved that no cruelty was intended. But I can see now, thinking over the school idea and my previous comments, how you must have taken it. But Yvette you do not seem to remember (now I am talking about an assertion made in one of your latest letters) that you yourself told me—the morning after the 2 a.m. doorbell ring—that you were in love with the dentist or had been. Also you decidedly admitted that you should not be expected to live for me alone and I have repeatedly agreed to that. For I feel that your temperament is tempestuous—anyone can see that.

But please lets not quarrel. I'll try & do better. You know that I care for you. I cannot see how I am to change as to that. And it may be that a more favorable set up will be achieved this fall. Living with Helen here is no more than living with her anywhere. She knows how I am. And she knows about you. There is nothing to be said. And except for an occasional quarrel nothing is said. Dont write any more angry letters.

As for that room. It sounds excellent. But rather high for you. Do you know that you can get a large room & bath with all service at the Ansonia for that. I've been intending to pay you fifty dollars for that translation, but I suppose that will not nearly solve your renting problems. But then you spending so much doing for others. And then take that car! What will you do with it in N.Y. Garage service is expensive. And you will not be able to use it much. It does seem with your salary & your allowance that you should make out better than you do. Just now I am running under a real strain. I have so many things to take care of. But if I sell a movie here as I confidently expect to—or do an original story for them—I'll have some money to turn on. And if so I'll give you enough to cover that extra rent. I should know by September 15th. If it doesnt go through though I'll be just where I am.

Oh, its hot here today. Dreadful. The one relief is the nights—for it begins to cool off & stays cool until 9 a.m. I'm hard at work on my philosophy book, which should be good if I get it done. But is a job. And I've had so little intelligent help, really none. Please think kindly of me & forget the letter.

T.D

I just saw a dreadful smack—two cars & four people in each. One 7 year old boy killed outright. Another—about 12—with a broken back. Two women (about 40 each) apparently dying. I couldnt tell. Horribly cut anyhow. And two men injured—(face, hands etc). Head on street corner crash!

* * *

Sept 5—1935

Yvette Dear:

What a lovely letter from Vermont! Anyone reading it can feel your presence in the place and the sweetness of it. The sufficiency and serenity. I have seen so many of them. It is New England. It is the Old South. It is Pennsylvania and Iowa and Kentucky and Texas. It is our true and only worthy tradition and should be respected & treasured as such.

I wondered where you were. I am here at my table—writing and making notes. I have just written something on memory (The Myth of Enduring Memory)[1] and seeing the sun come up & go down. George[2] is coming to dinner. He will be here soon. We will talk philosophy & go for a drive. Helen is planning to leave for Portland to be with her mother two weeks before we return. Pretty soon I should be back. There is nothing much here except quiet and the opourtunity for concentration. How long was your trip? Who went with you? I wonder.

Enclosed is a check for a dollar. Get those things out of the P.O. Tell me what this is (This 26th package). Translate this French letter from Russia and let me hear from you. Evidently you are planning a grand winter, and you know I wish it to be all of that for you.

T.D.

1. One of the chapters in "The Formula Called Man."
2. George Douglas.

* * *

Sept 10—1935

Yvette Dear:

It was I who suggested the Ansonia because you get so much for your money—mail service, linen, cleaning, all in telephone calls, messenger service. And of course I don't mind if you live there. It's a sensible place to live. Besides at any time, if you decide to move out there is no lease. They pro-rate the rent up to the day you leave. If you go there October 1st it means that you mean to stay there until May 1 or June 1—seven or eight months all told. This year you were yelling to get out in the country by May 1 & did so, which means seven months. Besides if I didnt want to come as you say—and proved that I didnt—at any time you could proceed to share it with a girl fifty-fifty I presume. If you did that it would make your rent $25^{\underline{00}}$. You could work the sister act.

Here's the other angle. Say—in order to permit you to live at the Ansonia alone for seven months I agreed to send you ten each month, I wouldnt send the whole seventy in advance because if I did you'd be back by Oct 1 or $15^{\underline{th}}$ asking for more. I know you. But I will do the ten a month for the number of months you reside at the Ansonia—providing as you say—"I continue to see you there"—and even if I dont.

Now as to the last paragraph covering all the women who visited me at the Ansonia. The following are a matter of record. (1) Yvette Szekeley. 2. Helen. (3) Marjorie. 4. Miss Light. 5. Miss Helston. 6. Mrs. Stewart who did economic studies for me. 7. Miss Clark of Philadelphia whom I helped to get a novel published. 8. Marguerite Tjader-Harris, wife of Magistrate Harris who did art investigations for me and copied library material for nothing because she is rich & likes me. At the same time she was living with a German ex officer and adored him.

You of course know that I have a lot of admirers. They hunt me up out here—or anywhere. At the hotel I had to bar most of them out. Some came with letters which could not be ignored. Some barged in—a French-Indo Chinese critic—aged 26 whose lover was a French artist and with her, a communistic secretary of the central committee, very intense, very graceful & very devoted. They used her deliberately to persuade me (or they thought) to do things. Miss Sayre (on a once in 6 months visit to New York)—wives & secretaries of publishers. What of it? All the time I was working. All of the time. I did my best to have free time for you. And I am not listing authors, editors, publishers, Hume,[1] communists, socialists, Townsendites, Hollywood producers, agents, lecture bureau people, etc, etc etc.

Think what you will. If you don't know now you never will.

What is the next subject before the House.

T.D

Now that you want to get out of Mt. Kisco it rains, snows, hails, tornados and raises hell generally. If you didnt want to get out it would be sunshine & flowers, regardless. Go to, Gemma—I know you.

1. Arthur Carter Hume, Dreiser's New York attorney.

* * *

Wednesday. [1935]

Yvette Dear:

I'm sorry about Helens letter. Its very savage I see. But then shes written me scores such and still does. I told you some time ago she was going to write you. She has written you before. If writing were sufficient to settle anything! But it isnt. Hard words break no bones. Besides if she were not jealous & hurt herself would she be writing you. There is nothing new in the situation and I have told her repeatedly that I cannot & will not live an exclusive life with her. I know its hard but it isnt any harder on her than it is on me. Shes talked of leaving & much more. But I am alive & so is she & you. Better forget it. I wrote you yesterday about the Ansonia. Write me if that is ok. Please translate that French letter from Russia.

T.D

And you can write it. One letter looked as though it had been opened & I accused her of it but she denied it furiously. If you would use long legal looking envelopes & typewrite the address it would be better. The papers here say its raining there.

* * *

Tuesday Sept 17 [1935]

Yvette:

Thanks for the translation. It is quite clear except in two places. But in those my knowledge of the facts helped to straiten it out. The trouble with Piscator is that he refuses to recognize the fact that he is only a co-author with Lina Goldschmidt, and he signed a contract with her as such.[1] He & she are receiving 50% of the American production if it comes to pass.

How are you? Moving? It can't be raining still. September and October are usually beautiful months at Kisco, as you know. Helen is in Portland. Has been for over a week—about 9 days. I saw your letter addressed to her up there. As for me, since last Friday I've been feeling wretched. A sudden change of weather here from hot to cold tied up my right wrist & shoulder. So—no write. Besides it was hard to move around—even to read. I'm all right today, but it truly was bad weather. I had only my Jewish typist and George Douglas—who came & went doing things. Now I'm hoping to stay put.

In a way I'm not sure it was wise to write Helen. Maybe so. Shes strangely temperamental—moody, principally. If only she had some creative outlet I think she would feel better. As for me here—my creative outlet is all right but intellectually L.A. is a barren place. Actors have no brains. And those former settlers either. At times you feel as if you were in a lotus-land beautiful to look at but nearly everybody doped. I question if I could ever live here. I'm really sure I couldn't. New Mexico is better.

I'm sorry not to have written but I'll make up now.

Love

TD

Have you selected your room at the Ansonia. I have a piano, piano desk, & typewriter table & chair there, being held for me.

1. Lina Goldschmidt, a German drama critic, had collaborated with Erwin Piscator on a dramatization of *An American Tragedy*.

* * *

Friday [Mt. Kisco, 1935]

Yvette Dear:

I'm sorry about the change & all it seems to mean to you now, but maybe it wont be for the worse. I have found that the things I have dreaded most have proved (often) for the best and the things I thought spelled success, advance, perfection resulted to my dissadvantage (often). You cannot tell. Frequently (generally I would say) change is beneficial. Personally I have a feeling you will grow & do better. . . . . And thanks for putting the big desk away. And keep the $15^{\underline{00}}$ against services rendered and future charges on the desk—for six or eight months anyhow. I miss you & want to come down but there is a veritable hell of details here—living as I do now & I am miles behind what I need to do. I wanted to get down yesterday, but it rained and I had to meet Hume at White Plains & for 3 hours discuss legal matters & today I have to go to Bedford Hills to protest the taxes on this place. And in addition do work here. One thing you'll approve of I've had Philgas brought to the log cabin (the oil stove was impossible) & now there is a three plate gas stove in the same corner which can be lighted instantly. It will also warm up the room. When I get around to it I want to fix that chimney so it will really draw, then the dampness can be shut out. Please dont quarrel if I don't see you this week end. I've asked to go to the Philadelphia Convention. But if I go I may arrange to have you come over for a night anyhow.

There is trouble here & I have things to tell you. But whether for good or ill I'm not sure just now.

Just now a telegram from Lillian Smith[1]—303 W. 154th St. asking me to dinner 7. P.M. Did you give her this address. You know I wouldn't go.

Anyhow, Love
& I'll see you
T.

1. Lillian Smith, a co-worker of Yvette's.

* * *

Monday [1935]

Dear Yvette:

I had to come down today—Monday. But just for the day. Going back now but expect to be down Wednesday. So sorry I couldn't see you. Got the bag & book & Humes sketch. Am taking it along to read. But oh, Lord I'm lonely. And that in the face of all I have to do—work, people, letters. Its almost fantastic, but its true. On Wednesday or Thursday I'll phone you if I can. Wish you could come out to Kisco & finish that bath-room & just play around. Helen lives in the idea I must live for her alone but it cant be done. I think so well of her and understand & sympathize with all of her virtues & charms—but even so. Write me here & to Mt. Kisco. Ill try & get an invite for you & whoever you care to bring—direct.

Love
T.D

* * *

Thursday 12—'35

Yvette Dear:

Would have come down today. But Sherwood Anderson who is leaving for months & Jasper Deeter are here for tonight & tomorrow A.M. Expect to get down Friday (tomorrow) P.M. but may be Sat. Leave door open. Enclosed is $\$10^{\underline{00}}$ on your rent. Wish you could be out here. Its all so mixed up and trying. Terribly so.

Love

TD

* * *

Thursday [1935]

Dear Yvette

Just now I came back from a walk up to mail box to find that Olga Jordan[1] of the Greek theatre had called up. I recognized the name. So I'm writing to say Ill be down some time Saturday afternoon and will be with you. But you are such a liar. Before calling on the house phone I knocked at your door. No answer. You'll say you were asleep. Always when I call Margaret I am informed you'll be back in half an hour—long enough to telephone to you, wherever you are. Its all allright—but your week-ends are plainly disposed of—and not at Margarets. Now I hear talk of a cruel suspicious mind—and that where there is so much suspicion and so little faith there is no need for honesty on anyone's part—since one gets no credit. But occasionally one does get credit when the evidence is credible. It does happen.

I think you are right though in thinking of letting me drift out of your life. You need continuous as well as happy association. You know with my work and the various things public & private that I cant provide that. I dont provide it here. I feel the unfairness to you and yet envy the other fellow—an anomaly which is composed of the impossible plus dissatisfaction.

Ah, the devil.

But I'll call you up probably—around $5^{\underline{30}}$ Saturday since I have three things (errands) which I have to attend to first. I can't do them Sundays.

Love

T.D

1. Olga Jordan was, among other things, a co-worker of Yvette's at the Department of Welfare.

* * *

[November 1935]

Dear Yvette:

I called Sunday afternoon twice at the hotel. The last time the girl gave me Margarets number. She engaged me in a conversation trying to get me to come up. I finally said I was going to Chicago. I'm not. Only to Detroit, Toledo to lecture. I'll be back Sunday—and if your home will stay there Sunday night.

I'm coming down tomorrow night, Tuesday, & will be with you. (If your in)

T.D

* * *

Mt Kisco—Jan 1—'36[1]

Yvette:

Here's a letter. I'm supposed to say what? I'm moved to write it because you said write me a letter. And yet I'm not moved by that wholly. I'm really moved by the thought of being with you Friday or Saturday—maybe today—Thursday. I'm moved by the good times we have together—the humor and gaiety and complaints and ills and whatever. The room you have made out of nothing much—out of yourself, really, in the Ansonia, I like and am moved by. To me its as good as any island in the South Seas or a peak in the Alps or the Andes—or streets or restaurants in Paris or Moscow. Its something alive and colorful and gay and healthy,—a place to go to and be in. So was your little room in Sullivan Street and the basement in Perry Street. And that rag tagle affair in 83rd. I loved it. I used to kid you about it and berate the surroundings. But you were there. And you made the room. And when you left it it was done for. Rooms, places are a reflection of you. Your plenty even without any room. You could set up a lovely livable world in a hall or a barn.

Now have I written all this because you asked me to write or haven't I?

Love,
T.D.

1. Dreiser drew an arrow pointing up at "36" from below.

* * *

HOTEL ANSONIA
Broadway at 73rd Street
New York City

March 1—[1936]

Yvette:

Here is the twenty for the translation. The reason I am through is that I know not only from external evidence but from recent personal contact with you that you are not only indulging in other affairs, but that you have and worse that you entertain what might be considered a tolerant friendship for me—possibly admiration but no more. Sex intimacy with me has been nothing to you for a long time. I have observed it. More you have grown in a brassy assurance which relates to your ability to put things over, trick people, make them believe what you like. It is a comfortable feeling as long as it lasts—as long as no traps spring—no longer.

But I am not in the putover class. I told you you would hang yourself. You have. Your letters are insincere—mere literary bursts intended to fool readers, not me. Dont forget your exotic burst of affection for the captain in my presence. Self assurance & brass can do no more.

Lets call it a day.

T.D

* * *

March 2nd 1936

Yvette:

You ignore the fact that for the last two months I have pointed out to you your emotional indifference to me. I saw it before I left for California—the time you admitted that you had been in love with a dentist & still cared. I let it go because imagined that you really cared enough to come back. After returning here I noticed a change & have pointed it out. You like me as a person—some one to associate with through good weather & bad, when you are in love with others & playing about or when you are out of luck. But as for me being or meaning more than that I know now that I am not. And since I do not want and have not wanted to share an alfresco sex affair with others you can certainly grant me permission to drop out. You will always be free and an adventuress. You cannot help it. You are too healthy, resourceful and attractive. You do not really need me and I am in no position to demand any sacrifices of you. The answer is to quit for I am not content to be a helpful friend and bystander. So thats that.

You will not kill yourself. You will go on to happy days & experiences and forget me. Anyone who can openly thrill over the arrival of a lover while yawningly suggesting the wisdom of reading something to second assumedly duped lover needs no particular advice or sympathy and I am not providing any. I am not angry or disliking you entirely—merely awake, as I should be, by now.

TD

* * *

Tuesday [1936]

Yvette

I judged it was you who telephoned largely because of the refined inquiries and the fact that no name was given. If it had been Helen who answered she would have known who it was. Yet while I am sorry that things have turned out as they have, I cannot help recalling the bored mood of you for some time past and especially of the evening when that particular call came. Just before that you appeared to me to be doing your best to make a feeble show of pleasure in my presence. When the call came your thrilled response showed where your great interest lay, and without any thought of the contempt for me involved!

As you can imagine while I might forgive that as an evidence of a compelled delight which you could not resist & which naturally excluded me, you cannot expect me to rejoice in the spectacle of myself as a secondary figure, serving as a stop-gap in the absence of your real love or first choice. If I were wanting in places to go or individuals to enthusiastically welcome me I might conceivably remain. But since I am not and more, with difficulty and neglect of others made the occasions which permitted us to be together, I naturally am unwilling to make myself the pathetic part of another such, shall I say uncomplimentary, scene. True you write now as though I were of more import than the last months have shown. But it is still plain to me that I am secondary—one of several, and as I said to you I am not willing to play that. If you had really cared you could not possibly have submitted me or anyone you liked to any such open and brazenly contemptuous insult. So, while I am worried if by any chance you are emotionally regretful, I cannot truly see how that could be or that I should forgive it.

The truth is I came to be a more or less useful play fellow, the spectre of a dead if in fact not wholly disagreeable romance. If I could say anything more consoling I would. But your action on that occasion and others does not permit it. My value had shrunk for you and you were neither kind or thoughtful or even diplomatic enough to conceal it. And so a genuine feeling was killed quite completely.

T.D

* * *

Wed. 26—'36

Dear Yvette:

I plan to come down Sunday night. I think we will use my car. If your room is vacant I may stay there. Or, if you are free maybe will go to a hotel. At any rate I will be down late in the afternoon & call you first at 251 W. 73rd. If your not there, then later at Margarets. Your letter reads as though you had become converted to class superiority & had deserted the mass entirely. And yet you havent had such a hard time—no worse if as bad as I had as a kid & later. But money never converted me to the conviction that luxury is much more than a bore to a live, thinking active person.

T.D

I hope you have found some simple place. I wont go where we are part of any group. What happened to the first place you had in mind?

* * *

Wed. night [1936]

Yvette Dear:

You mustnt think I'm completely indifferent. I'm not. I'm passing through a difficult period. Maybe it will come out for the best or at least satisfactorily work. The need to sell this place, to get back to the city or nearer it and the time it takes to get in and out figures in it. I did not leave here last week end. Spent Sunday in bed. The night I mailed that letter I went to the Russian Consulate and returned on the 10[30] train and I have been in since. I would like to see you, truly, but I must get this book out of the way and I'm worried.

Love

T.D

* * *

Wed 29—'36

Yvette Dear

Saturday is impossible. I have two engagements which I must keep. Why cant it be the following week—even some week day evening like Wednesday. Let me know. Because of things that have come up I doubt if I can see you Saturday at all. I see no way of fixing it now. If I can I'll wire you. Last Saturday was lovely but you didnt treat me right. This is not by way of revenge. Its political and scientific—people I want to meet and from whom I can get material.

T.

* * *

Saturday [1936]

Yvette Dear:

Please dont think that I dont care for you anymore or that I wouldnt like to see you. I will—and be happy doing it. And you dont have to prove your worth to me by achieving something. Your worth is in yourself—your temperament, your courage, your tolerance, kindness & good humor. Our affairs have been mixed from the beginning but the affection & friendship have come through unchanged & I fancy they'll last for some time. I want to see you this coming week—I hope Wednesday evening. What are you doing?

T.D

* * *

Saturday [1936]

Dear Yvette

It was nice of you to notify me of Schwarz's wish, but he also wrote me the next day & I have answered him. And thanks for the photos—though those of me with my feet almost concealing me are a little too out of drawing. I remain resentful of your visiting here without any word or warning. And I am not ready to accept the assertion that you desired to see if you could do anything for me, for you know if I needed you I would get word to you. It is this sort of thing that makes me resentful of anyone. And you well know it could cause trouble. More I asked you long ago not to mail letters addressed by hand. Your pleasure appears to be to make the handwriting as conspicuous as a sign. I ask why? Affection will not explain it. Some other things might easily.

T.D

* * *

Friday. [1936]

Yvette Dear:

Today I arranged with the New York–Mt. Kisco Express Co to call at the Ansonia, Monday a.m. between 10 & 12 to get the typewriter desk. I havent [illegible word] first name but please see him & tell him that the typewriter desk is being called for. I cant find the Helston list—but am still looking. When it shows up I'll collect what else belongs to me. As for the 200$^{\underline{00}}$ I cant do that now—not at 'this' time anyhow. I wanted to rent the house for 1800. It cost me $200 to put it in order again & at the last minute I was compelled to take $1100—really (considering the money spent) $900. If I successfully complete this book & arrange the right advance I may do something later. Possibly in Sept.

Always you talk of the chill of my letters. Yours are too often practical. I think your dreams are being metamorphosed into fiction—or will be. As for me I feel subdued just now and not a little old.

T.D

I may get into N.Y. next week. I'll let you know. Let me know about the piano desk.

* * *

Wed. [Oct. 1936]

Dear Yvette:

Sorry not to have been able to see you at three or after. But I came down to not only see Clark, but to get some letters out of my storage file & take them to Hume at Yonkers. I only reached his office at five—and after an hour with him came on out here. I'll see you another day. I liked Clark very much and imagine most anyone would. If he could over come his depression—(which he is likely to convey to anyone whom he is trying to persuade, but which he need not)—he could easily connect himself. He has a fine and persuasive presence which he should use to the full. If he does so he cannot fail of a valuable connection.

T.D

* * *

Friday—, June 18—'37

Dear Yvette:

Greetings, wherever you are. I doubt if this will reach you in time for you to take advantage of it. Anyhow theres a Miss Cook who runs a position securing bureau at 206 Broadway. A perfume house that imports French perfumes desires a receptionist <u>who can speak French</u> to meet and greet incoming buyers. She has to speak French well. With it goes a little secretarial work—not much. Salary $50^{\underline{00}}$ per week. If you were here and went down looking your smartest you might pick it up. Thought you'd like to know. Why not apply to several agencies for a position as a receptionist.[1]

Is it nice at Fire Island? Any whales?

1. After this sentence is a large rectangular hole in the letter where something was cut out.

* * *

THEODORE DREISER

Aug 17—'37

Yvette Dear:

I have moved out for a couple of weeks anyhow to the Long Island Biological Laboratory at Cold Spring Harbor Long Island. Expect to return Sept. 1. And I may be in town once or twice on business. Its as you know, about an hour and a half. I have rooms in what is known as the Old Fire House—because it was that before it was fixed up for biologists. Maybe you'll stop out some afternoon. I've left my things in storage at the hotel.

Love
T.D

* * *

Thursday [1937]

Yvette Dear:

They wont let any women visitors on the place after twelve midnight, unless they have registered & taken a room. Only wives of active scientists registered for work here as their assistants in the laboratories are allowed to stay permanently. The assistants have rooms assigned them in dormatories. If anyone is coming male or female to stay overnight, they have to be registered & paid for separately. I have two nice rooms & a bath—very cheap, but for myself alone. Yet anyone can come down for the day or afternoon or evening & stay until midnight. There is a midnight train to N.Y. from Sgassat—3 miles away. But this place isnt any further from N.Y. than is Mt. Kisco. They say here that people in their own cars make N.Y. in 55 minutes. Its only 3 miles East of Oyster Bay. Route 25a passes the gate—which is a mile west of Cold Spring Harbor. You come to it before you come to Cold Spring Harbor. If you wanted to drive out some afternoon after four you could stay until eleven or twelve as you wished.

Its very nice—right on the bay—but the meals are fierce. And the people scientific. They talk science or things they are planning to do together all of the time. Its very quiet & I work all day. There are two telephones here—neither convenient. One is in the Office—three houses away. That one is Cold Spring Harbor 2207 (Thirty cents for 3 minutes.) But by the time you got the person it might be 60 or 90 cents. Yet I'm usually here. The other is in what is called Blockford Hall, the main dining & reception building. The number of that is Cold Spring Harbor 619. Its about 2 N.Y. short blocks up the road. But you can telegraph—32 cents for 25 words I believe. If you write or wire for say Friday—or Monday or Wednesday I'll be here. I dont have to go to N.Y. & so dont. The road entrance is on the left, as you come along 25ª. Its marked Long Island Carnegie Biological Laboratory. You come to Blockford Hall first, as you enter. Then you can ask for me—in the Old Fire house.

Love

T.D

* * *

Wed. 13 [1937]

Yvette Dear

I'm mostly in bed up here—although yesterday I worked down stairs in the morning—reading & writing notes. This morning I'm down again—principally to report. I'm taking medicine three times a day—oiling my chest & resting. By Monday I hope to be able to return and decide on my next step. As soon as I get in town I'll call you. If I'm sure of the day I'll write you beforehand. The last three days have been very beautiful here & if I had felt better I would have been outside. My doctor still holds that I need a change. Its difficult to have to arrange for it all right now. Write me as I told you. Wish I could take dinner with you at your place. When I go I'm wondering if I could leave something with you—with full assurance that you wouldnt disturb them or let anyone do so. Are you sincerely capable of that much responsibility. I'm touchy about my papers. Besides that though I might ask you to take care of certain things that come up for which of course I would pay you. Are you all right? Im pretty irritable at times I know but there is still something between us.

Love

T.D

* * *

THEODORE DREISER

Dec 20—1937

Dear Yvette:

Heres to better and better days and years: and nothing off for bad behavior.

I wish though you'd give me an outline of Case 26. Id like to see if that couldnt be turned into some form of story. Even if you plan to use it—the way I would do it would never interfere with the method you would employ, I know.

Love
T.D

Check for 10 enclosed

* * *

Tuesday [1938]

Yvette Dear:

You are always looking for some entrance to the stage. Here is an idea. There is a theatre called The Free Theatre in 28th Street just East of Lexington Ave on the South Side of the street. It is conducted by a zealot & crank called Davenport.[1] No admission is charged. The actors are not paid. An expense collection (voluntary as in a church) is taken up. He stages many of the best plays, and actually a number of actors & actresses who could not break through in any other may have gotten their starts there. He is poor & often threadbare—but there are young boys & girls & men & women about there. Since there is never any money they do not stick—but some training and technic is to be picked up. Dont want to browse around there. My name will admit you to his presence I am sure. And if an intelligent group ever centered there—it would by degrees & in spite of him I think,—possibly even with him make some thing out of it.

I'm sorry about Sunday night. I had to go to Wm Sulzers for dinner. I expected to be out and away by 930. We didnt get loose until 10:40 and it was raining hard. But I'll be in this week & next Saturday night.

Meanwhile, why not look up this strange place. Crazy as it is I see it as an opourtunity for one who wants to make one out of it. Incidentally pick me up some local color there. I want to work a sketch.

T.D

1. Butler Davenport, playwright.

* * *

THEODORE DREISER
Mt. Kisco

April. 21—'38

Dear Yvette:

I received the poem and the letters, and everything is okay in so far as liking and being friends is concerned. But still I cannot help noticing the cavalier attitude into which you drop the moment I relax my personal & private conception of what—considering my affairs & obligations—I can or cannot do. I seem to become a utensil of sorts. I can be harried by demands. An arrangement can be requested by you & made by me—and the arrival from someone from somewhere sets it aside. However I know that if the arrangement with me were of any real importance no casual arrival could interfere with it. The answer is, of course that the arrangement is of no real importance at any time. So utensil it is—and remains.

I wish it were otherwise.

T.D

* * *

THEODORE DREISER

May 26—'38

Yvette:

I couldn't get down and I wanted you to look over the play—so I let Harriet[1] take it for me. But I'll be down some day next week after Wednesday and call you up. Harriet had a job of her own for Sue, if Sue would take it. But if she doesnt its ok with me. I dont want her to annoy either you or Sue.

Affectionately
T.D

The fire[2] here has caused me a lot of trouble and work—dreadful. Write me as to the scenes you think should be used. Also any changes you think might strengthen it or make it less <u>defective</u>.

1. Harriet Bissel, Dreiser's secretary.
2. On May 13, the central house at Mt. Kisco caught fire, causing considerable damage.

* * *

French Line — à bord, le Normandie
July 14—1938

Dear Yvette:

Here is how it happened. Last Sunday wires from the League of American Writers and The American League for Peace & Democracy began to arrive asking me to attend—all costs paid—the International Convention for International Peace to be held in Paris July 21-22-23. All

I had to do was to go and say I represented them and that I believed in Peace. That seemed easy so, since I needed a lot of peace just then I decided to do it. So here I am in the gaudiest candy box ever set afloat. It reminds me of an old time French box, inlay and guilt (I mean gilt—but I think guilt is better for general use). Anyhow full length on state room bed I'm catching up on peace (and that's spelled right) as fast as possible. Went to bed at 10 last night & got up at 10^{30} a.m. today. At that rate I'll soon be in Paris. The reason I said nothing is—rushed to death. (Members of the two leagues with instructions) Cables for ticket. Passport. Only got it 1 hr. before sailing. Reports. Two trips to Mt. Kisco about 10 hours work packing & getting my work and New York plans rearranged. But I hope to be back in three weeks. Hope to leave for L.A. early in August. You may drive me at that. I was not sure that I was going until Wednesday morning at 9^{30} and the boat sailed at noon. But anyhow heres the news. If I hadnt gone W^{ed} I would have been too late. And if I hadn't gone I'd have called you up—and we'd have gone to that nice bar at 40th St. & Broadway. Give my love to Sue. And say something nice to Margaret on my behalf. I'll see you when I get back.

Love

T.D

My Paris address is
18 Place Vendome,
c/o E. C. Leawellyn.
he represents the Central
Hanover Bank

* * *

Adresse Telegraphique
Lutétiaotel-80-Paris

HOTEL LUTÉTIA
43, Boulevard Raspail
Square du Bon Marche
Paris
July 28—'38

Dear Yvette:

I'm leaving here today for Spain, Barcelona.[1] Expect to go from there to London. I would have written you oftener but with all I had to do here it was impossible. Calls, Calls, Calls. Interviews Every hour on the hour. Meetings ditto. And the worst of it is while I like Paris I dont really. Once it had romance—for me. Today—? The French themselves are now too humdrum. I think they are discouraged—Let down, a sort of where do we go from here attitude. No writers. No poets. No musicians—a few fading artists. Dishonest international politics. Idle American rich. But the food is good & cheap. Rooms also. One can live on a very little—if you have the little. Otherwise its hard to get. In spite of the probable suffering a complete social upheaval would be good here.

But I'm not happy away from America. I'm not so very happy there either. But oh, Lord—sitting in a chair in front of a café is nothing either. I'd rather be working in a small room in N.Y.

Sorry I had to go but it was best, I needed a change—even this. And the radicals think I have done some good. We should change things in America so they say. But economics wont solve all our woes. Look at those who have money? Are they any happier—or, happy. George Eastman (Kodak) shot himself. So did the author of Grape nuts—leaving $30,000000 to a tow headed female secretary. No use writing me. I'll be back before it gets here at that. But be kind to dumb brutes.

Love,

T.D

1. Dreiser had been invited by Spanish Loyalists to visit Barcelona and see firsthand the destruction brought on by the war.

* * *

THEODORE DREISER

Nov. 24—'38

Dear Yvette:

Here's the Santini check.[1] You change the account to my name.

It was so nice to be with you yesterday. It seems to me you are nearly the only person in all I have known who meets life in terms of personal effort & good will and without endless recriminations. If I can find anything for you in L A I'll let you know.

Love & all my good wishes.

T.D

Have them receipt the bill & mail to me.

1. Dreiser was storing his furniture with the Santini Brothers firm.

* * *

253a West Lorraine
Glendale, Calif

Dec. 8—'38

Dear Yvette:

Yes—sunshine and flowers. Both right outside. But 90 in the sun also! 87 to 90 ever since I arrived. No flies. No mosquitoes. No ice water in the place yet. Mountains 3000 feet high begin right back of the garage. Noisy, restless Hollywood is 5 miles away. Here live simple people—like me. Shiny green black black birds; mockers that sing all night long—damn them. But I've gotten my desk in order; clothes & papers properly disposed. And so to work. No telephone. But I wont escape I know that, just the same. I have so many things to do first that I'm calling first, one hundredth and working back.

Anyhow thanks for the storage receipt. And if you get them to put it in my name & send me the bill I'll be grateful.

No word from Gingrich.[1] Thats strange. Perhaps Clark had better address him direct. I'm sorry Greenburger proved useless. He got me my Thoreau contract[2] and placed several people with Harpers. Yet he may be phony at that.

Love

TD

1. Arnold Gingrich, editor of *Esquire.*

2. Dreiser edited *The Living Thoughts of Thoreau* (1939). Sanford L. Greenburger was an agent for the International Literary Bureau in New York.

* * *

263 West Lorraine ______________________________ Glendale California

Dec. 28—38

Yvette Dear:

I have just come back from the mortuary services for Calvin Bridges in Pasadena. He died here at All Angels Hospital Tuesday morning at four a.m. I saw him alive at the hospital a week ago Sunday night, again on Monday and again on Wednesday. The first time he was wandering and I could only look at him. On Monday he was clear, but weak. Yet able to talk a little. He looked so wonderful too—like a great

Greek. On Wednesday he could recognize me at moments and speak my name. At other times he thought he was dictating to his secretary & told me to get my pencil. I loved him so truly. He was so great a man.

Well now he is gone—cremated. Not a relative present. (Too poor to come) Just scientists from the Institute of Technology in Pasadena. It made me very sad. I am so now.

Enlargement of the heart: Six weeks ago he walked in to the hospital, asking for a room. He went to bed and never got out again. The papers here all recite his distinguished achievements today. He was 11 days short of being 50 years old!

I enjoyed your letter so much—its realistic presentation of yourself and your work. I feel all the time what a relief and a satisfaction it would be to you to remove to this strange exotic world with its so different vegetation, its encircling mountains, its flowers and gardens and practically (not always) perpetual sunshine. Just before I came they had had 263 days without rain. And when I arrived for 3 days it was 87, 89, 92 Fh. Then came a solid week of rain, night & day, almost 8 inches! Now its bright again—day after day. Cool at night—about 65 from 9 am to $4^{\underline{30}}$. No flies. No mosquitoes. Almost no insects. So strange. And cars, cars, cars over 50 square miles—the ocean on two sides, the mountains on the other. Over this little bungalow fly most of the aeroplanes from New York and the East—not all of them noiseless. It depends how high up they are as they enter.

I am reading & working on the Bulwark. I eat very little, retire fairly early, get up early—and to work, day after day. If I feel stiff I get up & walk about this simple area, looking at the high mountains & the swell richly gardened cottages. The pepper & acacia trees, the poinsettias and pampas grass never tire me. Nor to see oranges and lemons growing in yards here & there. If only I had the means now I would certainly give you vacation just to let you see. If I sell anything to the movies this winter I will.

One can live cheaply here. This little bungalow, or Coast unit, costs only 40 a month, charmingly furnished. Telephone gas & electricity are much cheaper than in N.Y. (I'll say). The great open front markets carry everything & they are every where. I would love to see your pleasure in being here. You would like it so much.

I read what Gingrich or his office said of Kens work. They are so wrong. If he will get together twelve or fourteen stories I will get him a publisher and write an introduction. But you read & ok them first.

You think I do not miss you, that out of sight, out of mind, but you are never out of mind—never. Give my regards to Sue & Clark. Tell both to write me.

Love

T.D

* * *

Chapter 8: Final Years: 1939–45

THEODORE DREISER

Jan 10—39

Yvette Dear:

What a nice letter—charming but so sad. I think your spirit enriches itself but by reason of sorrow. You are so truly kindly, tolerant, affectionate and brave. If I had ever had real sensual appeal for you I think we would have gotten along famously but somehow I steadily sensed that you looked elsewhere for that. And of course you cannot be blamed for that—no Harriet is not here. I felt keenly that certain things needed straightening out—or to be ended—both between her & myself & Helen and myself. Helen is here for the time being but for how long I cannot say. She cares for me after a fashion—still. I think for practical reasons principally—companionship, support, to be in on somethings. But a deep love—no. And that was what I most desired to truly know.

Meanwhile, now that I am here, I am working hard on The Bulwark and, as an aside, my philosophy. Also, I am trying to sell a movie—and I may. If I do—but I'd better not count my eggs until they're hatched. But I'd like to present you with a trip out here—a vacation just so you could see how much you do like it. And then I could see you once more.

Dont think I forget. I never do. And I'll write you.

Why don't you bolt & take a room. I cant see Margaret unloading herself on you. Its such a hard—really commercial—proceedure. She hates you & really does this I think to pay you out & to prove to herself that she can use you & anybody. If you'd stand your ground I think she'd change.

But[1] its so nice to hear from you. Your letter rings so true—this one. And I like that. It goes with your kindness—your loving nature and your generous spirit. Write me.

T.D

1. In the margin alongside this paragraph Dreiser wrote his return address: 253[a] W. Loraine, Glendale Calif.

* * *

The letter addressed c/o The Hotel Benson, Portland, Oregon & marked "hold for arrival" will get me.

D

HOTEL OAKLAND
14th & Harrison
Oakland, California

Feb 9—'39

Yvette:

I got your letter just as I was leaving Glendale to deliver a few talks. I'm here today and night—tomorrow San Francisco. The Town Hall. After that Portland. Seattle. Salt Lake, Ogden, Lewiston, Idaho & so back to Glendale.[1] I'll be back by the 24th.

Your letters! You have such a pleasing way of putting down your reflections—cheerful and the reverse. It is too bad that you haven't a place—and the time—in which to present your interpretations in fiction or essay form. You'd find an audience, I know. You're as experienced and tolerant and better yet sympathetic because of understanding. If I could make a sale out here that would bring my head above water I'd give you a chance—a peaceful living for a year at least. So often I wish you were at hand, just to talk and, better, bathe in your temperament, for you are rest giving. I feel better for being with you. Wish me some luck.

I wrote Clark at Washington, but he hasn't had time to reply. He writes the most refreshing letters—so varied and electric. I am positive that with a little more time to feel out <u>his</u> method he will come through. If only he will be wholly serious and strive for a structure that—arrow-like—will drive home his point. I cant see how he can fail. Really.

As for me I'm so busy, 10 hours a day. Some days I'm all but a nervous wreck. I have such a swell thing to work out. Marvellous.

I got here last night & have given six interviews, been photographed four times and now—1 P.M. am leaving in a special car to look at the Worlds Fair Setup. Back by $5^{\underline{30}}$ & then the [illegible word] at $8^{\underline{30}}$. Tomorrow S.F. But here's the bell. I hafta go.

Love, T.D

1. Dreiser refers here to a lecture tour in which he spoke about "Life," which most often meant the state of world politics in 1939.

* * *

April 14—'39

Yvette Dear:

The trouble right now, is money. I havent turned anything here, yet—or finished anything other than an article or so. I know how you feel—and why you take on these burdens (craving for intimacies: to belong). But if they give you that sense they are worth something. And now that Clark is started he ought to do something. Its a sure thing—if he's got in with Gingrich[1]—he wont do worse as time goes on, but better. As for me, unless I turn something out here within a month or so I'm coming back to see what I can rig up there. $200 sent to you wouldn't give you anything out here. You must have a car. A little court bungalow or small house will cost $35^{\underline{00}}$ (furnished). But there is gas, light, telephone. Meals. Entertainment. And I would have to supply that and would want to. I need some ready cash. Just the same there isn't a day breaks but that I expect word as to one or another of my things. Now it is The Financier; now The Titan—Carrie. The "Genius"—and one may come through.[2] If and when—(and you'll read of it quick enough in the papers)—I'll provide you your trip, depending on the amount that comes to me. As for Clarks book—if he has fifteen really good stories I'll be glad to read them (not instanter but as quick as I can) and if they please me as much as most have I'll send them to a publisher and offer to write an introduction. As to the result—well—I'll let you know. Or I'll send them to you with a letter & you take them to the publisher—the package—with my letter. Then you'll know who has them & how long they are out.

It's very lovely here now, bright & hot (cool at night) but for two days I've been in bed with something like ptomaine poisoning. Cramps, weakness, headache, fever. But what did it I don't know. Tonight—any minute now—comes the doctor. Then to bed again. Tomorrow I hope to be better. This is a good old family man. What else is news with you. Did you try to read Thoreau?

Love
T.D

This month Esquire has an article about me by Masters.[3]

1. Arnold Gingrich, editor of *Esquire.*

2. Dreiser was trying to sell the film rights to one of his novels. The following fall he sold *Sister Carrie* to RKO for $40,000.

3. Edgar Lee Masters, "Dreiser at Spoon River," *Esquire* 11(May 1939):66, 146, 151–52, 154, 156, 158.

* * *

Hollywood
June 26
39

Yvette Dear:

The trouble is that I have been caught up with too many things to make it possible for me to conduct a regular or even a partial correspondence with anyone. I have had to do too much work getting certain ideas I had in mind for the movies (money-bait) to permit of little outside of that. And, as you know, Im always rushed by people & unsolicited correspondence. To help out Ive let Helen do some, but more has gone to a young physicist who has been taking science dictation and researching for me. Decidedly I was glad to hear of that week you had—and now this vacation—and if I had come into any money at all, I certainly would be glad to help, but as it stands I haven't yet. There is constant talk, and there was one week when I thought a real sum of money would be paid down, but it wasnt. So here I am working along, as I did in NY but on less money. And fortunately it takes less to live here. Aside from food and clothing, about 75$^{\underline{00}}$ runs this little little place, light, rent, heat, laundry, telephone and what not. Food is more. Clothing not nearly so much.

Since writing you last I have moved from Glendale. Lovely as it was over there & reasonable the cost of running a car was much—much more—about \$20$^{\underline{00}}$ for gas alone. The distance to anywhere was much too great. Over here, where I am now it is much more central for what I do—the distance to movies—their editors and agents nothing—five or ten minutes.

And its nice—the heart of Hollywood, in one way—residential. And quiet. And simple. The only thing I dont like is the absence of real intellectuals—and the stir that goes with them. In New York, you take them for granted,—run into them everywhere & enjoy them. Here you have to hunt them out. Mostly the young & old also are interested in sex—pursuing each other with one end in view. Dress, conversation, entertainment—all work to the same end. Real thought—non commercial, non sexual is wanting. The houses & streets and store windows are stuff with eroticisms—clothing, pictures, gestures all. Its a scream. I think it must be the climate. Libertinism tops everything.

But how is Clark. You dont even mention him. I still have such hopes for him. He should read William Saroyan if he hasn't.

As for your trip. <u>If</u> I come into any money between now & the time you start, Ill be glad to make good on what I said. But unless I do—and until—I cant promise anything. I'm too slim pressed. And I need so much just now—not to be. But wait two weeks. If anything breaks I'll let you know. Otherwise—well, I just dont see how. I may have to come back to N.Y. this fall & drum up a little trade. Just the same I'd like to see you. My new address is 1426 North Hayworth. (That's near Sunset and Fairfax. The telephone is Granite–7498. Let me hear more.

Love
T.D

* * *

THEODORE DREISER

Oct. 27—[1939]

Dear Yvette:

Never rage at the heathen. They are all lost souls.

Thinking of your new radio skill. Why not take one of my short stories—or character sketches—<u>Twelve Men</u>—<u>Gallery of Women</u> and show how one would run, radioized. It might start something. Last night I was sore, sad—irritated by a long, hard day. There have been times when I have done better—I will admit.

T.D.

Have you a copy of Clarks radio start on *Sister Carrie*?[1]

1. Ken Clark's radio script of *Sister Carrie* was never produced.

* * *

THEODORE DREISER

Nov. 13—'39

Yvette Dear:

Enclosed is copy of my introduction to Clarks remarkable *What Place Is This*.[1] Due to a lot of things—work, earlier promises of reading of new books I didnt get to it until last week. But when I did I couldnt set it alone, and was stopping a lot of things every little while to read another story. When I did I wrote the first two papers of this forth with. But thinking a second mind might be good, I handed it over to another writer (male) right around the corner. The result was the last page—a quotative. But he liked it too,—*much*. Rates the stories (most) high. I mailed a copy of the introduction to Clark at 333 East 17th & hope he gets it. This one goes to you. I'd be willing to send the ms on with this introduction to a publisher but I feel it would be better if Clark were to take it and get an additional opinion or two, and just leave it at Harpers or—preferably—one of the new Publishers. How about Norton. Or maybe Farrar & Rinehart. Or, if he chooses he can take it to S&S. They refuse to do anything for me but they might push him.

Anyhow its a fine book and I'm glad—very.

How are you getting along? Are you married? Me, I drift along working and wondering about life. The mystery still grows on me. And how I hate this war. There is so much downright brutality in life these days—terrible. It gets on my nerves. I think our American government scheme should be reformed to give the worker (not the shirker) a decent break.

Let me know—shall I send the ms to you or Clark? Write.

Affectionately

T.D

By the way I have a bill from Santini Bros. for that desk. It reads balance due to Nov. 19th '39—3^{00}. But back in July I paid them 10^{00}. That makes

13[00] for 12 months & you said it was 50 cents a month. Have they raised the tonage rate on me? Why cant I pay it through you?

1. Ken Clark's collection of short stories, "What Place Is This," was never published.

* * *

Saturday, Feb. 17—1940
1426 N. Hayworth

Dear Yvette:

Sorry not to be able to write before but I've been in bed exactly 3 weeks and 2 days—today. Not able to write any one. Pluritis—or some such thing. Even now I'm not strong but with a backboard and a small bed table I can write this and some other notes before I rest up. And heres how things stand. Clarks book came back from Farrar & Rinehart. (Their letter enclosed) The same day or a day later it went off to Harcourt, Brace with the same comment. No word since. But someone will publish them I think. Im also enclosing that additional $15[00] I promised. I havent altered in my views but I cant write much now. "Sister Carrie" has been transferred from Universal which took an option on it last spring to R.K.O. which now announces that Ginger Rogers is to play Carrie and probably Orson Welles Hurstwood.[1] We'll see. Its supposed to be exhibited next fall—October or November. I cant write anything more right now save that I'm getting better & hope to be up and doing presently.

Affectionately,
T.D.

1. When the film was released in 1952, Jennifer Jones played Carrie, and Laurence Olivier played Hurstwood.

* * *

1426 N. Hayworth

4/27—'40

Dear Yvette:

I'm sorry about Clark, of course—the publishing delay and his money needs. I feel that the stories should be sent to Viking Press—but personally to the publisher whose name is Ginsburg. He is wealthy and an idealist and might fall for Clark—hook, line & all. I think his name is Harold. I'm perfectly willing to write the same letter I did to Harcourt Brace. But dont send the ms here—I'll send a duplicate of the letter when I get Ginsburgs full name.

As for money—why not have Clark apply for a Guggenheim Fellowship. Harcourt Brace would endorse his request. I would. I'm quite sure Ginsburg—once he reads the ms would. He should get $2,500 there. Have someone look up the details. The Fellowship has a secretariat in N.Y. See telephone book. The Fellowship hands out scores of awards every year to dubs who are never heard of afterwards. Usually it refuses really able people, but no harm in trying. More, later. I'm rushed & tired today.

As ever

T.D

Clark ought to try his hand at a play.

* * *

1426 N. Hayworth

Hollywood

May—1940

Yvette, Dear

Whenever you bestir yourself to write a nice letter you do it so gracefully. It is like someone who decides to sing a little song—a sweet, plaintive one. And not because he or she is miserable but because it is sweet to think or write or sing and so hear a plaintive melody. You do it often, allowing, as you do so, little dreams and wishes to enter, quite as separate entities, and ride with you and the song as on a boat on a quiet stream. It is so lovely—a true poetic mood. And always, when you do so, you move me as does a song—a brief plaintive melody. And without willing but because of your sweet plaintive mood I find myself going back, here and there, with you—in one of your small but always gay rooms—as accross some field, or by some stream where we have been together—Staten Island, Long Island, Princess Bay—the moods & roads along the Hudson, some camp where you were—the log cabin at Mt Kisco—and you gayly naked in the rocky hidden Pool below it.

You must not think I forget, Yvette. I never do. Nor your brave, gay, hopeful, generous and forgiving spirit. Not I. You have lived many a lovely poem without ever noting that you were doing so. And in doing so have permitted others to share them. Me, for one. And I am not ungrateful. I wish truly that I might do some charming thing for you—some thing that would be in your mood and in mine. By the middle of July I hope to know that a second venture of mine here has turned the sale corner. If so I'll contribute to your vacation idea and gladly.

With love
T.D

* * *

Sept. 19—'40

Dear Yvette:

Here's the permit. And I certainly hope you had an interesting trip back East. How did you like San Francisco? And Salt Lake. It made me sad to see you suffer so just before you left and I was so glad you staid all night. That was something for me as well as for you. The little song you taught me runs in my head but I wish you would have some one copy out the music so I may hear it played & sung.

It's as fair and warm here as ever. No change. Every time I pass Kingsley Drive I think of your little place. My book is done—and gone.[1] And I have word that it is much liked. Writing it drove me nearly nuts.

Love
T.D.

Regards to Clark when you write him.

1. Dreiser is referring to *America Is Worth Saving,* which was published on January 20, 1941.

* * *

[Oct. 25, 1940]

Dear Yvette: Glad to hear from you & to know that you are all right. The only reason I didn't answer your letter is that I felt that the first part of it seemed a little stagey—not actually genuine. So I waited for a better type of letter. As for your visit to Mt. Kisco, I'm sorry I was mistaken as to what was in the little house. I could swear I left a rather nicely designed simple bed, a chair, some odds and ends in the closets, etc. I would much rather you had written me before going to Mrs. Stern to ask her about anything, since she is not responsible for what is or is not in the little cabin and should not have been bothered. She is entitled to be short or sharp-tongued if she chooses so to be. And I would rather hear from her direct as to what she desires—rather than through you. As for saying you were taking the place by the year, it would have been better to say I was letting you use it since that is the truth. And I will be glad to let you use it if it is a pleasure to you & of course, causes me no trouble. As for guaranteeing you the use of it for longer than next summer—if so long—I cannot do that since I desire to sell the rest of the place, and if I get an offer and the buyer would not tolerate a tenant why, I'd have to ask you to vacate—all though I try of course to arrange for you to keep it through the fall. I refused to rent the log cabin to Mr. Levy except from May to May. And the reason I did that was that buying offers come in the spring—not the fall. And, if I had an offer I would want him to vacate, that is if the buyer wanted him to vacate. So I can only say that if I get no buyer you can stay. As for Mrs. Stern, the worst of her action is that I did not want her to store anything in that cabin. She had no right so to do. But your inquiry gave her the opourtunity & she seized it. Now I cannot ask her to take those things out. In future, if you go up there keep away from her & Mr. Levy. At least do not discuss me—where I am, what I am doing, how I am, etc.

As for the piano desk I find I cannot use the big table in the big house out here. So plan to ship piano desk here. Am sorry as to that, but I haven't anything to take its place.

Yes, I received Clarks song book & mean to write him. Am, however, terribly pressed with work.

T.D.

P.S. Next to the cabin you wish to use is a private store-room. Please, if you go up there, let no one disturb the locks on it. I do not want it entered by anyone.

* * *

<u>1426 N. Hayworth Ave.</u>

Nov. 20—1940

Dear Yvette:

There is no reason why you shouldn't use the cabin as I suggested. All my furniture and belongings in Mt. Kisco and New York will shortly be transferred here. And my contact with the new owners of the house will be ended. I still own 23-acres of the ground and the right to use the road in and out. The old spring below the big house—west of the pool is on my property, so you would be entitled to take water from there—a long walk. I have to reserve the right to sell the place at anytime since I may need to. Now that I have stated my complaints I have no other feeling in the matter and you are certainly welcome to use it. For the next two weeks or so Miss Light[1] will be around there occasionally checking things out. Perhaps during that time you had better not be there. Helen is easily irritated by you—any word of your doings. After that there can be no trouble I am sure.

I am shipping the piano desk out here very shortly.

Regards

T.D

1. Evelyn Light, Dreiser's secretary.

* * *

Mch. 19—'41

Yvette, Sweet

I had to rush off as you know to Newark and then to Philadelphia and then to Washington and then to San Francisco (on a special mission to see J. B. McNamara before he died, only he died just as I got there). But I have been thinking how sweet it was of you to respond to a midnight call and come to me so generously. And I loved being with you. And if only I could endure New York as I once did you would see more of me. Or if ever you managed to move out here.

For there is, for me, something perpetually enticing about your mind as well as your body—a natural and poetic refinement which makes many of your letters dreamily phrased compositions on the contrast and the varying values of life. Naturally you percieve so much—lifes meannesses as well as its beauties. But you do not quarrel with it as I do. You are so tolerant and kindly and forgiving! Mayhap you feel you have things in yourself to forgive, but no matter. I doubt if a father confessor could demand much more than a few "Hail Marys"—six or seven at the most before you could go in peace. As for myself I love your laughter, your desire for love—as you once said "to belong to some one"—your kindly, smiling, amused and amusing accounts of the peccadilloes and little sins of others. But, dearest, belong to whom you choose, you will always belong to me. You cross me at times, as you know, but I get over it. And in due time return in thought as well as in affection and love to the sweet things that make you what you are—my Yvette.

Write me sweet and I will write you. And one of these days we will be meeting and loving as we did—and much more than you think.

With the sweetest memory of your coming and of us together—

T.D.

1015 N. Kings Road,
Hollywood
A long letter from Clark. I fancy you met and you told him about us.

Baddie

* * *

April 9—'41

Yvette Dear:

I'm a long time answering your letter, but I was glad to get it. And when your in the mood, I wish you'd write me again. I'm about as busy as anyone could be, day after day, and that heads off much correspondence of a social sort, but ours is different. And will be, I hope, for always.

I had to smile when you referred to yourself as older and different—more sober, less hopeful. You are a little more sober, that is true, but one thing you may not know and that is that it adds enormously to your charm. Ten years ago you were so extremely youthful and impulsive—a little wild socially and much less meditative. Now you have still the sweetness of a girl—much more than you had then—plus a truly poetic dubiousness concerning all things, which appeals to me. It is so truly mental and yet shaded with a rich emotion. You seem sweeter and more lovable than you were even in your playful, restless amorous youth. So——. I do not doubt that you are in contact with a male or two or three who tell you so. As for me I wish you were out here where I could see you. Meantime I wish you happy hours all the time.

Love—T.D

All my furniture, books, everything is out here now—stored or placed in various parts of a house I've rented and it saves me not a little in storage rent. The rosewood piano desk is here in my writing room & I'm writing on it. It becomes the room and the room it.

That 15 acres next to the cabin to which you have the key has been sold to a man by the name of Mann, and he & his wife are building a house there. It is the land that slopes down to the little swimming hole in the thicket. Too bad.[1]

1. With this letter is a typed copy of TD's thoughts on Sherwood Anderson that was read at Anderson's funeral.

* * *

June 18—1941

Dear Yvette:

Herewith the certified check for $50[00]. I have deposited your June 16th check for $25[00] for collection and am holding the Sept. check as you suggest. I have to warn you that financially things are looking decidedly black not only for me but you and everyone. These endless billions being shipped and given to Britain are going to be paid for by Americans—principally by Americans earning as little as $26[00] a week and from there on up. Out here land taxes, furniture taxes, food taxes are mounting daily and with this lunatic in the White House will continue so to do. My 1941 tax bill is likely to take all but a base living from me and so I cannot promise that I can do more. As I see it, it is time that every American definitely & violently protested in every way. My book *America Is Worth Saving*, has been completely suppressed—all book stores—(under threats from some where)—refusing to handle it. S & S have as completely suppressed my volumes as though I had no following at all—refusing to supply orders, even those from me.

I wish you pleasure of the cabin. If you can paint it, it certainly will aid in preserving it. . . . Regards to Clark. I know he is around.

T.D.

* * *

Wed. April 29, 42

Yvette Dear:

I'm sorry I didnt write you, but its not for want of thinking of you. I think of you so very often—our various and varied contacts like that last one, or the one out here. I'm working on The Bulwark and it isn't always easy going. No novel is. But I feel I'll get it done in good form. By the way be sure and see *My Gal Sal*—the movie about my brother Paul[1] which is going to be shown their shortly. Its in technicolor and beautifully done. I wrote the script, and by the way I'm in it for about 10 or 15 seconds as a little boy—only theyve taken a little slap at me by showing me crying about something. But the thing is clever—terribly. Its amusing, gay, had delightful songs including My Gal Sal, and On the Banks of the Wabash, and its done in technicolor. Rita Hayworth & Victor Mature are the stars—Mature playing Paul, and while they don't follow my text they borrow enough of it to give the right note: the period & the color of the period—the so called Gay Nineties. You'll love it I'm sure. Its too gay and comic and swift in action for you not to.

How's everybody. You. Sue. Clark. Your mother & Clarks boy. I'm wondering if you'd like to use the upper cabin this summer again. If so your welcome. Mr. Levi is staying in his log cabin until May 31 and maybe longer. If you go, tell me how things look up there.

Right now I'm not as well as I ought to be—intestinal flu which I had and from which I'm recovering. I found the cure for it but I lost weight and feel weak. I wish I might see you occasionally but I don't like N.Y. anymore and while this place is growing it doesn't attract all of the people I know, and so I have to make new friends here & there as best I can. And then, of course, the war depresses me not a little but it has to be borne.

I hope you're strong and well & keep your old spirit. You stand up better than most. I know that. If I had the money I'd invite you out here but things are too tough for words and the saving days have certainly come.

Love, of course. And thanks for the letters.

D.

What was that comment of yours on life that I liked so much.

1. Paul Dresser, the songwriter.

* * *

Monday, June 1—42

Yvette Dear:

I haven't answered your letter because, because—there are so many letters. I just dont even try to keep up. I did write you though to ask if you cared to use the upper frame cabin next to the resident who calls his place "floatin on the Crotin"! But no answer in so far as I can recall. The Log Cabin is to be vacant this summer and my sense of family ties calls me to offer it to Gertie[1]—now newly married and her husband Mr. Dorn. If they dont want it I'll let you know. I'm keeping the gas connected for the time being.

Love! Love! Love! Yes, I know. It is an intense thing but it involves so many jealousies and heartaches and obligations and duties that unless one is wholly ablaze like a frame house—and even so—one cannot endure for long. The devouring passion. The passion that can transform into hate in the twinkling of an eye. . . . . .

Yours, I will admit, has been of a more patient, poetic and philosophic—even courteous turn, but then you have never been wholly faithful either. And why should you be. You're probably like the rest of us—never had a wholly faithful lover. Sometimes I doubt if that animal exists or ever has. But when one is truly in love one is inclined to be a firm believer—unfaithful or faithful as the spouse may be.

Well, dear, so much for this morning sermon. I'm not feeling so hot and still I write. I like so much to see you & often enough I wish you lived or worked out here. Then with my car & you to drive it I could find you fast enough. As it is——well—you'd better write me about the Cabin.

Have you seen My Gal Sal? Everyone seems to like it even though my text was not a little altered. You'd better take a look at it.

And as for your letter it is sweet—very. But then you are a born poet when it comes to letters. You write exquisitely when you are emotionally moved. Better write a book or story that consists of letters only. Yours would succeed I feel sure.

Meanwhile write me and know that I truly wish you were here.

D

1015 N. Kings Rd.

1. Dreiser's niece, the daughter of his sister Emma.

* * *

Monday
June 8—[1942]

Yvette Dear:

It isn't that I dont read your letters at the time they arrive but I read so many. And many that I read—purely practical demands—

require an immediate answer. Others—as you know can be thought over—ones like coming out here for three months. If it weren't for H— the immediate defensive jealously that sets in—I'd say yes. H____ is jealous of anybody who could command my interest. And though nothing comes of it save a sombre, pervasive gloom, still that in itself is enough to darken a summer. Besides for you there is the long trip—roundtrip fare not less than $\$130^{\underline{00}}$ or more—with sleeper. And once here there is the matter of time I could give you. I am writing a novel—so many hours a day. Actually there is a free unused perfectly furnished room here which you could occupy—but gloom, suspicion, unexpressed anger. Certainly I could say to you come & occupy it—but unless you dine here (places to eat are rather distant in this area) and could help achieve an agreeable spirit? Otherwise I would truly have to command silence or compel her to leave.

If she were not here and did not do really competent secretarial work, as well as provide excellent suggestions on occasion I would have nothing to say. But she is and does. And if you have a room outside, well—work & all that takes time as you know—play time. I have a car which I cannot drive & once you were here, would prefer to go places & stay all night or a day or two. But——here is the novel, and all else that I have to contend with. So.

Of course, if you were in her place, you would be equally jealous or—if not entertained, you would play about with others and make me angry. And so the whole thing would end suddenly as such things do, for the creator who created sex arranged for all that—(discord)—perfectly. So, one finally resigns oneself or walks out & lives elsewhere, as I have and, no doubt, as you have. So, hanged if I can see how it is to be done peacefully & with pleasure for both. . . . If you see a way let me know. This sex and equity matter has baffled me all my life & will continue so to do, I am sure, unless once more I become a lone bachelor & arrange my hours & days to suit myself. Even so there is work—and lots of it. Let me know if you see how the problem is to be solved.

By the way, as to eating in that upper cabin—if you had a grain of sense you would collect some of those lesser sized stones around there, get some sand & plaster & build yourself an outside oven and cook your food outside. There is a sample down by the big pool & today every country place has one. I can take two good sized stones, place them side by side ten to twelve inches apart, secure a peice of heavy tin or iron for a cover, gather chips—not large pieces of wood, with which to feed a fire under neath & fry a steak, a fish or a chicken, and boil coffee or steep tea & there you are. Ham & Eggs & bacon & eggs & coffee on such a small contraption are as easily made as mud pies. As for bread, butter, cake, Ice cream, fruit, jelly——whats the matter with the grocery store?

Sues letter is delightful. What a quick, interesting, all knowing mind.

D

I wish I could have a month alone with you.

* * *

Oct. 16—'42

Yvette Dear

I am sorry to be so neglectful, but its not because I don't care for you—really because of an endless pile of work, correspondence (business letters) my novel etc. I'm always pleased to hear from you & I wonder sometimes,—considering the wages they pay—that you dont move out here & get in on war work. $\$30^{\underline{00}}$ to $50^{\underline{00}}$ a week appears to be average for so many. You cant get a girl to clean house for less than five a day. Endless stores are closing for want of female help—although want of male help plays a part in it too. I think of you often & wish I might see you but the distance and the fact that this climate suits me better makes the chance of doing it small. I had a rough time of it in Canada as you saw, but I didn't go there of my own accord.[1] Rather I was urged over & over to do—or rather come before I finally decided to do it. I was supposed to have so many friends there and no doubt I have but the pro-British authorities drove them all to cover. So I departed before they attacked me. Also in Chicago I caught a cold & still some of it left—not so very much.

But as to all else I'm ok and I wish you were for I always think of your saying once that your great need or desire was to belong to someone, to be able to feel as though you did. And that is so touching as well as so true of so many people—even at times of the strong and the seeming independent. For in so far as life goes we're all so small & weak and really need love & some care—each and every one. So— But you know the rest. I wish I might provide it for every living soul in distress.

As for you—if you were here, we'd manage to be together some—just as we were in N.Y.—17th St for one place.

D

1. Dreiser was invited to speak at the Toronto Town Forum, but his prespeech remarks, which were strongly pro-German and anti-British, led to the cancellation of the speech. Sentiment ran so strongly against him that he decided to flee Canada.

* * *

Mch 7—'43

Yvette Dear:

I'm sorry to be so slow about writing you. I enjoy your letters as you know and always feel guilty when I see one of your envelopes but the truth is as you know that I receive so much mail of all kinds—books, pamphlets, autograph requests, mail from organizations that want me to do this or that. Every so often I have requests from publications for articles on social and economic topics that I really should write about and occasionally do. Also ideas that I occasionally get for movies. And then of course my novel—chapter 35 of which I have just finished. Besides a person cannot stick at a desk all of the time. I like to have people drop in occasionally. Also I like to look up old New York friends—a lot of whom are out here now. And so—well I neglect a number of people whom I shouldnt—you for instance. Only in your case I pay up by worrying about it. Hence this explanation today. Yet I know if you were out here I'd find time to drop in on you—as you know. Also to spend the night. But at 3500 miles even mental contacts are not so easy and so.

Judging by your letters you are not really very happy—yet probably not any more unhappy than I am. The mystery and misery and incidentally the futility of life weighs on me not a little. I'm always wishing to feel better physically and mentally about it than, as a rule, I do. This war has weighed on me heavily. And so too the miseries of a lot of people whom I know and who have been badly shaken by it. Its only once in a long time that I spend a day and a night as comfortably mentally & in every other way as the one I did in New York with you. So you see what being so far away means. But I think of you just the same whether I see you or write. Temperamentally and in other ways you seem somehow a part of me. And will remain so—see or no see.

Incidentally that is a cute reminder card you sent me—quite the best for that purpose I have ever seen. If I had time to look up such things I'd have them on hand.

And so here's love and all good wishes. Let me hear how things are with you & Sue.

D.

* * *

Oct 11—'43

Dear Yvette:

Enclosed is my permission for you to occupy the log cabin on the estate anytime you manage to get up there. Mean while I want to say how nice it is of you (liberal) to offer me an introduction to your girl friend! And I'd like to meet her, and will—if she writes me? Meanwhile I want to tell you I'm pretty much down physically & mentally just now,—arthritis and a nervous depression that continues to accompany it, so that, in the main, I am actually confined to the house and occasionally to my bed even though betimes Im struggling to make progress with my novel. Its hard, very, but I do the best I can. Write me about the estate if you go up there.

T.D

Incidentally write me anyhow.

* * *

Monday, April 3 [1944]

Yvette Dear:

Yes its true that I was offered the American Arts and letters group award and accepted it.[1] I am supposed to be there May 14—not that I'm anxious to go for that but because apart from you I have several things that I must attend to—a conference with my publishers, the property at Mt. Kisco, my lawyer, etc. But most truly I would love to see you and will. Only one thing that interferes some what. H. is coming along. She has the property details in mind and since I may be able to sell it, she and the lawyer will have to work it out together. Besides there are my relatives—some six all told whom I'll have to see and I can't stay away too long from the job I have here. But I would like to see as much of you as possible. I've been intending to write of course,—but writing isn't like seeing. And since it's the seeing of you that I really crave, the writing always gets hard and so instead of that I prefer thinking of all the various things we did together—the little room back of the Ansonia, your room in the Ansonia, my visits to you when you were living with your mother in 91st St and so on. Different incidents and places stay in my mind—and revive themselves ever so often and will continue to do so—my last visit to N.Y. and your room in the Village. They make an exciting chain of things—like your room in East 17th St and mine in West 11th. Also in the George Washington. Now that I'm going to be able to see you again some how all these things come back, and I only hope I can arrange my time so that we can be together for a day or two or more. Only among other things, I have to go to Philadelphia and Baltimore, but I'll do the best I can. Mean while love and best wishes.

TD

1. The American Academy of Arts and Letters offered Dreiser its Award of Merit medal, together with a prize of $1,000.

* * *

CONGRESS HOTEL
Entrance to Hospitality

June-15—'44

Yvette Dearest:

I'm up here with Helen. Her mother is very ill. I'm leaving for LA. Saturday. You'll never know how sorry I was not to be able to get down there since I wished so much to be with you. I had appointments in Philadelphia & Baltimore and Westchester all of which I had to break—But—you looked so sweet and I was so anxious to have more of you. If you move out here I'd see you every other day sure. We've been attached so long! And your love is so real & so consoling. I wish now deeply that you weren't going to get married yet I know you cant waste more of your life on me.[1] So I can only wish that you were to be near me always.

Dearie that half hour was so darling. Your kisses so real. And our union. Ill not forget.

All my love to you, sweet. If I return to N.Y. soon will I get to see you? Your such a precious portion of my hurried & troubled life. Write me.

D.

1015 N. Kings Rd.

1. Dreiser is referring to Yvette's impending marriage to Ken Clark.

* * *

1015 North Kings Road

July 4—[1944]

Yvette Dearest:

That was such a comforting letter you wrote me for I was unhappy about the short visit I was able to pay. I had so many things to do—publisher problems, literary agents, contacts arranged for me by the Artists and writers guild that brought me to N.Y. In addition the sickness and death of my sister Mame who died five days after I arrived and I had to take charge of all that. Then there were the other members of our family, Sylvia, Ed—my sister Emmas 2 children Gertie & George, also Eds daughter Vera—quite a group calling on me for contacts—and their friends, critics who wanted to interview me and did. I never spent four more strenuous weeks. Incidentally there was the property at Mt. Kisco I had to look after—show it to three prospective buyers! And then you! And I wanted to see you so much—stay all night with you if I could. And yet only one contact! But how sweet that was! What was rushing me that day was the planned call of two publishers—or their representatives—Doubleday, Doran and Scribners. Yet—thank heaven—I reached you & you me in the old intense way. Those thrilling kisses. Your willing and intense union with me. My mind was full of your new charm that plainly had come through more world experience—your mental charm and then your developed physical charm. You never looked sweeter!—a gracious, meditative and more affectionate type of beauty. How I wished you lived near me now. It would be so helpful to be able to go to you and relax in your real affection—to be able to strengthen myself in the love that you have for me,—particularly now when I need it most. Depend on it—if I make another strike in the movies I'll give you enough to stay here for a year or two in order that you may connect in such a way as to be able to stay here for keeps—or until it bores you.

Honey I miss you. I wish we were in that room again—or I could go today—the 4th of July, wherever you are and stay all the day and night with you—play & talk. Do you know that with the exception of the time that Marguerite was trying to persuade you to bring an action against me I never spent a single unhappy hour with you. Always when we were together the room or the atmosphere in which we moved was so soothing. I relaxed and was happy and so it would be here.

Well, honey, have I said enough. Its so trying to be so far away and yet so helpful for a few moments to be able to write & tell you that, for I have been wishing so keenly since last we were together that I could be with you again.

Love & Kisses
T.D

* * *

July 15—[1944]

Yvette Dear:

Why not a letter? I feel so let down since I got back. Have you left N.Y. I think so much of our one brief contact and wish there were more! Did I tell you while I was there that my sister Mame died? She had developed a cancer of the bladder and had to be operated on which reduced her strength to nothing. All of the family did what they could and naturally her sickness and death & burial interfered with my other affairs greatly. One thing that helped a little was her telling me the day before she died that she was resigned to go—that she had lived long enough! And she was truly an interesting & resourceful person.

Well dear write me if you can manage the time. I was so pleased & cheered by that one hour.

D
with love

* * *

Aug 14—'44

Yvette Dear:

I love your—or is it my birthday card.

How sweet of you to think of me. But then I've been thinking of you—the fascinating type of woman you've grown to be. So wise! Kindly, understanding and forgiving. Enveloped really in an aura of love and tenderness for everything I think. And conveying it so effectually. Truly if just now or anytime I could walk to where you are, or invite you to some quiet place in order to sense that something different about you that you have always truly had: I see it now so clearly—love of life and kindness. Well, now I can only write you and think of you. And wish that I might hold you close in true affection. You are truly so sweet. And the golden hours you have made for me.

Well Babe—its hot here today. Stifling and I am working in my writing room. But I wish I were not. Rather (so much) with you. I'm going to send you a little present—not in this letter but the next one.

Love & kisses

D

The last words of Mame to me just before she died were "Not all the people of the [world] in combination and thought can make a single blade of grass. Yet God can carpet the fields!"

* * *

Aug 30 [1944]

Yvette Dearest:

Such a sweet, loving letter and so like you. I've reread it three times because somehow it brings you physically close to me—as though you were really here. And although I write so little, so often I recall the different times or occasions when we have been together—like the time you had the dark little basement room somewhere up on the west side—maybe West 87th or 88th St and how one day after walking & talking a little way in Central Park we went up there together and spent an hour or so loving and kissing. You were always so enticingly youthful and vigorous and so sensually provoking on that score alone. I remember Jerome Blum[1] saying to me once after he had seen you skipping along beside me some where—(I think it was in 57th Street) that I would give anything if he could have a girl like that—young and playful.

And he didn't know who you were and never found out from me. If he had he would have painted you I'm sure.

Dear—as to the Xmas gift I want a scarf for around my neck but not a woolen one unless it is very soft wool. Actually I'd much rather you pick out a bright peice of flowered cotton cloth—about a yard and one half long and a half or 3/4ths of a yard wide so that it could be folded lengthwise and so make a scarf that would go twice around my neck and leave enough length over so that I could tuck the ends under my coat. A scarf like that is very useful here in the winter months. The principle thing with me is brightness of color—mixed colors—red brown blue green—anything you wish. And it doesn't need to be of silk at all. A soft cotton will please me just as much. I have a silk one that I rarely use before. I have a cotton length that I like better. But you use your own judgement.

Sweet I'm busy this a.m. & will write you later. But how I do wish you were here. How I'd hold you in my lap and kiss and pet you and tell how delightful it was to be with you. If I come to N.Y. anytime again I'll arrange my time to have at least a week with you—or all the hours you can spare. I think your so human, kind tolerant and wise as well as esthetic, artistic and philosophic—just the type of girl that any wise life-loving man would care for.

Here's thinking of you Babe. And use this money order to buy yourself a nice gift.—Love and kisses,

D

1. Jerome Blum, the painter.

* * *

Sept. 20—44

Yvette Dear:

Marguerite[1] didnt come here to work on the book alone. I have a series of articles and a book of philosophy to clear up if I can. Helen has in the past year found it more than she can keep up with and when I was in N.Y. I found Marguerite so efficient and energetic that when I made the remark that I wished I had someone out here who was as efficient, she instantly volunteered to undertake the work for the winter at least and at a very low wage—object not matrimony but to see Los

Angeles & the west coast. Also to put her son Hilary, who lives here with her, in an engineering school in which same he now is. Not that M. wouldnt have an affair with me or any of a long list of others if she were so moved but she seems truly to be interested in working on the book and the philosophy as well. Also in escaping another New York winter. Whether she said I could not finish the book without her or not cuts no ice with me. I would not like to mention it even, since I sincerely doubt if she said it, and besides given time enough, I think I can finish it.

The nicest part of your letter is your explanation of your attitude toward me which is so like you. Long ago though as you know you and I have forgiven each other a number of things, and I still feel for you just as I have written you. There has always been something so very relaxing and comforting in every contact I have ever had with you and there will continue to be. I can't dismiss your genuine sweetness of heart, your loving and forgiving attitude toward all types and conditions—your pity for the inadequate and the defeated. Away or with you I feel all this and will continue so to do and its so comforting to read this latest proof. Truly I wish I might see you sweet—walk in and hold you in lap and my arms. I sincerely wish you were out here but I dont imagine you would like M____s job. It is very difficult—reading, rearranging, editing & retyping—a dreary business. As it is M____ only plans to stay until May if she can possibly accomplish enough to satisfy me by then. Her salary is very small because she has an adequate income of her own. Also because she looks on this as an exploratory west coast trip.

D—with love

1. Marguerite Tjader Harris was working with Dreiser on *The Bulwark.*

* * *

Nov. 1—'44

Yvette Dear:

What I had in mind for you to do was a fifteen or eighteen hundred word sketch of your childhood—the formative years between five and eleven or twelve—the period in which all of us register our first impressions of this strange new world into which we came through no willing of our own. For then, for the first time we register totally strange figures moving about us—mother and father (maybe), brothers and sisters, strangers, the family doctor, cats and dogs to say nothing of birds and chickens, horses, cows, sheep, pigs, and those still stranger things—the sun, moon, stars, storms of wind or rain, or both—thunder, lightning, beautiful trees and flowers, the strange and unexplained moving traffic of life which as we live and grow and for some unknown reason take for granted like houses, churches, schools, stores, dealers in this and that, police, the art of cooking, hunger and thirst—in sum a whole world of things into which the use and enjoyment and—or—difficulties of which, by degrees, we fit ourselves—learn how to do, use or avoid etc etc etc—until, by degrees, we come to be what we are—craftsmen or doers of this or that, but still never knowing (any of us) how or why it all comes about.

The reason I wrote you about it was that one day it suddenly occured to me what an interesting set of short articles,—a series of say six, all told, such a group would make:—six or seven different people from as many different lands or cities or states or small town homes or farms such a group would make,—the differing deductions and viewpoints the different writers of the same would present. And recalling your youth, the interesting things you told me I decided to see if I couldnt stir up six or seven different individuals to each do one. And so I sat down and wrote to you because I know yours would be interesting and I might use yours as an illustration of what I meant—show in one or two instances to others.

Anyhow, Sweet, above is the idea. The general title for the entire six or seven might be—My Native Heath or My Natal Environment. May be you could think of a better title. My idea is that I should get at least $\$200^{\underline{00}}$ per article—possibly $125^{\underline{00}}$. Each writer should or at least is free to sign his or her own name. If any do not wish to—(one has already refused) then each can use a pseudonaym and I will appear merely as the originator of the idea—and—or—editor. What do you think, honey. Let me know. Personally I'm not feeling so well—(a bad cold is annoying me.) Just now I'm all alone & how I wish you were here to look after me a little—to be close to me through the night & day. You have so much understanding and so much poetry of mind. I feel it always when I am near you. Only you are not near me. Love & all good things to you.

D

* * *

Jan 17—'45

Yvette Dear: Where are you? I see where your beloved Budapest is being pounded to bits by the Russians in order to get rid of the Germans! I miss hearing from you and often I feel that you might do better out here than there in N.Y. For one thing I believe that you & I might do an occasional film together which would sell. You have such a romantic and at the same time realistic touch which I feel might be productive of an original and attractive film, and if you were here we could work on it together. Anyhow I keep thinking how profitable such industry might prove. Also whether you are doing any writing on your own. That sketch you sent me is so good and if and when the set of six is sold you will get your 6th of the total set-price. Meantime I'm thinking of you. If by any chance I get to N.Y. by May and it now looks as though I might could we by any chance spend a few days together in or out of N.Y. Let me know. And heres my love and best wishes always.

T.D

* * *

Feb. 20—45

Yvette Dear:

I am so sorry about your mishap. Its just too bad for you certainly deserve an easy period in your life—one devoid of the stress and strain that you have endured through your youth and up to now. I wish very, very much that I were in a position to relieve the financial burden of all this even though I am not the one who should look after you. But for the entire year past I have been straining over The Bulwark and doing little else to bring in the necessary subsistence here. It is true that by August or September I'm likely to have it done—in which case my financial circumstances are likely to change but right now I am carrying all that I can. Just the same—if curiously—I wish I were the one whose infant were on the way. I'd like to see what we'd make of it, how much true pleasure and comfort we would be able to see or experience in having it together! Lord! Lord! this world! and what wishes & sorrows it presents us with.

Just now I have a disease of my own—a painful rash of sorts that itches & burns and compels me to apply a salve externally which is presumed to drive it away but does not. Only yesterday I was told that there is an epidemic of the same which in many cases results in external ulcers! Yet at least I have none of those. When I get a little better I'll see if I cannot write you something more cheerful for I am hoping to sell that series "I remember, I remember" in which case your contribution should bring you $60[00] or $70[00]. I'm sending them on to Gingrich of Esquire today.

Love and my sympathy and all my good wishes! You know how unchangingly I feel about you & always will. Love

T D-

* * *

1015 N. Kings Road

Los Angeles
April 6— 45

For one thing I've been working hard on my novel—The Bulwark which I expect or rather will finish in the next 3 weeks. Its only 300,000 words long! Next within the last two weeks I had to under go an operation principally related to my genito-urinary organs.[1] It was very painful and absorbed 3 days of my time. I'm better and am hoping I will not have any more trouble. This letter is the first letter I have written since my surgical trouble began and I'm hoping it will rub out my seemingly criminal silence. I wanted to write and have thought of you plenty, wishing that I might come east for a while. Then I would be with you. You always write such kind, forgiving letters and I love you as much as ever as you know.

Out here after a long stretch of damp and chill it has turned hot and I fancy will stay so for a time. 96 degrees Fh. in June or July is no trick for the weather man to pull here. I've experienced 88[Fh] in June here.

Aren't you sorry for your seemingly attractive town of Budapest? I am. I wish I could see you.

Love and kisses,
T D

I've thought much concerning your operation and have been wondering how you were getting on.

1. Dreiser suffered from prostatitis, and he was treated for it with, among other things, a metal rod inserted into his urinary tract.

* * *

May 5—[1945]

Yvette, Dear

Just thinking of you and wishing I might see you. Truly hope you are ok. Have just finished my new novel The Bulwark.[1] It will go to the publishers in a day or two. Wish you were here to read it and give me your opinion. Love & all good wishes—best wishes.

T.D

1. *The Bulwark* was published posthumously on March 21, 1946.

* * *

June 16—'45

Yvette Dear,

Before you begin scolding me please take into consideration the fact that I have been working on two books this long time—the Bulwark and the Stoic and except for some minor corrections have finished The Bulwark (its in the hands of Doubleday Doran—accepted and to be published this fall). As for The Stoic its within two chapters of its end and it also goes to Doubleday-Doran.[1] The Bulwark is a novel all on its own—no connection with any other, while The Stoic is really volume III of my Trilogy of Desire of which my The Financier published long ago was volume I and The Titan volume II. So now The Stoic makes volume III of this trilogy. All three volume are to be boxed in one box and sold as a set. I'll see that you get a set when it comes out. Meantime for nearly the whole of this last year or since I saw you I've been working I cannot tell you how hard—writing and dictating & correcting and incidentally feeling anything but strong and for the most part non-creative. I cannot tell you how often I have wished you were out here and working for me—only alas, practical and some emotional difficulties or objections stand or have stood and still do in the way, not only that but physical ills of one type and another at one time and another have interrupted and delayed me. In fact it is only now or in the past six weeks that I have begun to feel as though things were easing up a bit. Even so I see no immediate opourtunity for a vacation—none at least until the Stoic is done and gone and my final corrections that the Bulwark needs are made and done with. Then if I get a sufficient advance I may show up in N.Y. and ring your door bell. Oh that that may be. I'd like to loaf and play with you for a few weeks anyhow. Meantime—until then—

So this is why I want you to get over being mad at me—to see or hear my story (the above). Physically today I feel down—I can't say why—actually as though I ought to be in bed and be taking some good tonic. As things stand I feel bad & I wish you were here to cheer me as you always do. Meantime with love & all good wishes I'll be thinking of you and your ever colorful and poetic reactions to life—good, bad or indifferent as it may be.

D

1. *The Stoic* was published posthumously on November 6, 1947.

* * *

July 10—'45

Yvette Dear:

Such a poetic, Lovely letter from you this morning July 10th. You are off on a hill somewhere—up near Brewster,[1] and you fairly sing of the heavens and the earth which considering all you have to do and your unchanging sense of duty always impresses me. I marvel that you dont at least verbally rebel against the conditions that have almost always made you earn your own way. So often I feel that it might be a relief to you if you were to write an honest forth right book like Black Boy[2] and in it have your say concerning all the things you have had to endure and so what you think of life. It would be colorful and more dramatic and I feel it would sell, yet not only the data but because of the beauty of your prose. Why not.

As for myself, although I have practically completed two books I am not feeling nearly as well as I should. Most of the time I feel so tired,—so ready to go to bed and stay there for a period—weeks I should say. Also I yawn so much day after day—so much so that I am thinking of consulting a doctor.—Yet I dont—too weary almost to bother. And yet I wish I knew the answer. The one nice thing that comes occasionally and for all that I cant keep up with my mail relieves me is a letter from you—a letter like this one from Brewster. Somehow it joins in with my wishes and my sense of beauty—my wish to be with you seeing the beauty that you see. Oh, Yvette—truly yours is a lovely temperament—poetic & helpful. I wish I were there now. I think I might get well.

Love & all good wishes
D

1. Brewster is in upstate New York.
2. Richard Wright's autobiographical *Black Boy* (1945).

* * *

Oct. 3 [1945]

Yvette Dear:

Whether I seemed to change or didn't at one time or another I always carried in my mind thoughts (many) of various phases of your temperament that did appeal to me and still do,—understanding—a clear, poetic, forceful mind balanced by charm,—the sweetness of your temperament as well as your looks. Plus your face and form and your generous consideration always of the lacks and errors and often enough the meannesses of the others. Always, as I long ago noted, you were always working hard yourself and yet were never jealous or envious even—in so far as I could see—of the comforts and privileges—even the luxuries—of others. The one thing that used to anger me most—quite the only thing I think—was the attraction you had for men and what seemed to me your willingness to go with now one and now another when I—of course and jealously and selfishly enough—did not want you to have any other than me. That way you could pay me out and did as you once confessed—only paid out or not I could never think of wholly giving you up, or feel that you were wholly willing to give me up.

And so we have gone on,—month after month, year after year. And always I have found myself coming back to this quality and that in you—principally wisdom and sweetness of heart in you—and always thinking how pleasant it would be to live with you—how life would most probably flow on in a gracious world of forbearance on your part—whatever mine might be—and yet I can never think of myself as quarrelling savagely with you, let alone enduringly, for I am always conscious of the basic sweetness and tolerance and courtesy and kindness of your innate affectionate self.

And so it stands. And although I know you go with others and satisfy yourself as best you can—still there you are—the innately wise and kindly and poetic Yvette and so you will remain. And if I were only near you you would see much more of me than you think assuming that you wished it so, for I would be coming to you in search of peace and quiet, and the somehow delicate sweetness of your moods—and would certainly find happiness in them if you continued to find happiness in me.

So with love and all good wishes I am closing for just now. But your temperament and your sweetness of heart will be with me. And I'll write again.

Dont trouble much over the Xmas present. If you want change to a 40 inch belt or whatever do so. But the scarf still appeals to me as a good idea.

* * *

Los Angeles,
Dec—1945

Yvette Dear: Thanks so much for your letter of Dec 6. You always write so wisely and so kindly and so tolerantly, so much so that you make life seem so much better than it often truly is—so much so that often I think of you as the most tolerant and generous of all the people I have met. Also to cause me to feel that if ever I strike it financially, I will wire you not only the means but the request that you dispose of your nice little apartment and come out here where I at least can contact you. As it is I can only write and that in the face of two long novels—The Bulwark and The Stoic on which I have been working for the past two years,—slaving is a better word.

However, as you will be pleased to know I have finished both. One, The Bulwark has been accepted by Doubleday Doran who intend to issue it on March one. The other is The Stoic which will be distributed about May 1. Apart from these I have been showered with requests for a lot of articles on my personal opinions as to this and that which same I could never find time to write as you can well guess. But meantime here I am again, this time with a check for 15^{00} which is your Xmas present since you know best what you want to buy. And when I get more I'll send you more. Meanwhile dear dont forget me. I so much like to hear from you & to feel that you still care. And as I dream if a certain windfall arrives you are to come out here or at least you are going to get the means so to do, as well as my wish that you will be moved to favor me that much.

And meanwhile think of me. And here is my merry Xmas to you.

Love as ever

TD

Index

This book has been set in Baskerville and Bellevue typefaces. Baskerville was designed by John Baskerville at his private press in Birmingham, England, in the eighteenth century. The first typeface to depart from the oldstyle typeface design, Baskerville has more variation between thick and thin strokes. In an effort to insure that the thick and thin strokes of his typeface reproduced well on paper, John Baskerville developed the first wove paper, the surface of which was much smoother than the laid paper of the time. The development of wove paper was partly responsible for the introduction of typefaces classified as modern, which have even more contrast between thick and thin strokes.